THE LAST DAYS OF SOCRATES

PLATO (C. 427–347 B.C.) stands with Socrates and Aristotle as one of the shapers of the whole intellectual tradition of the West. He came from a family that had long played a prominent part in Athenian politics, and it would have been natural for him to follow the same course. He declined to do so, however, disgusted by the violence and corruption of Athenian political life, and sickened especially by the execution in 399 of his friend and teacher, Socrates. Inspired by Socrates' inquiries into the nature of ethical standards, Plato sought a cure for the ills of society not in politics but in philosophy, and arrived at his fundamental and lasting conviction that those ills would never cease until philosophers became rulers or rulers philosophers. At an uncertain date in the early fourth century B.C. he founded in Athens the Academy, the first permanent institution devoted to philosophical research and teaching, and the prototype of all western universities. He travelled extensively, notably to Sicily as political adviser to Dionysius II, ruler of Syracuse. Plato wrote over twenty philosophical dialogues, there are also extant under his name thirteen letters, whose genuineness is keenly disputed. His literary activity extended over perhaps half a century: few other writers have exploited so effectively the grace and precision, the flexibility and power, of Greek prose.

HUGH TREDENNICK was born in 1899 and educated at King Edward's, Birmingham, and Trinity Hall, Cambridge, where he got a double first in Classics. He was Professor of Classics at Royal Holloway College from 1946 until 1966. He was Dean of the Faculty of Arts at London University from 1956 to 1960, and joint editor of the *Classical Review* from 1961 to 1967. His translation of Xenophon's *Memoirs* of Socrates is a Penguin Classic, and he also edited and translated works by Aristotle. He died in 1982.

HAROLD TARRANT was born in Slough, England, in 1946, and studied at Cambridge and Durham universities. He has taught at the Department of Greek (subsequently Classics) at the University of Sydney since 1974, and is currently a Senior Lecturer. His publications include *Scepticism or Platonism?* (1985) and *Thrasyllan Platonism* (1993). He has received recent grants from the Australian Research Council for work on an annotated translation of Olympiodorus' *On Plato's Gorgias* and on the chronological unity of Plato's dialogues. He is also an officer of the NSW Chess Association and a keen bush-walker.

PLATO

THE LAST DAYS OF SOCRATES

EUTHYPHRO · APOLOGY · CRITO · PHAEDO

Translated by
HUGH TREDENNICK AND HAROLD TARRANT

Introduction and Notes by
HAROLD TARRANT

PENGUIN BOOKS

PENGUIN BOOKS

Published by the Penguin Group
Penguin Books Ltd, 27 Wrights Lane, London w8 5tz, England
Penguin Putnam Inc., 375 Hudson Street, New York, New York 10014, USA
Penguin Books Australia Ltd, Ringwood, Victoria, Australia
Penguin Books Canada Ltd, 10 Alcorn Avenue, Toronto, Ontario, Canada m4v 3b2
Penguin Books (NZ) Ltd, Private Bag 102902, NSMC, Auckland, New Zealand

Penguin Books Ltd, Registered Offices: Harmondsworth, Middlesex, England

This translation first published 1954
New edition, with additions, 1959
Reprinted with revisions, 1969
Revised translation with new introduction and notes 1993
13 15 17 19 20 18 16 14 12

Filmset in 9.5/12 pt Monophoto Sabon
Typeset by Datix International Limited, Bungay, Suffolk
Printed in England by Clays Ltd, St Ives plc

CONTENTS

PREFACE

Hugh Tredennick's *The Last Days of Socrates* has helped introduce these works of Plato to countless readers. It has been part of an important project which has made great literature accessible to all sorts of readers. Since 1954, however, much has changed in Platonic studies; as a result the original volume was being outshone by many of the newer Plato translations in the Penguin series. I have tried to write a more extended general introduction, taking account of modern directions in the study of Plato, but without straying into the kind of technicalities which the general reader would find problematic. I have divided the translation into segments in order to give the reader 'signposts' marking a dialogue's development. The footnotes and the introductions to the individual dialogues have also been rewritten and to some degree expanded. As for the translation, I have altered chiefly what I thought needed to be altered, and in the *Apology*, *Crito* and *Phaedo* most of the credit must still go to Tredennick. In the *Euthyphro*, where the tone of the original translation seemed to me less suited to Socrates as there depicted, I have included much more original material.

It is extremely useful to have the *Phaedo* in the same volume as the other three works, though because of its literary qualities and philosophic rigour it may seem to have deserved a volume of its own. There have been several annotated translations dedicated to that work alone, and yet there is merit in refusing to be drawn too far along the path towards producing a full commentary. Many readers will not need in-depth discussion of Platonic metaphysics in order to appreciate a work of this power; some will find too much commentary tedious. I have tried to steer a middle course here between unhelpful shallows and mystifying depths. The reader who is still ready for a further challenge will find a number of suggestions in the bibliography.

Sydney   HAROLD TARRANT
March 1992

GENERAL INTRODUCTION

PLATONIC LITERATURE

The works of Plato, with few exceptions, are fully philosophy and fully literature. He therefore presents a double task for the interpreter, and at times a more complex task still. For his works abound with mathematical examples, illustrations from a variety of walks of Athenian life, quasi-religious myths and quasi-rhetorical speeches. The true interpreter must somehow try to match Plato's tremendous breadth of interest as well as his philosophical depths. Ideally he will see himself as a philosopher, mathematician, historian, speech-maker, literary critic *and* as a moral and religious being. It is not surprising that over the ages interpreters have failed the test. Platonic scholarship is still moving, and still for the most part moving forward, but there will always be a further challenge: more to do, more to understand.

Yet whereas the ideal Platonic interpreter is as remote an ideal as Plato's Ideal State in the *Republic*, there are countless numbers who are attracted to his works because they have one or more of those interests which coincide with his. Because he can appeal to us as literature or as philosophy or as religion or as a source for Greek society, etc., he attracts a multitude of readers with a variety of special interests.

His works have the qualities which allow them to be interpreted, and reasonably interpreted, in many ways and from many points of view. This has much to do with the fact that they take the form of dialogues, rather than treatises addressed to the reader. We are not directly asked to believe anything; we are not required to take anything on trust. We are asked to be spectators at an occasion, whether historical or fictitious, when lifelike characters talked on real issues, issues which are sometimes remote from us but which we can feel were pressing ones for them. We are asked to react to human experience and human ideas, for which we, as human beings, have some understanding. We are asked to listen to the arguments critically; we are also asked to respond to the personalities of those participating. We may be encouraged to learn certain lessons and to form certain conclusions as a result; but many of the problems superficially seem left unresolved, and we are not bullied into taking the author's line. Consequently Plato's dialogues have continued to have appeal over the ages, and have survived numerous changes of intellectual and religious fashion, for somebody has always found something of value within them.

The term 'dialogue' in fact embraces a wide variety of works. We shall meet in this volume the *Apology*, which in most respects resembles other law court speeches which have come down to us; it is essentially a monologue, interrupted only by a short cross-examination of the principal accuser, Meletus. But cross-examination also occurs in other forensic speeches,[1] and the skilful characterization of Socrates has parallels in the contemporary speeches of Lysias, which are likewise tailored to bring out (in the most attractive and sympathetic light possible) the character of the speaker. The *Menexenus* has a brief dramatic introduction, but is otherwise little more than a mock funeral-speech for a public burial, apparently parodying the Periclean funeral speech from Book 2 of Thucydides. In the *Critias* another short dramatic introduction leads into something more like a novel – except that it is a novel without any individual personalities. In the *Symposium* dialogue provides a frame for seven related speeches; in the *Phaedrus* it is a frame for a rich mixture of speeches, myth and argument.

Perhaps the earliest fundamental division of Plato's works to be widely accepted was that into dramatic and narrative works.[2] A 'dramatic' work, in this technical sense, was one in which the main conversation was written in a form rather like a drama. Only the words supposedly spoken were written down. The speakers were identified by the way in which they frequently named each other as they conversed. There were limitations inherent in this kind of presentation, in so far as every time the writer wanted to draw attention to actions or to the appearance of the participants, he had to have one of the speakers comment upon what was happening. It is also difficult to handle many characters simultaneously within the 'dramatic' dialogue, for one might easily lose track of who was supposed to be speaking. Consequently, where Plato has to handle a large number of characters, as for example in the *Protagoras* or the *Symposium*, or where the argument is to be accompanied by a great deal of action, he inclines towards presenting the conversation in the form of a narrative. This narrative often, but not always, emerges out of a short 'dramatic' introduction where the narrator converses with somebody eager to hear the tale, as in the *Phaedo*.

Dialogues were not exclusive to Plato. They were written by a number of followers of Socrates, and it was a natural form for these writers to adopt. They wanted to depict Socrates in action, i.e. in conversation: for Socratic philosophy can only be truly realized through question and answer. We have plenty of examples of Socratic conversations in the works of Xenophon, most notably his *Memorabilia*.[3] These are all in the narrated form, even though Xenophon does not exploit the advantages of that form in the way that Plato can. It is very likely that the narrated form was favoured by other well-known writers of Socratic dialogues, such as Antisthenes and Aeschines.[4]

A famous passage of Diogenes Laertius (3.48) gives Plato the credit for the introduction of the philosophic dialogue, allegedly after he had developed great enthusiasm for the 'mimes' (brief non-philosophical dramatic sketches) of Sophron. A fuller parallel passage in an Oxyrhynchus papyrus published by M. Haslam in 1976 (*P. Oxy.* 3219, fr. 1) makes it clear that it is the *dramatic* dialogue which is supposed to have owed so much to Plato.[5] We may suppose that with his great dramatic talents, which may at one time have been encouraging him to write tragedies, Plato was able to inject extra life into bare dramatic sketches, which, like other prose works, were probably read aloud by the author in the first instance. To read a narrated work one only had to play one character, the narrator; to read a dramatic work one had to become a minimum of two.[6] Playing such a double role seems to have been considered educationally dangerous at *Republic* 394b ff., but all the same *Theaetetus* 143c speaks as if Plato had begun to see the perpetual inclusion of such phrases as 'I said' and 'He agreed' as unnecessarily cumbersome. Dramatic works often have a freshness and immediacy about them. We enter directly, often quite suddenly and with little or no introductory conversation,[7] into the world of Socratic debate. The *Euthyphro* and *Crito* are examples of such works. By contrast, narrated dialogues, particularly the *Phaedo, Symposium* and *Parmenides* where setting of the introductory dialogue is remote from the action, ease us gradually into the world of Socratic legend.

It should be clear to virtually any reader that Plato greatly enjoyed writing, and enlisting his literary powers in the service of philosophy. We are confronted, however, with a well-known passage of his *Phaedrus* (275c ff.) which questions whether written compositions have any serious purpose. Certainly Plato valued face-to-face teaching more than any written message which he left behind, but an important part of his criticism of the written word concerns its habit of addressing all alike; moreover the literature criticized always says the same thing when the reader tries to ask it questions. The dialogues, however, are asking *us* the questions, and as we change ourselves so do the answers. For an author who had a fear of the finality of the published word, Plato did at least choose the most flexible form of composition possible, and the effort which has gone into many of his compositions clearly demonstrates that he usually took his activities as an author with considerable seriousness.

Seriousness, of course, does not mean that the dialogues are all serious in tone. A work like the *Euthydemus* is distinctly comic for the most part, and the *Euthyphro* is another work with important comic elements, ridiculing not only Meletus and Euthyphro, but 'Daedalan' Socrates as well (see 11c–e). Even in the sombre setting of the *Phaedo* there is room for the occasional joke. Irony and caricature play their part from time to time. Humour spices the dialogues, as do some of Socrates' grotesque analogies and charming tales. Humour invites the reader in, and sometimes an erotic element plays this role. But once we have been captured Plato does not waste the opportunity to make us think. He may even try to persuade us to adopt his own beliefs.

Plato's principal tool of persuasion is of course argument. There are two particular terms which are often used in this context, *elenchus* and *dialectic*. The former is Socrates' means of examining the soundness of the views of others. Typically an interlocutor will make a moral claim that Socrates cannot accept. He then secures the interlocutor's assent to some further proposition or group of propositions, and, accepting these, proceeds to demonstrate that they are inconsistent with the original claim. It is a tool for the exposure of problems with beliefs and inconsistencies in sets of beliefs rather than for demonstrating what is true and what is false.[8] It makes considerable use of inductive arguments. It is the weapon employed in the *Euthyphro* for example, or in the cross-examination of Meletus in the *Apology*. It is not, however, characteristic of the *Crito* or the *Phaedo*. In the latter work Socrates is not trying to expose the false beliefs of others so much as attempting to give a thoroughly argued justification of his own deep-rooted beliefs. To such reasoned justification the term 'dialectic' would apply. The term is derived from the verb 'to converse', and need mean no more than 'conversational art' – not the art of polite conversation, but the art of employing person-to-person discussion in such a way as to come nearer to the truth of a given issue. The teaching of dialectic is to constitute the culmination of the education of the Guardians in Book 7 of Plato's *Republic*.

Even dialectic is conceived more as a means of legitimate persuasion than as a means of proof. In the *Gorgias* there is talk of 'arguments of iron and adamant', but it is denied that they have led to knowledge (508e–509a). In the *Phaedo* Socrates wants the argument to suggest to him that its conclusion is true (91a); he seeks for sound and trustworthy arguments, and for the skill in argument to be able to recognize them. The medium of language (*logos*), and presumably of argument in particular, is thought to provide in a sense a *reflection* of the truth rather than a guarantee of it (99e–100a).[9] The concept of formal validity is not yet in evidence, though already the connection between dialectical and mathematical procedure is present.[10]

Whatever Plato himself thought of the proof-giving powers of argument, his readers were bound to be cautious; hence the appeal to those who have trusted in unsound arguments (and regretted it) not to become detesters of argument (*Phaedo* 89d ff.). After an age in which sophists and orators had discovered the art of arguing convincingly for all sorts of conclusions, and often for contradictory ones, it is possible that many of Plato's readers viewed argument more as a tool of deception than as a source of truth. Others still would have mistrusted their ability to recognize a good argument. So argument could not be Plato's only tool of persuasion. Sometimes he will use character as a catalyst to belief, exposing flaws of character in those who expound the views which he rejects, and showing Socrates to have the kind of qualities which are both trusted by the reader and somehow consonant with the line that he takes. The credibility of the argument and the credibility of its promoter were inextricably related.

Another important device is myth. Myth appeals to the reader's cultural identity and to deep-seated beliefs and feelings. We might view these feelings as culturally conditioned; Plato would have seen many of them as dim traces of innate knowledge. Myths may be placed at the end of such works as the *Gorgias* and *Phaedo* in order to induce some spark within us to give its sub-rational assent to the argument's conclusions. Lesser myths, like simpler imagery and metaphor, subtly condition our reading and assist in eliciting a positive response from us.

Often, of course, Plato is more concerned to discourage certain beliefs than to promote any particular ones himself. The elenchus will then be an important tool, as will satire. The exposure of the beliefs of the interlocutor will be accompanied by his exposure as an incomplete moral being.

THE GROUP *EUTHYPHRO–APOLOGY–CRITO–PHAEDO*

Early in the first century A.D. Thrasyllus, who was not only the astrologer of the Roman Emperor Tiberius, but also a polymath and devoted follower of Plato and Pythagoras, accepting that Plato had arranged his works in groups like the tragic playwrights, argued that these were groups of four. As the first of these groups he postulated the 'tetralogy' *Euthyphro–Apology–Crito–Phaedo*. The rationale was simple enough: the works all had a dramatic setting at around the time of Socrates' trial and death, and they all contributed to a paradigm of how the philosopher should live and die.[11] All manuscripts of Plato stem from exemplars which employed Thrasyllus's order, and thus there has been a strong tendency to keep these works together even today. Certainly they provide a satisfying sequence, and combine to shed considerable light on the circumstances surrounding Socrates' death – or Plato's view of those circumstances.

The *Euthyphro* depicts a professedly worried Socrates about to face a preliminary hearing of the impiety charges against him – and consequently most anxious to discover at last what piety really is. The *Apology* shows Socrates speaking in court, not merely when defending himself, but also when proposing a possible punishment after conviction and when responding to the news that the jury have voted for his death. The *Crito* shows Socrates in prison, responding to an eleventh-hour plea by Crito that he should let his friends arrange his escape. The *Phaedo* shows him conversing with his friends on his last day, arguing for the immortality of the soul, and attempting to reassure them about his fate.

In spite of the fact that they make an attractive sequence, modern theory would resist the suggestion that Plato composed these works as such, or even that he published them as such. It is usual, in the English-speaking world at least, to regard the *Euthyphro*, *Apology* and *Crito* as early works of Plato, written within a decade or so of Socrates' death, and the *Phaedo* as belonging to his 'middle period' (a decade or so later), when Plato had reached his peak as a literary artist and was already putting his own distinctive doctrines into the mouth of Socrates. This chronology is less secure than is often pretended, but one ought not to believe that the works necessarily constitute a compositional unit.

PLATO'S SOCRATES

Socrates was a character who took on many guises in literature, being transformed by the individual author's perception of his character and his activity. Among scholars of ancient philosophy Socrates is often taken to be Plato's 'Socrates' as he figures in those dialogues of Plato which they would label 'Socratic'. There has not, however, been much unanimity about which dialogues ought to be so labelled. All that tends now to be agreed is that in certain middle- and late-period works, the character called Socrates becomes more of a mouthpiece for Plato's own doctrines and less 'Socratically' characterized. The *Phaedo* is normally classed among them, even though it certainly offers a number of insights into

Plato's view of the real Socrates. Chronology is important, not because Plato forgot what his mentor and source of inspiration had been like, but (i) because his concerns developed and changed in such a way that it would have been unnatural to limit himself to examining problems from a Socratic perspective, and (ii) because the conventions of Socratic writing were shifting in such a way that it was no longer expected that one's character 'Socrates' would only say what Socrates himself could have said.

The shifting conventions are illustrated by observations at the beginning of Xenophon's *Apology of Socrates*, in which it is noted that all who had (so far) written about the trial and death of Socrates had managed to capture his defiant aloofness, but that they had thereby made him look rather imprudent because they had not additionally gone into his reasons for preferring to die at this stage than to live. The unanimity of these writers was indeed an indication of historical fact in Xenophon's eyes, but was he criticizing them for not having gone beyond Socrates' actual words to explain that aloofness? The Socratic writer, it seems, did not merely have to say what Socrates said and did, but also had to put it in an attractive perspective. This of course is what Plato would do in the *Phaedo*, a work which actually contains a new defence speech, this time delivered to his own friends and explaining (in a much more philosophical manner than Xenophon) why the philosopher must welcome death (63e–69e).[12]

One might detect in the *Phaedo* a Platonic response to the challenge of another Socratic writer, Xenophon. Likewise one might see in the *Euthydemus* an attack on those who present their Socratic philosophy in too 'eristic' a manner, striving for victory in argument at the expense of truth;[13] and scholars often suspect a Platonic response to his fellow-Socratic Antisthenes in various passages. Certainly Antisthenes attacked Plato in his work *Sathon*, whose title is a crude, lisp-like perversion of Plato's name. As dialogues became a polemical tool for carrying on debate between rival Socratics, the character of 'Socrates' must progressively have been used to present the author's own side of Socratic philosophy; and the less one saw of the real Socrates in the works of rivals, the more justified one would feel in remodelling him to suit one's own ends. There was not one Socrates in the literature, but several.[14]

What I have to say here, then, concerns Plato's Socrates, as he appears in supposedly early dialogues or in later passages which seem intended to shed light on the historical figure. Socrates' investigations are referred to in the *Apology*, and Plato shows us his investigative technique in works like the *Euthyphro* which appear to be examining what an interlocutor either should know or would claim to know. Discussion usually arises, at first sight, from Socrates' desire to remedy his own deep-seated ignorance of the subject which the other understands; we suspect, though, that his real desire is to expose the ignorance of the other and in so doing to draw attention to difficulties inherent in the subject which every would-be expert must be aware of. Sometimes, however, as in the *Charmides, Lysis* and *Meno* where his interlocutors are young men in need of guidance, his purpose in exposing ignorance is more constructive and tailored towards encouraging them to pursue philosophy. Always there is a sense in which the examination of the person's theories constitutes an examination of their life and character, as *Laches* 187e–188a shows. For as we have seen, Socrates' method of argument, the elenchus, exposes inconsistencies in the moral beliefs of the interlocutor, inconsistencies which are likely to be reflected in their lives.

It is well known that Socrates claims not to teach, not to give instruction to the interlocutor. It is essential that the interlocutor himself should either volunteer or assent to each premise and each step in the argument. Socrates does, however, lead. There are occasions when he makes helpful suggestions which keep the argument going. There are many more when his questions introduce aspects of the problem which will have to be considered thereafter. He can be constructive, but he recognizes that the only secure construction in education is a construction freely built upon the learner's own experience. In time the elenchus itself fades from the scene. It is not much in evidence in the *Crito*, and is no longer the means of investigation in the *Phaedo*; for in both it is Socrates' beliefs rather than those of the interlocutors which must be justified. Still, the assent of the interlocutor to every step remains important; he must not be bullied into assent, but gradually led on to see that he too must accept the logic of Socrates' position. Socrates emerges as extremely astute in debate, but too dedicated to his educational purposes and to his quest for the truth to become either a showman or a shifty deceiver. Though there are

times when we may suspect that he is being unnecessarily contentious and altogether too reluctant to try and understand his
opponent's position, it is not Plato's intention to depict him as
petty or malicious in his questioning.

As far as the action of the dialogues is concerned, Socrates
seems to play very little part in it, other than arriving at and
departing from the scene of the debate. In the action of the
Euthydemus, for instance, Socrates is initially seated alone; the
others take up their positions, act and react. Socrates usually
argues quietly, leaving others to be provoked into actions, though
he does get up to leave when debate temporarily breaks down in
the *Protagoras* (335d). In a way, Socrates is most famed for his
inaction: in the *Symposium* for his spell standing in a neighbouring
porch (175a–b) or his failure to respond to Alcibiades' advances
(219b–d) or his immunity to wine (220a, etc.). It is the same
Socrates who holds only routine offices in Athens, resists illegal
measures and refuses to escape from prison. The action tends to
move around him, as round the centre of an eddy.

The figure who remains sure and unmoved amidst the turmoil
of life might seem to some to be a man who has founded his life
upon beliefs which are unusually secure and unassailable. The
reader of the *Apology* will feel that Socrates is such a person at the
same time as being confronted with Socrates' own claim that the
only way in which his wisdom exceeds that of others is that he
recognizes the state of his ignorance. The Socrates of the putative
'early dialogues' (as also of the putatively late *Theaetetus*) is
indeed a person who makes much of the yawning gaps in his own
knowledge. His investigations generally arise out of his claims that
he does not know the answers to seemingly everyday questions,
such as 'What is courage?', 'What is rhetoric?', or 'Can virtue be
taught?'. These works tend to end either inconclusively or with
some conclusion so counter-intuitive that it could convince nobody.
Euthyphro would be an example of the former kind, *Hippias
Minor* of the latter. The occasional passage where Socrates does
seem to be openly propounding his doctrine, such as *Protagoras*
345b–c, tends to be so contentiously presented that it seems to be
not so much an expression of belief as a challenge to those who
would prefer not to believe. Socrates never sets himself up as an
authority upon any matter relating to morality,[15] nor upon any

matter traditionally taught by Presocratic philosophers or by the sophists. For that matter he does not set himself up as a master of investigative technique or in the expulsion of false beliefs, for these skills are attributed to the guiding hand of Apollo or some other divine inspiration rather than to any systematic knowledge.[16]

That Socrates is not an expert may be difficult for the reader of the present works to accept. Socrates seems like an expert handler of the elenchus in the *Euthyphro*. He seems to be telling the jury what justice and the juryman's oath demands in the *Apology*, a work which also has him tell of his defiant refusal to become implicated in unconstitutional measures likely to lead to unjust deaths. He seems to be equally certain about the requirements of justice and lawfulness in the *Crito*. And he is about as convinced as one could be of the immortality of souls and some of the related theories in the *Phaedo*. This last work is less of a problem, in so far as it is acknowledged to be a middle-period work, but one feels that Plato is writing partly to explain the complete equanimity with which Socrates faced death (see 58e), an equanimity which was for him based upon Socrates' deep-rooted beliefs.

There are various possible ways of attempting to reconcile Socrates' disavowal of knowledge with his attitude of great certainty. Firstly, there is the sceptic way. The ancient sceptics, who like many others saw Socrates as a predecessor, believed that the untroubled state of mind was best achieved by avoiding coming to conclusions. Socrates could be seen as a true sceptic, and his equanimity in the face of death a result of his success. This does not help to explain his little lectures to the jury and to Crito. Then there is a chronological approach. The *Apology* and *Crito* are set at the end of Socrates' life; also from this period are his refusals to act unconstitutionally. There is no need to suppose that he always had the convictions which he demonstrates in the last few years of his life. The very success of his examination of others may have persuaded him that he did have some of the answers himself. Yet the Socrates of the *Apology* does not suggest that he is abandoning his disavowal of knowledge. Even at his firmest, he still talks about what he *thinks* or what seems just to him (30c–d, 35b–c). Above all, the profession of ignorance is still strong in the *Euthyphro*. We might discount this as being the product of Socrates' irony, but it is not the function of Socratic irony to tell direct lies.

Irony would rather involve telling half-truths, toying mysteriously with the interlocutor and keeping your real meaning hidden.[17] Thus the chronological approach meets with only limited success.

Another possibility is to distinguish between senses in which Socrates does know, and senses in which he does not. For instance he may have that kind of limited knowledge which is open to mankind, but falls short of full knowledge, something traditionally reserved for the gods.[18] If this is Plato's view of Socratic knowledge, he certainly does not make it obvious. The Socratic message is that men do not have that kind of knowledge to which they *as men* aspire. Euthyphro would not be put out nearly so much by the thought that he might know his subject with slightly less precision than Zeus.

The most depressing aspect of Socrates' disavowal of knowledge is the fact that his best-known doctrine (I should prefer to call it 'theme') is that virtue is knowledge. The result would be that neither Socrates nor anybody else with whom he is familiar can be virtuous – unless of course knowledge of one's own ignorance can suffice to yield virtue.[19] As for others, Plato's Socrates does not encourage the belief that any of them were virtuous in the preferred sense of the term, but Plato surely wants us to believe that Socrates was himself virtuous in some very meaningful sense.

The burning question, of course, is the nature of knowledge itself. What is it to know? How does one test knowledge? How does one recognize it? It is because this question was so central that Plato's main treatment of it did not appear in its final form until the *Theaetetus* – fairly late in his career. There Socrates is 'unproductive of wisdom' and 'has nothing wise' to offer (150c), but yet he possesses the crucial skill of investigating and evaluating the ideas of others, and above all of distinguishing the true from the false (151b–d). He knows, Plato would have us believe, not just his own ignorance, but also whether others know or do not know. And with this knowledge he ought to be able to declare true or false all propositions which an interlocutor had submitted to him for testing. Can he know that a proposition p is true without knowing that p? This is by no means unthinkable. Let us pursue the consequences.

If others can produce the rational true beliefs required as a basis for knowledge though they have no ability to test them, while

Socrates has the ability to test their truth or falsity while not having the necessary true beliefs, it is clear that the process of discovery – of coming-to-know – can only take place when Socrates tests the beliefs of others. It must emerge through some dialectical exchange between Socrates and correct believers. This will explain why Plato's devotion to Socrates' conversational methods is greater than his devotion to what we see as Socratic doctrine. Others have some beliefs which are true, but unfortunately wallow in ignorance because they do not have the means to identify which ones; Socrates can help them, but relies upon their cooperation in providing ideas for scrutiny.

If this assessment of Socrates' contribution to knowledge has any merit, then it is clear why he professes his ignorance – he remains dependent on the suggestions of others; but it is likewise clear why he can be extremely confident on certain questions which he had regularly examined with the experts. The conclusions to which his investigations have consistently come, whether that a given proposition is true or that it is false, are propositions known from experience to have passed the test. To doubt the results of these investigations would not be to doubt his own abilities; it would rather be to doubt the generosity and good will of the divinity from whom he had received his powers and the command to use them.[20] That would be a case of impiety. Socrates cannot doubt many of the findings of his quest, because he cannot doubt the prophetic gifts that propel him on that quest and assist him to undertake it. His confidence is partly a product of his alleged divine inspiration;[21] he does not have the same confidence in *any individual's* power to discover the truth on his own through his ordinary cognitive powers.

This being the case, it is clear also that time contributes to Socrates' later confidence, for that confidence is dependent upon his experience of the results of his questioning. Even so, we should see comparatively little of it if it were not for the openness with which Socrates speaks in parts of the *Apology*, as well as *Crito* and *Phaedo*. This is because Plato's Socrates was a master of irony, a master of mystification said by Alcibiades to 'spend his whole life playing the ironist and toying with mankind'.[22] Alcibiades is contrasting Socrates' external self, which one does not and should not take seriously, with an internal self whose splendour (by 416 B.C.) had only been revealed to those who knew him closely. It is possible to see Socrates' non-serious mask as a defence mechanism – one which had long prevented the Athenians regarding him as a threat. But his own involvement in the political turmoil in 406–403 B.C. had forced him to reveal his hand. Without that mask public suspicion of his activities increased, forcing him all the more to talk plainly. The *Euthyphro*, with its dramatic date just before the trial, shows the mask breaking down and shows also how those who saw him as a friend and ally could come then to detest him. The *Apology* shows the mask being deliberately lifted. The *Crito* and *Phaedo* show the mask virtually gone.

There is one other aspect of the *Crito* and *Phaedo* which is of relevance in this context: Plato appears to be quite deliberately portraying Socrates as a man whose powers of vision had reached their peak just as he is about to die. In the *Crito* revelatory forces associated with Apollo are operating with considerable impact upon Socrates. At 44a–b we are told of a prophetic dream, in which a lady in white appeared to him, and suggested through a Homeric quotation that it would be two more days before he died; and at the end of the work the voices of the Athenian Laws, which have charmed his ears like the Sirens, seem to be regarded as part of the machinery employed by Apollo to lead Socrates to his death. We are not meant to see this as entirely typical of Socrates; rather we must see it as characteristic of Socrates in his final hours.

The *Phaedo* actually supplies the theory which underpins the picture of a man on the brink of divine knowledge. At 84e–85b Socrates compares himself with the swans, fellow-servants of Apollo, god of prophecy, who according to his account sing their swan-songs just before death not out of any sorrow, but out of joy at what they know is to come.[23] Socrates has extra powers of insight as a result of his impending death, and so the familiar ironic Socratic elenchus has given way to a new and unfamiliar song which reaches its climax in the visionary account of the higher and lower regions of the world in the myth. The increase in Socrates' visionary powers is likewise explained by the theory that the philosopher avoids the pleasures and pains of the body, striving to separate his soul *gently* from the body, practising being apart from the body so that the intellectual powers may reach their peak (cf. 65–8). The gentleness with which Socrates' soul leaves his body after drinking the hemlock (117e–118a) testifies to the close proximity to the other world – and to its truth – that he has already achieved.

The *Crito* and *Phaedo*, then, portray a Socrates who has achieved, when close to death, the maximum possible proximity to a divine knowledge of the truths of the other world. It is not surprising here if he speaks with unfamiliar voices and with an unfamiliar confidence. It is not surprising that Socrates' earlier belief that death is either the end of all sensation or the beginning of a new journey (*Apology* 40c) has changed to confidence in that new journey. For it is no longer Apollo's social critic who speaks, but the voice of Apollo speaking through him. Or so Plato would have us believe.

SOCRATES' CAREER AND HIS LAST DAYS

Socrates was born in 470 or 469 B.C., a decade after the Persian Wars had concluded and at a time when Athens was well on its way to a period of military, economic and intellectual hegemony of Greece. The son of Sophroniscus, a stonemason according to tradition,[24] he would not have had any very special education. During his youth Presocratic philosophy flourished, concentrating on the origin, nature and workings of the universe and mankind's place within it. Still in its infancy was the sophistic movement, piloted by Protagoras and other itinerant intellectuals who usually taught more practical skills, geared to the needs of ambitious young men and founded upon anthropocentric principles.

Socrates must have become reasonably well known before the age of forty, not necessarily because of any overt philosophic activity, but rather because he was very much a man of the city and its public places. The earliest dramatic dates of works which show Socrates handling the conversation,[25] those of the *Protagoras* and *Charmides*, belong to the later 430s B.C. Socrates in both works is keen to ensure that the youth are correctly educated – with due concern for the quality of their 'souls'. He is a man with obvious erotic feelings towards the most sought-after young men of this period, Alcibiades and Charmides, even though (if we are to believe Plato) his erotic relationships followed a rather unusual course. His feelings were perhaps tempered by his even greater thirst for knowledge which caused him to seek out professional intellectuals, though he had little money to take their formal courses[26] and a preference for drawing them into conversation. He moves already in the company of men of pretensions, already knowing the future oligarchic leader Critias very well, but also being familiar with men prominent in the democratic camp. There seems to be some surprise at the beginning of the *Charmides* that Socrates had managed to survive a hard-fought campaign in Thrace, perhaps because his lapses into other-worldliness (immortalized in the *Symposium*) were already well known.[27] In fact his qualities as a soldier earned him the admiration of others famed for their bravery.[28] The *Charmides* and the *Protagoras* both paint a plausible youthful picture of Socrates; the former (155e–157c) has him delighting in a piece of blatant deception required to lure the attractive Charmides into conversation, while the latter shows him somewhat more contentious and headstrong in both argument and tactics than he will seem in works set at a later stage. Though he has already become something of a cult figure among young men (*Charmides* 156a), it seems that he has not yet acquired a reputation for wisdom: the young Hippocrates does not think of Socrates as a wise man in the same sense as Protagoras (309c–d), and the sophist himself suggests that he will not be surprised if Socrates *becomes* famed for wisdom (361d–e).

The reputation for wisdom is acquired sometime during the next decade or so. It is interesting that in the *Laches*, set in or around 420 B.C., the old man Lysimachus, because he had been spending most of his time indoors recently, had not connected the Socrates whom the young men are always praising with the son of Sophroniscus. The year in which Socrates came to great prominence was probably 424 B.C., as two comedies in which he played an important role, Ameipsias's *Connus* and Aristophanes' *Clouds*, were presented early in 423. Could the Delphic oracle recently have declared him to be wisest?[29] Possibly, though we get no hint in the *Clouds* as we have it that Socrates was engaging as yet in any programme of moral questioning of the kind that the Delphic oracle is said to have provoked, nor do we receive the impression that the Delphic response story was well known at Athens. What we do find Socrates engaged in at this time is the seeking-out of teachers. While Aristophanes depicted Socrates as already running a school of miscellaneous learning himself, Ameipsias was showing him rather as the over-age pupil of a music-teacher-cum-sophist, Connus.[30] Another musical expert with whom Socrates is associated was Damon, who features as somebody who had learnt much from the sophist Prodicus in the *Laches* (197d), and as an expert on verse metres at *Republic* 400b4–5 – a passage surprisingly reminiscent of Socrates' line 651 in Aristophanes' *Clouds*.

What picture of Socrates' current interests and pursuits does the *Clouds* suggest? Socrates is in charge of a weird school of philosophy, but this hardly implies that he did ever run such a school. It might, perhaps, have been inferred that his purpose in taking up all sorts of quasi-sophistic studies himself had something to do with the desire to set up such an institution. Aristophanes might have been giving an exaggerated and highly comic account of where he guessed Socratic activities might lead. In the background (at least of the extant version) hides the figure of Chaerephon, Socrates' accomplice, who seems to attract at least as much venom as Socrates himself and is treated elsewhere by Aristophanes as a thief and cheat. It would be a reasonable guess that Chaerephon was the man whom Aristophanes judged to be promoting Socrates, especially in view of the fact that it was Chaerephon who at some stage asked the Delphic oracle about Socrates' wisdom. Socrates himself remains an other-worldly type, and seems to show little interest in the payment which his school is being offered or in the uses to which his pupils intend to put their new-found knowledge. It is not he who had the entrepreneurial skills to turn philosophy into a profit-making business.

When it comes to his picture of Socrates' interests, they are indeed fairly broad, but contain nothing of any moral or practical significance. His concerns are for the heavens above, the earth below, for the study of language, poetry, argument and problem-solving. There is much here that is Presocratic, and it seems to rely fairly consistently on the cosmology and biology of Diogenes of Apollonia;[31] there is much else that seems indebted to the teaching of the sophists, particularly that of Prodicus, with whom Socrates was much associated and who is mentioned in line 361 of the play. Only in the much-used theme, crucial to the plot, that there are two arguments on every topic is the influence of Protagoras obvious.[32] Likewise absent is any strong indication of particular influences from the Presocratics Anaxagoras and Archelaus, with whom Socrates is associated in the *Phaedo* (96b, 97b–c). Now clearly Aristophanes must have had easy access himself to the doctrines of Diogenes, and in that case one assumes that Socrates did as well: from whatever source. Was there some representative of Diogenes' philosophy at Athens whose expertise Socrates was also trying to tap at this time?

Whatever the answer, I think it is clear that Socrates did consult various experts with strong connections with philosophic or sophistic views during the late 420s. The section on Socrates' early career in the *Phaedo* says nothing to question such a belief. He once was an enthusiastic inquirer into various Presocratic theories, including those of Archelaus, Empedocles, Diogenes, Heraclitus and Alcmaeon of Croton (96b), but soon found that they raised more questions than they answered. Eventually he heard somebody reading from a book of Anaxagoras about Intelligence being the arranger of the universe (97b–c), and thought it might be possible to solve Presocratic questions by asking, 'How is it *best* for things to be arranged?' Curiously, he had already learnt much from Archelaus (a significant Athenian follower of Anaxagoras), but he had not at that stage encountered Anaxagoras's famous doctrine of a cosmic Intelligence. Nor was it an aspect of Anaxagoras's thought which played an important part in Archelaus. It is quite reasonable to suppose that it had not been Anaxagoras's mature doctrine by which Archelaus was influenced.[33] Anaxagoras probably died around 428 B.C., and it may have been then that his mature work was brought to Athens and made public there. This could have prompted renewed interest in Presocratic philosophy on the part of Socrates, primarily in those Presocratics who made use of intelligent governing principles. This is what Diogenes did rather better than Anaxagoras, relating the cosmic intelligence to crucial aspects of man's environment such as the seasons and the weather (fr.3), and modelling man's intelligence on the divine intelligence (fr.4) so that it might control his sensations and thought (A 19). It is clear that he did not do this well enough to retain Socrates' interest in cosmology and biology, but it is a reasonable bet that it was Diogenes, not Archelaus as is usually supposed, who had brought Anaxagoras's work to Athens, and had inspired Socrates with temporary hopes of solving Presocratic problems.

I conclude that it is extremely likely that Aristophanes, when he wrote the *Clouds*, was aware of Socrates' studies not only with Prodicus and with musical theorists who had pronounced sophistic leanings, but also with Diogenes and with Anaxagorean doctrine as Diogenes presented it. It is often held that Aristophanes is a non-discriminating anti-intellectual who adds nothing to our knowledge of Socrates.[34] But scholars are becoming increasingly dissatisfied with that view. His picture of Socrates is in many ways a sensitive one, and he was an intellectual of great cleverness himself.

Study of the role of intelligence in the world and in mankind would have acted as an appropriate launching-pad for study into human wisdom and human excellence in general. It explains why Socrates placed so much emphasis on our need for knowledge to guide our actions, for if cosmic intelligence automatically did what was best for the world then human intelligence would likewise do what was best for the human being. It shows too why the stimulus of the Delphic oracle (*Apology* 21a) should have sent him on a fruitless search for a wiser man, the man of intelligence, a search which in time became a mission to expose the vanity of others' claims to expertise.

The Socrates of the *Clouds* and just after belonged to an Athens which, though war-torn, was optimistic. Over the next two decades he was to witness his state involved in the most notorious recklessness, impiety and injustice. Implicated in the impiety scandals of 415 B.C. were his friends Phaedrus, Eryximachus and Alcibiades; leading the injustices of the Thirty (404–3 B.C.) were his friends Critias and Charmides. He survived these troubled times, not as a result of apathy but because disappointment in others helped him remain aloof – and to resist strong pressures to participate in the injustices of 406 and 404 B.C. (*Apology* 32b–c).

Remaining aloof was no longer safe under the restored democracy of 403 on. It must have been evident to all at his trial, if not before, that he did not share the popular confidence in the new order, its institutions, or its people; he saw there neither piety nor justice. Such a man could scarcely promote the new sense of working together. With cooperation from the popular politician Anytus and the little-known Lycon, Meletus brought the notorious impiety charges, claiming that Socrates failed to acknowledge the city's gods, substituting his own private ones and undermining the moral fabric of the young. Tried before a huge jury, he lost his case by a small margin and the punishment of death proposed by the prosecution was chosen (by a greater margin) as more appropriate than the fine which he had proposed to pay. Execution, usually following rapidly upon sentence, was delayed while a religious mission to Delos was observed. Eventually, however, in spite of great efforts by his friends to have him escape, he drank from the official cup of hemlock poison.

SOCRATIC PIETY AND SOCRATIC JUSTICE

This is not the place to try and offer a reconstruction of Socrates' moral philosophy, but various important points may nevertheless be made. Both piety and justice were classed as virtues in Socratic thought, and the virtues themselves were in some sense one. They tended to coalesce in one individual, and though one thought of them as manifesting themselves in different spheres of conduct they were all founded upon some basic moral knowledge, a knowledge which was sufficient to ensure correct conduct. The virtues of justice and piety (or holiness) were considered to be especially close, as one observes in the *Euthyphro*, *Protagoras* and Xenophon's *Memorabilia* 4.6.

The *Euthyphro* can be seen as a struggle between two competing conceptions of piety, one which places enormous emphasis on the acceptance of religious traditions – both religious beliefs and religious duties such as prayers, sacrifices and purification ceremonies, the other which seems to follow no prescription, relying instead on the individual's power to discriminate between right and wrong both in theological belief and in action.

The *Apology* might also be viewed as a struggle between two conceptions of piety, one which sees one's religious duty as integrated with one's duty to the traditional values of the city – not merely participating in its religious ceremonies but also respecting its political institutions and social principles, and that of Socrates who follows at all times whatever divine orders he believes he is receiving (28e–29a, 31c–d, 37e): which must surely be a recipe for social breakdown were it to be followed by everybody. As Socrates concludes his defence speech (35c–d) he asks the jury not to expect him to do what he does not think honourable, just or holy; this is because, in soliciting an act of impiety from the jury, he would be convicting himself of overlooking the gods. He as an individual pleads the right to follow his own interpretation of divine law, an interpretation sufficiently original to give credence to the notion that his gods were not the gods of the city. In order to understand the importance of this dispute between Socrates and Athens we may refer to the *Euthyphro* once more. Euthyphro claims at 14b that piety as he conceives it preserves both private households and cities. The benefits of holiness and the disastrous effects of impiety were supposedly felt by families and by whole cities. The common good could be undermined by one dissident individual. Did Socrates have the right to follow his own private piety when the common good was at stake?

Socrates himself, however, believed that any transgressions can cause genuine harm only to the individual. Divine law does not permit the better person to be harmed by the worse (*Apology* 30b–c). No amount of impiety or injustice on Socrates' part would genuinely damage his family or state if they were not at least as guilty as he. *Gorgias* 474d–480d (like the *Republic*) depicts injustice as first and foremost a divisive quality within the soul, tearing the individual apart. Punishment is useful *for the criminal* in so far as it relieves him of injustice, the worst of all evils. So justice is a salutary quality in the soul, a quality which determines that the individual will act justly. Like other virtues it is associated closely with moral knowledge, and as such it must be allowed to determine what is just. To act contrary to one's intuitions of justice will itself promote injustice within the soul, the greatest of human evils. The individual, if he thinks he knows what is just, becomes the arbiter of what is just for him, an arbiter whom no legal or judicial body can – in his eyes – override.

Not surprisingly for one brought up in an age when Presocratic philosophers and sophists made their mark at Athens, Socrates conceived of justice as a natural corrective force, operating throughout the cosmos and in the minds of men, not as a man-made institutional one. It was easy to see such views as subversive, and the *Crito* helps counter this impression. The *Crito* places great emphasis on Socrates' acceptance of his obligations to Athenian law, not because that law is authoritative *per se*, but rather because higher law requires obedience to just agreements justly made, and an individual has agreed to abide by his city's laws in choosing to reside there. It is left to the *Apology* (37e) to make it quite clear that the higher authority, associated with God and with the individual's perception of what is right, takes precedence over this derived authority of the city's laws.

SOCRATES THE ATHENIAN

How then did Socrates rate as an Athenian? Like many of his fellow-citizens he expressed admiration for the government of Sparta,[35] but other passages suggest that he thought well of his own city.[36] He had no illusions about the dangers of democracy because he had seen too many of its excesses, and his philosophy tended to suggest that a chosen few would rule better than the many; but this translated into typically Athenian free expression of his ideas, not into the choice for some alien regime. Religions not traditional at Athens had a fascination for him, but he did not have an un-Athenian devotion to them.

When it came to war the *Apology* (28e) shows how Socrates supported Athens in all that was expected of him. When it came to applying his principles in public duties he was just as firm (32a–d), and he expected others to be firm too (35c–d). He had no ambition for political leadership, but he offered intellectual leadership instead. And just as he saw death as the inevitable outcome of principled political endeavour, so it became the outcome of his social endeavours too. We cannot see him as a poor Athenian simply because he fell into disfavour with the Athenian people – so did Pericles, so too did Alcibiades. To be a great Athenian he had to be an inspiring figure, to fight at times against the tide, to risk being seen setting oneself above the governing people. Socrates was an outstanding Athenian, and he paid the price for being one.

But was it not particularly un-Athenian to get oneself condemned for deserting the city's religion? As Michael Morgan has recently said, 'The Athens of Socrates' final years ... was the scene of extreme religious heterogeneity and of intense unresolved conflict. The old and the new mingled. Festivals were celebrated with new sincerity by some, with offhand perfunctoriness by others.'[37] In Socrates that conflict is mirrored – resolved even – in a single individual, who captures uniquely the spirit of his city in those turbulent times.

HOLINESS

SOCRATES IN CONFRONTATION: *EUTHYPHRO*

INTRODUCTION

THE *EUTHYPHRO* AND THE DEATH OF SOCRATES

Discussing the type of dialogue of the *Euthyphro*, and the other works with which it is allied, may be more productive than trying to fix upon the date of the work.[1] In terms of its dramatic date it belongs to the group set in the days between Socrates' having learnt of the charges of Meletus and his actual death. The *Theaetetus*, a discussion on the nature of knowledge, is set before he has gone to meet the charges before the King Archon; the *Euthyphro* finds him already there. The *Sophist* and *Politicus* are set the day after, but their placing seems to be due to their relationship to the *Theaetetus* only. Then come *Apology*, *Crito* and *Phaedo*. Together with the *Euthyphro*, but unlike the sequence *Theaetetus–Sophist–Politicus*, these works have an important role to play in explaining Socrates' trial and death, and in defending his role throughout.

Of the two charges against Socrates, one maintained that he was corrupting the young men of the city, the other that he was replacing the city's gods with 'gods' of his own. Plato does not seem to tackle the corruption charge head on in any one particular work, though several works (notably the *Euthydemus*, *Protagoras* and *Gorgias*) compare favourably the effects which Socrates had on his young friends with the effects of other intellectuals upon their pupils. The *Euthyphro* examines skilfully the nature of Socrates' questioning of religion, and compares it critically with a narrow religious 'fundamentalism' as propounded by Euthyphro. It does so in such a manner as to leave most readers ready to accept that Socratic doubt is more truthful and more valuable than unreasoned religious dogmatism. This is achieved in the course of a work which sets out to explore possible definitions of holiness, asking precisely the kind of difficult question that Socrates had become unpopular for.

The Virtue Dialogues

Holiness or piety was one of five Greek virtues whose close relationship or possible identity was explored in the *Protagoras*. The others were justice (with which it is closely related here too), prudence (moderation, temperance), courage, and wisdom (or knowledge). Plato explores the difficulties of defining these concepts in *Republic*, *Charmides*, *Laches* and *Theaetetus* respectively. Possible definitions of 'the fine' (a partly ethical, partly aesthetic quality) and 'the friendly' are explored in the *Hippias Major* and *Lysis*. There is no need to regard all these works as part of the same project, let alone as close in date. But the virtue group in particular seem to have a great deal in common:

1. Introductions are generally on the long side, setting the scene and bringing before the reader at least one person who might be expected (by less acute observers) to possess the virtue concerned.[2]

2. Socrates finds some excuse for demanding an explanation of that virtue, whereupon the interlocutor gives one or more examples which seem to illustrate the concept, thinking first and foremost of the way in which the virtue manifests itself in himself.[3] Socrates explains that the explanation of the virtue given cannot cover all instances of the good quality concerned.

3. The interlocutor then tries to give a universal definition, but in the first instance he generally casts the net too wide; at any rate the definition will fail to capture the essence of the *definiendum* because it misses its fundamental *goodness*.[4] Often this will result in an attempt to qualify the definition, but the essence will still elude the speakers.

4. Eventually a position is reached which appears to bear some resemblance to what Socrates is expected to have held: a muddled Socratic position. This may be done by Socrates leading the way, as in the *Euthyphro*, until the virtue can be seen as some kind of knowledge; through the mediation of some friend of Socrates (Critias in the *Charmides*, Nicias in the *Laches*) or of an opponent who perverts the Socratic position (Thrasymachus in the *Republic*); or by the interlocutor half-remembering something which Socrates is able to fill out, as in the *Theaetetus*.

5. Whatever the true Socratic position may be, the interlocutor is not able to defend this version against the assaults of Socrates himself, and the dialogue (or book, in the case of the *Republic*) ends without any satisfactory definition *or explanation* of the good quality being reached.

Within this group there are various levels of complexity. The argument is simplest in the *Laches*, probably, followed by *Euthyphro*, *Charmides*, *Republic* and *Theaetetus*.[5] Presentation is simplest in the *Euthyphro*, which confines itself to two speakers; all other works have three significant contributors.[6] *Charmides* and *Republic* 1 differ from the rest in having the dialogue set in a narrative told by Socrates; the others are 'dramatic' dialogues, containing nothing but the actual words given to the participating characters. *Charmides* and *Republic* 1 (this latter because its ultimate purpose is to introduce a major work on the nature of justice) seem less interested in exploring the correct way to arrive at a definition than the other works, though it is doubtful if any show as much interest in this topic as the *Hippias Major* or the early part of the *Meno*.

Three of this group produce imaginative comparisons between Socrates and other persons: the *Euthyphro* likens him to Daedalus, the *Charmides* (156d ff., 175e ff.) to a Thracian healer, and the *Theaetetus* (149–151, etc.) to a midwife of ideas.[7] In each of these dialogues the comparison recurs with dramatic effect.

What did Socrates think?

One question which the reader inevitably asks on reading these dialogues is: What does Socrates himself consider the virtue in question to be? Simple answers to such questions are now no longer in fashion. Undoubtedly the theme that virtue is knowledge was closely associated with Socrates, and we are in a sense approaching a Socratic position in the latter part of *Euthyphro*, *Laches*, and *Charmides* where the word knowledge (or 'understanding': *episteme*) features in definitions being discussed. But the lack of a conclusion, I suggest, is not wholly contrived. This may be because, in accordance with another Socratic theme that the virtues are one, no satisfactory division of knowledge can be established which will mark one virtue off from other virtues.[8] But it would be foolish to suppose that other definitions in a dialogue, and other features quite apart from the argument,[9] are not meant to make the reader or listener think about significant aspects of the virtue. One should not forget that Socrates wanted to make us think out for ourselves what the virtues are after taking all the most relevant material into consideration. These works invite us to use our own minds, not to identify and hence accept the Socratic position.

In the *Euthyphro* the notion that holiness is a division of justice concerned with a man's relation to the gods is not incompatible with its being some kind of knowledge, science or understanding (assuming that justice is thought to be also). The idea that holiness can be *defined* in terms of what the gods approve of, however, is never likely to have attracted Socrates or Plato; it is a bit like defining justice in terms of what a ruler or ruling class approves, and this would have worried Plato immensely. Plato's *Timaeus* has God himself acting in accordance with what he recognizes as good, not decreeing goodness to be whatever he approves. The question which excites the Socratic mind is how anybody, man or god, can *recognize* any action as an instance of goodness. What is the standard, and in what terms can we express it?[10]

On this question it must be said that the *Euthyphro* fails: the standard is not divine approval, apparently, but it will not help to say that holiness is part of justice unless we understand how to recognize an instance of justice.[11] Nor is it of much practical use to reduce holiness (in persons) to some kind of knowledge, and holy actions as those which result from such knowledge. What one must aim at is discovering the primary object of that knowledge: the standard which it must keep in mind when calculating how to act piously in any given situation. To accept that holiness is knowledge is to accept only that the would-be holy person must continue his search for the basis of the knowledge concerned. And it is this very search that Socratic philosophy is all about.

EUTHYPHRO

Introduction: in 399 B.C. a meeting takes place before the court of the King Archon.[12] *Two litigants discuss their respective cases.*

EUTHYPHRO:[13] What's come over you, Socrates, that you've 2a deserted your usual pastimes in the Lyceum,[14] and are now lurking here by the King's Porch? It surely can't be that you too have a suit before the King as I have?

SOCRATES: No indeed, the Athenians don't call it 'suit', Euthyphro, but 'prosecution'.[15]

EUTHYPHRO: What? Somebody's prosecuting you, I gather; I'll b hardly accuse you of prosecuting somebody else.

SOCRATES: No indeed.

EUTHYPHRO: Somebody's doing it to you?

SOCRATES: Quite.

EUTHYPHRO: Who is he?

SOCRATES: I don't even know the man at all well myself, Euthyphro; he's obviously some young unknown; but they call him Meletus,[16] I believe. He's from the deme of Pitthus – you might recall a Meletus from Pitthus with straight hair and not much of a beard, but a rather hooked nose.

EUTHYPHRO: I can't recall him, Socrates; but what's the prosecution he's brought against you? c

SOCRATES: What is it? No trivial one, in my view. To have discovered, as a young man, a matter of such magnitude is no mean thing. For he knows, as he claims, how the young men are being corrupted and who it is that's corrupting them. The chances are that he's a clever sort of fellow, who has noticed how – in my ignorance – I'm corrupting his contemporaries,[17] and goes to the city, as if to his mother, to tell on me. He seems to me to be the only one in politics to approach the subject correctly, because it's d quite right to make young men and their future excellence your first concern [18] – just as a good farmer is likely to concern himself first with the young plants, and only then with the others. And so Meletus too, perhaps, is first weeding out people like me who corrupt the young shoots of youth, as he puts it; then he'll evidently move on to looking after older persons and be responsible for countless great benefits to the city – the logical outcome for one who has made so promising a start.

EUTHYPHRO: I should like to think so, Socrates, but I'm very fearful of the opposite outcome. In my view he is beginning by striking at the very heart of the city in trying to harm you. So tell me, what is it he says you are doing to corrupt the youth?

SOCRATES: Heavens! Strange things, my man – if we take him literally at least. He claims I'm a manufacturer of gods, and he says this is why he's prosecuted me, that I create new gods and don't recognize the old ones. [19]

EUTHYPHRO: I see, Socrates; it's because you claim that the divine sign keeps visiting you. [20] He's launched this prosecution on the grounds that you improvise on the subject of the gods, and so he's off to the lawcourts to present you in a bad light, knowing that such things are easily misrepresented before the general public. They ridicule me too, whenever I say something in the Assembly about matters divine and predict the future for them, saying that I'm crazy! Yet in all my predictions I've spoken the truth; they just have a grudge against all of us who are inclined that way. One shouldn't be bothered about them – just meet them head on.

SOCRATES: You may be right, Euthyphro, that it's no matter to be ridiculed; you see, I don't think the Athenians are particularly concerned if they believe somebody to be clever, as long as he's not inclined to teach these skills of his. [21] But if they think anybody makes others as well just as clever, they get angry with him, perhaps because of a grudge, as you say, perhaps for some other reason.

EUTHYPHRO: I've no appetite for testing how they feel about me in this matter.

SOCRATES: Perhaps it's because you appear to make yourself scarce, and refuse to teach your skills; but I fear that I, because of my generosity, appear to them to communicate whatever I've got indiscriminately to anybody – not just without a fee, [22] for I'd even be glad to tip anybody willing to listen to me. So, as I said just now, if they were just going to ridicule me as you say they do you, it would be pleasant enough to pass the time in court jesting and laughing. Whereas now, if they are going to take things seriously, where it will all end is clear to no one but you soothsayers.

EUTHYPHRO: Oh well, perhaps it won't be such an ordeal, Socrates, and you'll contest your suit according to plan,[23] as I think I'll contest mine.

SOCRATES: And what is your suit then, Euthyphro? Are you prosecuting or defending?

EUTHYPHRO: Prosecuting.

SOCRATES: Whom?

EUTHYPHRO: Once again, it's somebody I'm supposed to be crazy to be prosecuting.

SOCRATES: What? Are you after a wild goose in flight?[24]

EUTHYPHRO: He's very far from flying – in fact he's really quite elderly.

SOCRATES: Who is this person?

EUTHYPHRO: My father.

SOCRATES: Your own father, Euthyphro?

EUTHYPHRO: Exactly.

SOCRATES: What's the charge? What's the suit for?

EUTHYPHRO: For homicide, Socrates.

SOCRATES: Heavens above! It's certainly beyond the masses to know the right course, Euthyphro. I mean, I really don't think it's an action to be taken by the man in the street, but only by somebody already far advanced along the path of wisdom.

EUTHYPHRO: Far advanced for sure, Socrates.

SOCRATES: Then is the man who died at the hands of your father one of your household? I suppose it's obvious; you wouldn't have prosecuted him merely for the sake of an outsider – not for murder.

EUTHYPHRO: It's laughable, Socrates, that you think it makes some difference whether the dead man was an outsider or a relative, and not realize that it's this alone which one must watch, whether or not the killer killed with justification. If so, let him be; otherwise proceed against him – even if the killer shares your hearth and table. Your pollution is as great as his if you live with such a person in the knowledge of what he has done, and fail to purge both yourself and him by taking legal proceedings against him. As a matter of fact, the deceased was a hired hand of mine, and, when we were farming on Naxos,[25] he was labouring there for us. Well, he got drunk, became angry with one of our servants, and slit his throat. So my father bound him hand and foot, threw him into a ditch, and sent a fellow here to find out from the Interpreter[26] what he should do. But in the meantime he took no

d interest in the prisoner, and neglected him in the belief that he was a murderer and that it was no concern of his if he died – which is exactly what happened. What with starvation, exposure and confinement, he died before the messenger got back from the interpreter. So both my father and my other relatives are all the more annoyed at this, because I am prosecuting my father for homicide on a murderer's behalf. They claim that he didn't kill him, or, even if he'd killed him outright, I still shouldn't be concerned about that type of person, because they think it's unholy for a son

e to prosecute his father for homicide – badly mistaking the position of divine law on what's holy and what's unholy.

Section A: Euthyphro is induced by ironic flattery to reveal to Socrates what he believes holiness really is. He offers his own (and similar) conduct as an example of holiness, supporting his statement with references to popular myths. Socrates expresses bewilderment at this kind of religious story, and repeats that he requires a general standard against which he may assess the holiness or otherwise of any given action.

SOCRATES: My word, Euthyphro, does that mean that you think you understand religion so exactly, matters holy and unholy that is, that you have no misgivings about the circumstances you describe? Aren't you afraid in taking your father to court that you too might turn out to be doing an unholy deed?

EUTHYPHRO: No, I would be of no use, Socrates, nor would

5a Euthyphro differ at all from the common herd of men, if I didn't understand the details of all things of this sort.

SOCRATES: Remarkable, Euthyphro! In that case it would be best for me to become your pupil; before I defend this prosecution against Meletus I could challenge him on this very point – I'd say that for my part I'd always, even in the past, considered it of great importance to know about religious matters, and that now, since he claims that I'm at fault in improvising and innovating on questions of religion, I have naturally become a pupil of *yours* – 'And presuming, Meletus,' I could say, 'that you admit that Euthyphro is an authority in such matters,[27] you must accept that my beliefs are true too, and not bring me to court; if you don't admit it, then bring a suit against that teacher of mine before you tackle me – for being the ruin of his elders, me by what he teaches me and his own father by the criticism and punishment that he metes out to him.' And if he doesn't do as I say, and either drop the suit or indict you instead of me, I'd better deliver this same challenge to him in the lawcourt.

EUTHYPHRO: Goodness yes, Socrates, if he should try a prosecution on me, I'd discover where his weak spot is, and he'd be on the defensive in court long before I was!

SOCRATES: I realize that as well as you do, dear friend; that's why I am anxious to become a pupil of yours. I know that Meletus here among others does not seem to notice you, whereas he observes me with such ease and such acuity that he's indicted me for impiety. So for heaven's sake tell me now what you were just then affirming you knew: what do you say piety and impiety are, be it in homicide or in other matters? Or isn't holiness the same in every sphere of activity, and unholiness too – the opposite of everything holy and the same as itself, so that everything to be called unholy has one standard[28] which determines its unholiness?

EUTHYPHRO: Completely so, Socrates.

SOCRATES: Tell me then, what do you say holiness is, and what is unholiness?

EUTHYPHRO: Well, I say that holiness is what I am doing now, prosecuting a criminal[29] either for murder or for sacrilegious theft or for some other such thing, regardless of whether that person happens to be one's father or one's mother or anyone else at all, whereas not to prosecute is unholy. Take a look, Socrates, and I'll show you clear evidence of divine law – the law that one must not let off the perpetrator of impiety whoever he should happen to be. I've already used it to show others that this would be the right way to proceed. You see, people themselves do in fact acknowledge that Zeus is the best and most just of the gods, and they admit that he imprisoned his own father because he had unjustly swallowed his sons;[30] and the latter too had castrated *his* father for similar reasons. But in my case they are annoyed with me for prosecuting my father for his crime, and so they make contradictory assertions about the gods' conduct and about mine.[31]

SOCRATES: Could this be why I'm defending a prosecution, Euthyphro, that whenever somebody talks like this about the gods, I find it very difficult to accept? That would be a natural reason for somebody to claim I'm in error. So now, if their view is shared

b even by you who understand such things, then evidently the rest of us are going to have to agree. What more could we say, when we admit for ourselves that we know nothing about them? But be a good fellow and tell me, do you really believe that these things happened like this?[32]

EUTHYPHRO: These and still more wonderful things, Socrates, which ordinary people do not know.

SOCRATES: Then do you think that there is really civil war among the gods, and fearful hostility and battles, and so on – the kind of

c thing described by the poets[33] and depicted by fine artists upon sacred artefacts, not least upon the Robe[34] at the Great Panathenaea which is brought up to the Acropolis,[35] covered in decorations of that kind? Are we to say that it's all true, Euthyphro?

EUTHYPHRO: Not merely that, Socrates, but (as I said just now) I'll tell you much more about divine beings, if you like; I know you'll be stunned by it.

SOCRATES: I shouldn't be surprised. But you shall tell me that another time when we have leisure. For the time being, try to

d answer more clearly what I asked you just now. You see, when I asked you before what holiness is, you didn't adequately explain it, but you said that what you are doing now, prosecuting your father for impiety, does happen to be holy.

EUTHYPHRO: Yes, I was telling you the truth, Socrates.

SOCRATES: Possibly. But look, Euthyphro, you do say that there are many other things too which are holy?

EUTHYPHRO: And so there are.

SOCRATES: Do you remember, then, that this wasn't what I was asking you to give me – one or two examples from a multitude of holy things? I asked you for that special feature[36] through which all holy things are holy. For you were in agreement, surely, that it was by virtue of a single standard[37] that all unholy things are

e unholy and all holy things holy. Or don't you remember?

EUTHYPHRO: I do.

SOCRATES: So explain to me what this standard itself is, so that when I observe it and use it as a means of comparison,[38] I may affirm that whatever actions are like it – yours or anybody else's – are holy, while those not of that kind are not.

EUTHYPHRO: Well, if that's what you want, Socrates, that's what I'll give you.

SOCRATES: Indeed, it is what I want.

Section B: Euthyphro offers a universal definition of holiness, satisfying Socrates in form but not in content. To define holiness in terms of what the gods regard with favour seems difficult for those who accept traditional tales of disputes among the gods, for the same action will please one god and annoy another. Euthyphro retreats to a position that 'the holy' is that which all the gods approve of, only to be confronted with the problem that, since what is 'divinely approved' is determined by what the gods approve, while what the gods approve is determined by what is holy, what is 'divinely approved' cannot be identical in meaning with what is holy. (Where A determines B, and B determines C, A ≠ C.) This argument has been much analysed, and is a powerful weapon against those who believe morality can be explained purely in terms of God's will.

EUTHYPHRO: Right then: what is agreeable to the gods is holy, 7a and what is not agreeable is unholy.

SOCRATES: Simply splendid, Euthyphro, you've now answered in just the way I asked you to. Admittedly I don't yet know whether you're *correct* or not,[39] but obviously you'll go on to demonstrate the truth of what you say.

EUTHYPHRO: Certainly.

SOCRATES: Come then, let's examine our thesis: for any action, or person, if it is 'divinely approved'[40] it is holy, and if it's 'divinely disapproved' it is unholy; and they're not the same, but exact opposites,[41] the holy and the unholy. Is that it?

EUTHYPHRO: That's quite right.

SOCRATES: And does it seem well stated?

EUTHYPHRO: I think so, Socrates. b

SOCRATES: Haven't we also said that the gods have quarrels,

Euthyphro, and disputes with one another, and that there is enmity among them, one with another?

EUTHYPHRO: It has.

SOCRATES: And what is the subject, please, of those disputes which cause enmity and anger? Let's look at it like this. If you and I were in dispute about which of two numbers is greater, would our dispute about this turn us into enemies, and make us angry with each other? Or should we quickly settle our differences by resorting to arithmetic?

c   EUTHYPHRO: Certainly we should.

SOCRATES: And surely, if we were in dispute about the relative size of two things, we could quickly bring an end to our dispute by resorting to measurement?

EUTHYPHRO: That is so.

SOCRATES: And weighing, I imagine, would be the way for us get a case of relative weight decided?

EUTHYPHRO: Of course.

SOCRATES: Then over what might we dispute and fail to find some solution? What could we become enemies over and get angry

d   about? Perhaps you have no ready answer, but I'll make a suggestion – consider whether it's over what's just and unjust, or fine and despicable, or good and bad. Aren't these the things over which we quarrel and can't come to an adequate means of resolution, leading us at times to make enemies of each other – you, me and everybody else?

EUTHYPHRO: Yes, it's that sort of dispute, Socrates; those are the issues.

SOCRATES: What of the gods, Euthyphro? If they disagree at all, wouldn't they disagree for just these reasons?

EUTHYPHRO: Inevitably.

e   SOCRATES: Then among the gods too, my fine fellow, your account suggests that different parties think different things just – or fine or despicable or good or bad – because they would not, apparently, be quarrelling with one another unless they were in dispute about this. Right?

EUTHYPHRO: That's correct.

SOCRATES: Surely those things which each party regards as just and good it also approves of, and they disapprove of the opposite kind.

EUTHYPHRO: Quite.

SOCRATES: But then again, according to your claim, the same things are considered just by some, unjust by others – those matters of dispute about which they quarrel and make war on one another. Is that right? 8a

EUTHYPHRO: Right.

SOCRATES: Then the same things, it's likely, are both disapproved of and approved of by the gods, and the same things would be 'divinely approved' and 'divinely disapproved'.

EUTHYPHRO: Likely enough.

SOCRATES: Then the same things would be both holy and unholy according to this account.

EUTHYPHRO: I suppose so.

SOCRATES: Then you've not answered my question, Euthyphro. I wasn't asking what turns out to be equally holy and unholy – whatever is divinely approved is also divinely disapproved, apparently. Consequently, my dear Euthyphro, it would be no surprise if, in trying to punish your father as you do now, you did something approved by Zeus and offensive to Kronos and Uranus,[42] or approved by Hephaestus and offensive to Hera;[43] and so on for any one of the gods who who disagrees with any other on the subject. b

EUTHYPHRO: Well it's my belief, Socrates, that not one of the gods disputes with another on *this*; that whoever kills someone unjustly should pay the penalty.

SOCRATES: What about men? Have you ever yet heard any human disputing the claim that a person who killed unjustly – or did anything else unjustly – should pay the penalty? c

EUTHYPHRO: There's no way they ever stop disputing these things, particularly in the courts; though they've committed a host of crimes there's nothing they won't do or say in their efforts to escape the penalty.

SOCRATES: And do they also admit they've done wrong, Euthyphro, and in spite of their admission still claim that they should not pay the penalty?

EUTHYPHRO: There's no way they do that!

SOCRATES: Then they don't do or say *everything*; for I don't think they have the nerve to argue that they should not pay the penalty even supposing they've done wrong. I think they deny they've done wrong. Is it so? d

EUTHYPHRO: That's true.

SOCRATES: So at least they're not disputing whether the wrong-doer must pay the penalty; but perhaps what they dispute is who the wrongdoer is, or what he did, or when.

EUTHYPHRO: True.

SOCRATES: Then don't the gods go through the same experience, if they really do quarrel about what's just and unjust as you say, and some of them say others are in the wrong, while those others

e   deny it? But even so, my friend, surely no one, neither god nor man, has the nerve to say that the actual wrongdoer should not pay the penalty.[44]

EUTHYPHRO: Yes, what you're saying is true, Socrates, in principle at least.

SOCRATES: But in each case, Euthyphro, I think the disputants — both men and gods, if gods really dispute things — are disputing what has been done; they quarrel about some deed, and one party says it's been done justly, the other unjustly. Right?

EUTHYPHRO: Quite so.

9a   SOCRATES: Come now, Euthyphro, my friend, teach me too — make me wiser. What proof have you got that *all* gods regard as unjust the death of that man who, as a hired hand, was responsible for somebody's death; was bound by the master of the man who was killed; and died from the conditions of his imprisonment before his imprisoner heard what he should do from the Interpreter? What proof have you that it is correct for a son to bring a prosecution on behalf of *this* kind of person, and to denounce his

b   own father for homicide? Come, try and show me some clear proof that this action, beyond a doubt, is thought by all gods to be correct. And if you show me to my satisfaction, I shall never stop acclaiming your wisdom.

EUTHYPHRO: Well, it's no small task probably, Socrates: though I *could* show you perfectly clearly.

SOCRATES: I understand: you think I'm a slower learner than the jurymen,[45] because you'll obviously give *them* a demonstration that it was unjust and that all the gods disapprove of such things.

EUTHYPHRO: With absolute clarity, Socrates, as long as they listen to what I say.

c   SOCRATES: They'll listen, as long as they think you're making sense. But here's a question which I thought of while you were speaking. I ask myself: 'However well Euthyphro were to teach me that all the gods in unison think that such a killing is unjust, what more have I learnt from him about what the holy and the unholy are?' All right, so *this* action would apparently be 'divinely disapproved', but you see, it appeared just now that what was holy and what was not were *not* distinguished in 'this way – for what was 'divinely disapproved' also appeared to be 'divinely approved'. So I'll let you off this, Euthyphro: if you like, let all the gods think it unjust and let them all disapprove of it. But what about this *d* correction that we are making to our account – to the effect that what *all* the gods disapprove of is unholy, what all approve of is holy, and what some approve of and others disapprove of is neither or both – is this how you would like our definition to run concerning the holy and the unholy?

EUTHYPHRO: What is there to prevent it, Socrates?

SOCRATES: Nothing to prevent me, Euthyphro, but you look at your own position, and ask yourself whether, on the basis of this assumption, you will most easily teach me what you promised.

EUTHYPHRO: Well, I should certainly say that what's holy is *e* whatever all the gods approve of, and that its opposite, what all the gods disapprove of, is unholy.

SOCRATES: Are we to investigate further, Euthyphro, and see if it's well stated, or are we to let it be and to accept something from ourselves or from another, agreeing that it is so if somebody merely states that this is the position? Or should we examine what the speaker means?

EUTHYPHRO: Examine it. But I myself think that this has now been excellently stated.

SOCRATES: We'll soon be in a better position to judge, my good *10a* chap. Consider the following point: is the holy approved by the gods because it's holy, or is it holy because it's approved?[46]

EUTHYPHRO: I don't know what you mean, Socrates.

SOCRATES: Well, I'll try to put it more clearly. We speak of a thing 'being carried' or 'carrying', 'being led' or 'leading', 'being seen' or 'seeing' – and you understand that all such pairs are different from each other, and how they are different.

EUTHYPHRO: I certainly *think* I understand.

SOCRATES: Is there not also something which is 'approved', while *b* that which is 'approving' is different from it?

EUTHYPHRO: Of course.

SOCRATES: Then tell me, is what's carried *being carried* because it *gets carried*,[47] or for some other reason?

EUTHYPHRO: No, for this reason.

SOCRATES: And what's being led is *being led* because it *gets led*, and what's being seen is *being seen* because it *gets seen*?

EUTHYPHRO: Certainly.

SOCRATES: Then it is *not* the case that because it's 'being seen' it 'gets seen', but the opposite – because it 'gets seen' it's 'being seen'; nor that because a thing's 'being led' it 'gets led', but because it 'gets led' it's 'being led'; nor that because a thing's 'being carried' it 'gets carried', but because it 'gets carried' it's

c 'being carried'. Isn't it obvious what I mean, Euthyphro? I mean that if something is coming to be so or is being affected, then it's not the case that it *gets to be so* because it's *coming to be so*, but that it's *coming to be so* because it *gets to be so*; nor that it *gets affected* because it's *being affected*, but that it's *being affected* because it *gets affected*. Or don't you go along with this?[48]

EUTHYPHRO: I certainly do.

SOCRATES: Then isn't *being approved* an example either of coming to be so or of being affected by something?

EUTHYPHRO: Certainly.

SOCRATES: Then this too is comparable with the previous cases: something does not *get approved* because it's *being approved* by those who approve of it, but it's *being approved* because it *gets approved*?

EUTHYPHRO: Necessarily.

d SOCRATES: Well then, what is it that we're saying about the holy, Euthyphro? Surely that it gets approved by all the gods, on your account.

EUTHYPHRO: Yes.

SOCRATES: Is that because it's holy, or for some other reason?

EUTHYPHRO: No, that's the reason.

SOCRATES: Then it *gets approved* because it's holy: it's not holy by reason of *getting approved*?

EUTHYPHRO: Presumably.

SOCRATES: Whereas it's precisely because it *gets approved* that it is approved by the gods and 'divinely approved'.

EUTHYPHRO: Of course.

SOCRATES: Then the 'divinely approved' is not holy, Euthyphro, nor is the holy 'divinely approved', as you say, but it's different from this.

EUTHYPHRO: How so, Socrates?

SOCRATES: Because we've admitted that the holy *gets approved* for the reason that it's holy, but it's not because it *gets approved* that it's holy. Right?

EUTHYPHRO: Yes.

SOCRATES: But then again the 'divinely approved', because it *gets approved* by the gods, is *divinely approved* by this very act of approval: it is *not* the case that it *gets approved* because it's *divinely approved*.

EUTHYPHRO: That is true.

SOCRATES: But if the 'divinely approved' and the holy were really the same thing, Euthyphro my friend, then: (i) if the holy were *getting approved* because of its being holy, then the 'divinely approved' too would be *getting approved* because of its being 'divinely approved'; whereas (ii) if the 'divinely approved' were 'divinely approved' on account of its *getting approved* by the gods, then the holy would be holy too on account of its *getting approved*. But as things are you can see that the two are oppositely placed, as being altogether different from each other;[49] for the one is 'such as to get approved' because it *gets approved*, while the other *gets approved* precisely because it's 'such as to get approved'. And perhaps, Euthyphro, when asked what the holy is, you don't want to point out the essence for me, but to tell me of some attribute which attaches to it,[50] saying that holiness has the attribute of being approved by all the gods; what it *is*, you've not yet said.

Interlude: Wandering arguments

So if you don't mind, don't keep me in the dark, but tell me again from the beginning what on earth the holy is, whether it gets approved by the gods or whatever happens to it (as it's not over this that we disagree). Don't hesitate: tell me what the holy and the unholy are.

EUTHYPHRO: But Socrates, I have no way of telling you what I mean; whatever explanation we set down, it always seems to go round in circles somehow, and not to be willing to stay where we positioned it.

SOCRATES: It's as if your explanations, Euthyphro, were the
c work of my predecessor Daedalus.[51] And if it had been me who
was putting forward these ideas and suggestions, you might perhaps be having a joke at my expense – you'd say that I too had
inherited from him the tendency for my verbal creations to run off
and refuse to stay wherever I'd tried to position them. But as
things are, the fundamentals of the explanation are yours – that
means a different joke is needed, for it's you they won't stay put
for, as you yourself appreciate.[52]

EUTHYPHRO: What I appreciate is that what we've been saying
demands more or less the same jibe – because its property of going
round in circles and never staying put was not conferred on it by
d me. Rather it is you who are the Daedalus; if it were up to me it
would stay as it is.

SOCRATES: Perhaps, Euthyphro, I've turned out cleverer than
him in my craft, in so far as he only made his own products
mobile, while I apparently make other people's mobile as well as
my own. And surely this is the most ingenious feature of my art,
that I don't want to be so clever. I should prefer our explanations
to stay put and be securely founded rather than have the wealth of
Tantalus[53] to complement my Daedalan cleverness.

*Section C (i): Socrates helps Euthyphro along by suggesting in
effect that holiness is a species of justice. Euthyphro agrees, but is
then required to say* which *species of justice.*

e But enough of this! Seeing that you seem to me to be taking
things easy, I'll try to help you find a way of explaining holiness to
me. And don't you withdraw exhausted before the finish! See
whether it doesn't seem necessary to you that everything holy is
just.

EUTHYPHRO: It seems so to me.

SOCRATES: Then is all that is just holy? Or is it the case that all
12a that's holy is just, whereas not all that's just is holy[54] – part of it's
holy and part of it's different?

EUTHYPHRO: I don't follow your question, Socrates.

SOCRATES: But surely you're younger than me no less than
you're wiser! As I say, you're taking it easy, basking in the wealth
of your wisdom. Make a bit of an effort, Euthyphro; it's actually

not hard to grasp what I mean. I am really claiming the opposite of what was said by the poet[55] who composed the lines:

But to speak of Zeus, the agent who nurtured[56] all this,
You don't dare; for where is found fear, there is also found shame.   *b*

I disagree with this poet. Shall I tell you how?

EUTHYPHRO: Certainly.

SOCRATES: I don't think it's true that 'where is found fear, there is also found shame', as it seems to me that many people, in fear of disease and poverty and other such things, *are* fearful but *aren't* at all shameful of these things which they fear. Don't you think so?

EUTHYPHRO: Certainly.

SOCRATES: But where there is shame, at least, there is also fear; for does anybody, feeling shameful at, or ashamed of, some deed, fail to take fright and feel apprehensive of an unsavoury reputation?

EUTHYPHRO: He's apprehensive, certainly.   *c*

SOCRATES: Then it's not right to say 'where is found fear, there is also found shame', but where is found shame, fear also is found, though shame is not found everywhere where fear is. For I imagine fear has a wider distribution than shame, because shame is a division of fear like odd is of number, so that it's not true that where there is number, there is also found odd, but where there is odd there is also found number. You follow me now, surely?

EUTHYPHRO: Certainly.

SOCRATES: Then this was also the kind of thing I meant in the case of my earlier question. Is it 'where is a just thing, there is also a holy one', or 'where is a holy thing, there is also a just one, but not a holy   *d* one everywhere there's a just one', the holy being a division of the just? Shall we put it that way, or do you take a different view?

EUTHYPHRO: No, that's it; your explanation seems correct to me.

SOCRATES: See what comes next, then. If what's holy is a division of the just, it seems that we must then discover the precise kind of division of the just that is holy. If you had asked me a question about what came up just now, for instance what kind of division of number even is – what this type of number actually is – I should have said that it's number that can be represented as two equal limbs rather than as unequal ones.[57] Don't you think so?

EUTHYPHRO: I do indeed.

e SOCRATES: Now it's your turn – try to give me the same type of explanation of the kind of division of justice what's holy is; then I can tell Meletus too that he should no longer be unjust to me and prosecute me for impiety, because I've already learnt well enough from you what is pious and holy and what is not.

Section C (ii): Euthyphro says that holiness is that part of justice which looks after the gods. Socrates worries that this might imply that the gods are improved by holiness. Euthyphro explains 'looking after' in terms of serving them. Socrates worries about the purpose to which such a service contributes.

EUTHYPHRO: Well, I believe that *this* is the part of the just which is pious and holy, the one concerned with looking after the gods, whereas that concerned with looking after men is the remaining part of the just.[58]

SOCRATES: Yes, I think that's a good answer, Euthyphro; but I still
13a need one little thing to be cleared up – I don't understand what it is you mean by 'looking after'. You wouldn't be meaning that we also look after the gods in the same way as we look after other things. We do speak that way, I suppose; for instance, we say that not everybody knows how to look after horses, only the groom, right?

EUTHYPHRO: Quite so.

SOCRATES: Because the groom's art is looking after horses.

EUTHYPHRO: Yes.

SOCRATES: Nor indeed does everybody know how to look after dogs; only the kennel-master.

b EUTHYPHRO: That's so.

SOCRATES: Because the kennel-master's art is looking after dogs.

EUTHYPHRO: Yes.

SOCRATES: Whereas the cattle-farmer's is looking after cattle?

EUTHYPHRO: Quite.

SOCRATES: But holiness and piety is looking after the gods, Euthyphro? Is that what you claim?

EUTHYPHRO: I certainly do.

SOCRATES: Surely any case of 'looking after' has the same effect. I'll put it like this: it's for the improvement and benefit of the thing looked after, just as you can see that horses are benefited and improved by grooming. Or don't you think so?

EUTHYPHRO: I do indeed.

SOCRATES: And dogs presumably are benefited by the kennel-master's art, cows by the cattle-farmer's, and so on in all other cases. Or do you think that things are looked after to their detriment?

EUTHYPHRO: No indeed, I don't.

SOCRATES: For their advantage then?

EUTHYPHRO: Of course.

SOCRATES: Well then, is holiness too, *qua* 'looking after' the gods, of benefit to the gods? Does it make them better? And would *you* agree to this, that whenever you do something holy you're improving one of the gods?[59]

EUTHYPHRO: No indeed, I wouldn't.

SOCRATES: No, nor do I think you mean that, Euthyphro, far from it; it was for this very reason that I asked you what you meant by 'looking after' the gods – because I didn't believe you meant anything like that.

EUTHYPHRO: And you were quite right, Socrates; I don't mean anything like that.

SOCRATES: Let's get to the point: what kind of 'looking after' the gods could holiness be?

EUTHYPHRO: It's like slaves looking after their masters, Socrates.

SOCRATES: I get it – it would be a kind of service to the gods, perhaps?

EUTHYPHRO: Of course.

SOCRATES: Could you then tell me, what goal does 'service to doctors' help to achieve? Don't you think it's health?

EUTHYPHRO: Certainly.

SOCRATES: What about service to shipbuilders? What goal's achievement does it serve?

EUTHYPHRO: Obviously a boat's, Socrates.

SOCRATES: And service to builders, one supposes, helps to achieve a house?

EUTHYPHRO: Yes.

SOCRATES: Tell me then, please, to what goal's achievement would service to the gods be contributing? It's obvious that you know, seeing that you claim that no one knows more than you about religion.

EUTHYPHRO: Yes, and I'm telling the truth, Socrates.

SOCRATES: Tell me then, in heaven's name, what ever is that marvellous work [60] which the gods accomplish using us as their servants?

EUTHYPHRO: A multitude of good things, Socrates.

14a SOCRATES: And so do generals, my friend, but all the same you could easily state their principal aim by saying that they achieve victory in war. No?

EUTHYPHRO: Of course they do.

SOCRATES: Then again, farmers also achieve a multitude of good things. But still their principal achievement is food from the earth.

EUTHYPHRO: Certainly.

SOCRATES: What about the multitude of fine things that the gods achieve? What's the principal aim of their endeavour?

Section C (iii): Euthyphro becomes impatient, and explains holiness as knowing how to pray and sacrifice in a way that will please the gods. Socrates reduces this to a knowledge of how to trade with the gods, and continues to press for an explanation of how the gods will benefit.

b EUTHYPHRO: Only a while ago I told you, Socrates, that it was too great a task to learn with accuracy what all these things are. However, let me tell you this without further ado: if one knows how to say and do things gratifying to the gods in prayer and in sacrifice, this is what's holy, and such conduct is the salvation not only of private households but also of the public well-being of cities. And the opposite of what is gratifying is impious, and turns everything upside down, and wrecks it.

SOCRATES: You could have told me the principal thing I asked for in far fewer words, Euthyphro. The trouble is, you're not c really trying to teach me – it's obvious. Even now you turned aside when you were on the point of giving the answer, by which I could have learnt well enough from you what holiness is. So now, because a lover can't help following where his beloved's whim leads, what is it again that you are calling 'holy' and 'holiness'? A kind of science of sacrifice and prayer, isn't it?

EUTHYPHRO: That's my view.

SOCRATES: Surely sacrifice is making a donation to the gods, while prayer is requesting something from them.

EUTHYPHRO: Yes indeed, Socrates.

SOCRATES: Then holiness, on this account, would be the science   *d*
of requests and donations to the gods.

EUTHYPHRO: You've understood well what I meant, Socrates.

SOCRATES: That's because I'm a zealot, Euthyphro, zealous for
your wisdom, and I'm keeping a close eye upon it, so that what
you say does not fall unfettered to the ground. So tell me, what is
this service to the gods? You claim that it's asking from them and
giving to them?

EUTHYPHRO: I do.

SOCRATES: Then wouldn't the correct kind of asking be to ask
them for those things that we need?

EUTHYPHRO: Of course.

SOCRATES: And again, the correct kind of giving would be to   *e*
bestow upon them in return what they happen to need from us? It
wouldn't be a case of skilled giving, I assume, to give somebody
things of which that person has no need.

EUTHYPHRO: Quite true, Socrates.

SOCRATES: Then holiness would be a kind of skill in trading
between gods and men.

EUTHYPHRO: A trading-skill, if it makes you happier to put it
like that.

SOCRATES: Well, I'm no happier unless it turns out to be true.
Show me what benefit for the gods eventuates from the donations
which they receive from us. It's clear to anybody what they   15*a*
contribute, because nothing is good for us except what comes
from them;[61] but how are they benefited by what they receive from
us? Or do we come off so much better than them in this trade, that
we get all good things from them, while they get none from us?

*Coda: Euthyphro affirms that the gods receive no benefit from our
service, only gratification. Socrates recognizes that explaining holiness in terms of the gratification of the gods is similar to explaining
it in terms of their approval. The argument has now gone round in
a circle. Socrates demands a fresh start, but Euthyphro has had
enough.*

EUTHYPHRO: Do you really suppose, Socrates, that the gods are
benefited as a result of what they get from us?

SOCRATES: Well, whatever could these gifts of ours to the gods
be, Euthyphro?

EUTHYPHRO: What else, do you think, but honour and tokens of esteem, and, as I said just now, *gratification*.

b SOCRATES: So it is something the gods have found gratifying, Euthyphro – the holy – but not what's beneficial or approved by the gods.

EUTHYPHRO: In my view it's the most approved of all things.

SOCRATES: Then the holy is again, it seems, what's approved by the gods.

EUTHYPHRO: Absolutely.

SOCRATES: Then will you wonder, when you say this, that your stated views are shown to be shifting rather than staying put, and will you accuse me of being the Daedalus who makes them shift, when you yourself are far more skilled than Daedalus and are making them go round in circles? Or don't you see that our account has been going round and has arrived back at the same

c place? Surely you remember that earlier in the discussion the holy and the 'divinely approved' did not appear the same to us; they were different from one another. Or don't you remember?

EUTHYPHRO: I do.

SOCRATES: Well, don't you realize that you're now saying that the holy is what's approved by the gods? Surely that's what's 'divinely approved', isn't it?

EUTHYPHRO: Certainly.

SOCRATES: Well, either our conclusion then was wrong, or, if it was right, our present position is not correct.

EUTHYPHRO: Apparently.

SOCRATES: Then we must inquire again from the beginning about what the holy is, as I'll not be willing to play the coward before I

d learn. Don't make light of me, but apply your mind in every way and do your best to tell me the truth. For if any man knows, you do, and, like Proteus,[62] you're not to be let go until you speak. For if you didn't know clearly what holiness and unholiness are there's no way that you would have taken it upon yourself to prosecute your father, an elderly man, for a labourer's murder; but you would have both been worried about the gods and ashamed before men if you took such a risk, in case you should be wrong in doing it. As it is, I know well enough that you think[63] you have true

e knowledge of what's holy and what's not. Tell me then, most worthy Euthyphro, and don't conceal what you think it is.

EUTHYPHRO: Another time, Socrates; right now I have an urgent engagement somewhere, and it's time for me to go.

SOCRATES: Look what you're doing, my friend! You're going off and dashing me from that great hope which I entertained; that I could learn from you what was holy and what not and quickly have done with Meletus's prosecution by demonstrating to him that I have now become wise in religion thanks to Euthyphro, and no longer improvise and innovate in ignorance of it – and moreover that I could live a better life for the rest of my days.[64]

16a

JUSTICE AND DUTY (i)

SOCRATES SPEAKS AT HIS TRIAL: THE *APOLOGY*

INTRODUCTION

The *Apology* purports to give us a version of what Socrates said in
court when facing a public prosecution for impiety on the grounds
that he was failing to acknowledge the city's gods, introducing
new divinities, and corrupting the youth. It gives his main defence
speech, his *epitimesis* (estimation of the correct penalty) and his
final address to the jurors after condemnation to death. It covers
matters which had taken place in an open Athenian court before a
very large jury (traditionally said to have been 500 or 501), matters
which were therefore public knowledge. This placed restrictions
on the extent to which Plato could have invented any of the
principal themes of the speech, and Xenophon's rival *Apology*
(1.1) confirms that the tone of uncompromising aloofness was
actually adopted by Socrates. Consequently it has sometimes been
thought that in this work we have the most faithful picture of the
real Socrates that we possess.

Nobody, however, neither Plato nor one of his readers, could
remember every word spoken, and we might seriously question
whether Plato wanted simply to reproduce what Socrates had said.
He was undoubtedly concerned to ensure that Socrates was remembered in the best possible light, and the actual speech was not
conspicuous for its success. The essence of what was said had to
be turned to better use. Thus debate continues as to how accurate
Plato's picture of Socrates can be. It is very different from Xenophon's picture, and it may have been just as different from that
portrayed by other Socratic writers.

Two unknowns greatly complicate this question: the date of the
Apology and Plato's 'publication intentions'. Though we can
accept that the work is early, estimates do not always put it within
a decade of Socrates' death.[1] The later it was written, the fainter

men's memories and the greater the likelihood that details were manipulated to suit a changed intellectual climate. Further, if for apologetic reasons Plato wanted to circulate a written version among literate Athenians, then he would be defeating his purpose if he did not visibly present the Socrates they had known; whereas if he intended the work for private readings in intellectual circles, (i) it is unlikely that the apologetic purpose was so important; and (ii) his audience might very well have been used to seeing a different side of Socrates from that which had been visible in court and in other public places.

THE LANGUAGE OF THE *APOLOGY*

The *Apology* is unusual in so far as the speaker actually draws attention to his delivery. Socrates is concerned that the jurors should accept quietly his conversational manner (17c–18a, 27b). Less unusual is his alleged unfamiliarity with the speech of the courts – in fact the prologue has seemed to most commentators to be a parody of forensic rhetoric, using device after device that we have come to associate with court speeches.[2] Professions of inexperience in speaking were commonplace, and this profession, one suspects, might be another element in the parody. It is characteristic of Plato, when making Socrates resist or criticize the methods of others, to show in passing that Socrates did in fact have as much ability to utilize them himself if he wanted to.

Some passages of the *Apology* do sound somewhat rhetorical, others sound typical of Socrates' familiar manner; there is a chunk of Socratic cross-examination, some story-telling and some lecturing. The work is thus something of a literary *tour de force*, giving plenty of scope for Plato to demonstrate a variety of skills. Works like the *Phaedrus* and *Menexenus* show that he enjoyed imitating the manner of the orators. No translation can match the changes of style.

THE TREATMENT OF MELETUS

No reader of the *Euthyphro* would expect Meletus to be well treated in the *Apology*, but it would be difficult to have anticipated the dismissive tone which is found here. The charges against Socrates were grave, and one would have expected him to take them seriously and to look upon his accuser as a serious opponent. He would have been expected to attack the accuser directly, doing his best to return like for like. This was not Socrates' way. Rather he sneers at his opponent, suggesting not that he is lawless or lacking in public spirit, but rather that he is deficient as a moral being. Meletus undergoes the kind of Socratic cross-examination that so many Athenians had experienced, and it is not difficult to feel that he too has been unjustly treated – not difficult to imagine oneself in a similar situation. The cross-examination provides a vivid illustration of what Socratic interrogation could be like.

At various points (24c with note on the text, 24d, 25c, 26b) there is a crude play on Meletus's name. He is 'refuted' by Socrates on the basis of Socratic thought, which seems somewhat counter-intuitive (25d–26a). He is led into denying that Socrates acknowledged any god at all (when taking the question to refer to any real god), and then shown that if Socrates introduces new divinities he acknowledges either (real or imagined) gods or other beings implying the existence of (real or imagined) gods. The jury will feel not that Meletus is lying, but rather that he is not sharp enough to be able to deal with Socrates' sophistry.

Finally, at the end of the cross-examination, Socrates declares that he doesn't need to refute at length the actual charge brought by Meletus. He had devoted six Stephanus pages to defending the imaginary charges of the old accusers; he devotes only four to Meletus's accusations. Another seven and a half pages follow in which little is said that has any direct bearing on the charges of Meletus.

Meletus, like the other two accusers, does not suffer the usual outright attack on his past and on his character, as if Socrates acknowledges that such matters ought not to be taken into con-sideration. But still Socrates has taken as unpleasant a line as possible, being unpleasant in an indirect manner, and he has made no attempt to see any redeeming features in what Meletus has done. It is typical that after the vote to condemn Socrates has been taken, he makes a jibe about Meletus's not having earned one fifth of the votes himself.

DID SOCRATES REPLY TO THE CHARGES OR CONFIRM THEM?

In the second century A.D. Maximus Tyrius wrote a treatise entitled 'Did Socrates do the right thing in not responding to the charges?' Maximus's sources are Xenophon, Aeschines and, above all, Plato. The title suggests that Socrates was acknowledged to have made no serious attempt to defend himself. There is much contemporary debate about how far this was correct, with Stone (1987) taking the view that it was, and Brickhouse and Smith (1989) denying it. There is much that is left unsaid in Plato's *Apology*, but we must bear in mind (with Brickhouse and Smith) the *possibility* that certain aspects of the defence were left to others, who spoke on his behalf. All the same, some things had to be said by Socrates if they were to be said at all, principally that he did in fact acknowledge the gods whom the city honoured, and that the oddities like his divine sign did not conflict with his basic acceptance of the religion sanctioned by the State. At no time did he state this. Frequently during his speech he makes claims relating to religion which would certainly have been at odds with Athenian views, and would have appeared to confirm that his beliefs had some other religious foundation.

By contrast the claim that he corrupted the young would seem to have been answered reasonably, except that we do not quite know what the accusers had based their claims upon. They may very well have regarded him as a considerable early influence on Charmides and Critias, both of whom participated in the discredited regime of the Thirty Tyrants. But they may not have openly said so, and Socrates was hardly going to mention such names. His blanket claim that he had never been the formal teacher of anybody, and could not be held responsible for any misapplication of his methods, would seem to answer any suspicions of his links with these two.

The curious thing about the *Apology* is that a very large part is given over to Socrates' attempts to dispel the long-term prejudice against him, while the tactics adopted were most likely to increase that prejudice. The cross-examination of Meletus is not a good advertisement for the elenchus. The unyielding attitude to proposed illegal measures in the past might have stood in his favour but for the unyielding attitude he was now taking to a legitimate court of Athenian law. Socrates' limited claims to wisdom might have been appreciated more had he not at the same time been suggesting a powerful ignorance among the rest of mankind. His mission in turning any conversation into a deep moral examination of the interlocutor would have looked better if he had not allowed his defence speech to change (some would say deteriorate) into a deep and critical examination of the Athenian courts themselves – and of juries in particular.

Could it not be that Socrates' so-called divine mission was really subversive rather than corrective? What kind of an example was it to the young men of the city to be showing a respect for the authority of the courts which was less than the respect for a God which he, as an individual, believed was speaking to him? Could they not make appeals to their own private religious ideas, and exempt themselves from the authority of the democratic institutions too? Socrates' very conduct in court could be taken as proof that his conduct in general promoted insubordination and a lack of respect for any authority. He had himself shown that he had no respect for the politicians, poets and skilled craftsmen, and one might readily guess that his followers would show no such respect either. Socrates *was* a problem; he did breed attitudes which were difficult for the city to handle. His exposure of ignorance had no positive results for the city's ambitions, and might rather have been suspected of undermining people's much-needed confidence during a critical period of reconstruction.

Socrates can be accused of convicting himself; likewise the jury can be accused of convicting an innocent man on false charges. Looked at from Socrates' point of view, there was little he could do without surrendering his principles, and there was no reason why they should be surrendered. He thought himself called by God in a given direction, and nothing would persuade him to change. But if one did not accept the God of Socrates, only the gods of the city, then Socrates had produced no reason whatever why he should not submit to the good judgement of the court. Neither side was in any position to budge. We have the classic situation of a Greek tragedy, where a person of high moral principle is confronted step by step with a situation from which there is no escape, often through conflict with some other person or persons whose principles are no less understandable, and may frequently – as in Sophocles' *Antigone* – represent the perceived interests of the state. The tragic potential of the situation is unlikely to have been lost on Plato, a man of great dramatic capabilities.

THE APOLOGY

Introduction: Socrates starts in rhetorical fashion, answering his opponent's claim that he will try to mislead the jury. He promises the truth, and begs to be allowed to speak in his own conversational style, into which he now slips.

What effect my accusers have had upon you, gentlemen, I do not know, but for my own part I was almost carried away by them; their arguments were so convincing. On the other hand, scarcely a word of what they said was true. I was especially astonished at one of their many misrepresentations: the point where they told you that you must be careful not to let me deceive you, implying that I am a skilful speaker. I thought that it was peculiarly brazen of them to have the nerve to tell you this, only just before events must prove them wrong, when it becomes obvious that I have not the slightest skill as a speaker — unless, of course, by a skilful speaker they mean one who speaks the truth. If that is what they mean, I would agree that I am an orator, and quite out of their class.

My accusers, then, as I maintain, have said little or nothing that is true, but from me you shall hear the whole truth; not, I can assure you, gentlemen, in flowery language like theirs, decked out with fine words and phrases; no, what you will hear will be improvised thoughts in the first words that occur to me, confident as I am in the justice of my cause; and I do not want any of you to expect anything different. It would hardly be suitable, gentlemen, for a man of my age to address you in the artificial language of a student exercise. One thing, however, I do most earnestly beg and entreat of you: if you hear me defending myself in the same language which it has been my habit to use, both around the trading stalls of the market-place (where many of you have heard me) and elsewhere, do not be surprised, and do not make a fuss

d because of it. My situation, you see, is as follows: this is my first
appearance in a court of law, at the age of seventy; and so I am a
complete stranger to the language of this place. Now if I were
really from another country, you would assuredly excuse me if I
18a spoke in the manner and dialect in which I had been brought up;
and so in the present case I make this request of you, which I think
is only reasonable: to disregard the manner of my speech – it
doesn't matter how it compares – and to consider and concentrate
your attention upon this one question, whether my claims are just
or not. That is the first duty of the juryman, and it is the pleader's
duty to speak the truth.

*Section A: Ignoring the court charges for the moment, Socrates
talks of the origins of his unpopularity in people's belief (i) that he
is one of those who seek physical explanation rather than divine
ones for everyday phenomena (i.e. a typical Presocratic philosopher), and (ii) that he is adept at pleading the poorer case more
powerfully than the better one (i.e. a typical sophist).*

The proper course for me, gentlemen of the jury, is to deal first
with the earliest charges that have been falsely brought against me,
b and with my earliest accusers; and then with the later ones. I make
this distinction because I have already been accused in your
hearing by a great many people for a great many years, though
without a word of truth; and I am more afraid of those people
than I am of Anytus and his colleagues,[3] although they are formidable enough. But the others are still more formidable; I mean the
people who took hold of so many of you when you were children[4]
and tried to fill your minds with untrue accusations against me,
saying, 'There is a clever man called Socrates who has theories
about the heavens and has investigated everything below the earth,
c and can make the weaker argument defeat the stronger.'[5] It is
these people, gentlemen, the disseminators of these rumours, who
are my dangerous accusers; because those who hear them suppose
that anyone who inquires into such matters does not also believe
in gods.[6] Besides, there are a great many of these accusers, and
they have been accusing me now for a great many years; and what
is more, they approached you at the most impressionable age,
when some of you were children or adolescents; and they literally

won their case by default, because there was no one to defend me. And the most problematic thing of all is that it is impossible for d me even to know and tell you their names, unless one of them happens to be a playwright.[7] All these people, who have tried to stir up convictions against me out of envy and love of slander – and some too merely passing on what they have been told by others – all these are very difficult to deal with. It is impossible to bring them here for cross-examination; one simply has to conduct one's defence and argue one's case against an invisible opponent, because there is no one to answer. So I ask you to accept my statement that my critics fall into two classes: on the one hand my immediate accusers, and on the other those earlier ones whom I e have mentioned; and you must suppose that I have first to defend myself against the latter. After all, you heard them accusing me at an earlier date and much more vehemently than these more recent accusers.

Very well, then; I must begin my defence, gentlemen, and I must try, in the short time that I have,[8] to rid your minds of a false 19a impression which is the work of many years. I should like this to be the result, gentlemen, assuming it to be for your advantage and my own; and I should like to be successful in my defence; but I think that it will be difficult, and I am quite aware of the nature of my task. However, let that turn out as God wills; I must obey the law and make my defence.[9]

Let us go back to the beginning and consider what the charge is that has made people so critical of me, and has encouraged Meletus to draw up this indictment. Very well; what did my critics b say in attacking my character? I must read out their affidavit, so to speak, as though they were my legal accusers. 'Socrates is committing an injustice, in that he inquires into things below the earth and in the sky, and makes the weaker argument defeat the stronger, and teaches others to follow his example.'[10] It runs something like c that. You have seen it for yourselves in the play by Aristophanes, where Socrates is lifted around, proclaiming that he is walking on air, and uttering a great deal of other nonsense about things of which I know nothing whatsoever.[11] I mean no disrespect for such knowledge, if anyone really is versed in it – I do not want any more lawsuits brought against me by Meletus[12] – but the fact is, gentlemen, that I take no interest in these things. What is more, I d call upon the greater part of you as witnesses to my statement, and I appeal to all of you who have ever listened to me talking (and there are a great many to whom this applies) to reassure one another on this point. Tell one another whether any one of you has ever heard me discuss such questions briefly or at length; and then you will realize that the other popular reports about me are equally unreliable.[13]

Section B: Socrates denies that he is a professional teacher.

The fact is that there is nothing in any of these charges; and if you have heard anyone say that I try to educate people and charge
e   a fee,[14] there is no truth in that either – though I think that it is a fine thing if a man has the ability to teach, as in the case of Gorgias of Leontini, Prodicus of Ceos and Hippias of Elis.[15] Each one of these is perfectly capable of going into any city and actually persuading the young men to leave the company of their fellow-
20a citizens, with any of whom they can associate for nothing, attach themselves to him, pay money for the privilege, and be grateful into the bargain. There is another expert too from Paros who I discovered was here on a visit. I happened to meet a man who has paid more in sophists' fees than all the rest put together – I mean Callias, the son of Hipponicus;[16] so I asked him (he has two sons, you see): 'Callias,' I said, 'if your sons had been colts or calves, we should have had no difficulty in finding and engaging a trainer to
b   make them excel in the appropriate qualities; and this trainer would have been some sort of horse-dealer or agriculturalist. But seeing that they are human beings, whom do you intend to get as their instructor? Who is the expert in perfecting the virtues of people in a society? I assume from the fact of your having sons that you must have considered the question. Is there such a person or not?' 'Certainly', said he. 'Who is he, and where does he come from?' said I, 'and what does he charge?' 'Evenus of Paros,[17] Socrates,' said he, 'and his fee is 500 drachmae.' I felt that Evenus was to be congratulated if he really was a master of this art and
c   taught it at such a moderate fee.[18] I should certainly become a proud and gentlemanly figure if I understood these things; but in fact, gentlemen, I do not.

Section C: Socrates explains what his own activity has been. The oracle of Apollo has declared that he is the wisest of men, and he has been trying to find men wiser than he is as part of his search for the god's meaning. The section begins in Socrates' conversational manner, but the narrative which follows is stylistically very like that of other Athenian speeches for the lawcourts.

Here perhaps one of you might interrupt me and say, 'But what is it that you do, Socrates? How is it that you have been misrepresented like this? Surely all this talk and gossip about you would never have arisen if you had confined yourself to ordinary activities, but only if your behaviour was abnormal. Give us the explanation, if you do not want us to draw our own conclusions.' This *d* seems to me to be a reasonable request, and I will try to explain to you what it is that has given me this false notoriety; so please give me your attention. Perhaps some of you will think that I am not being serious; but I assure you that I am going to tell you the whole truth.

I have gained this reputation, gentlemen, from nothing more or less than a kind of wisdom. What kind of wisdom do I mean? Human wisdom, I suppose. It seems that I really am wise in this limited sense. Presumably the geniuses whom I mentioned just now are wise in a *e* wisdom that is more than human – I do not know how else to account for it, because I certainly do not have this knowledge, and anyone who says that I have is lying and just saying it to slander me. Now, gentlemen, please do not interrupt me even if I seem to make an extravagant claim; for what I am going to tell you is not a tale of my own; I am going to refer you to an unimpeachable authority. I shall call as witness to my wisdom (such as it is) the god at Delphi.[19]

You know Chaerephon,[20] I presume. He was a friend of mine from boyhood, and a good democrat who played his part with the *21a* rest of you in the recent expulsion and restoration.[21] And you know what he was like; how enthusiastic he was over anything that he had once undertaken. Well, one day he actually went to Delphi and asked this question of the god – as I said before, gentlemen, please do not interrupt – what he asked was whether there was anyone wiser than myself. The Pythian priestess replied that there was no one. As Chaerephon is dead, the evidence for my statement will be supplied by his brother here.[22]

b   Please consider my object in telling you this. I want to explain to you how the attack on my reputation first started.[23] When I heard about the oracle's answer, I said to myself, 'What is the god saying, and what is his hidden meaning? I am only too conscious that I have no claim to wisdom, great or small; so what can he mean by asserting that I am the wisest man in the world? He cannot be telling a lie; that would not be right for him.'[24]

After puzzling about it for some time, I set myself at last with considerable reluctance to check the truth of it in the following way. I went to interview a man with a high reputation for

c   wisdom, because I felt that here if anywhere I should succeed in disproving the oracle and pointing out to my divine authority, 'You said that I was the wisest of men, but here is a man who is wiser than I am.'

Well, I gave a thorough examination to this person – I need not mention his name, but it was one of our politicians that I was studying when I had this experience – and in conversation with him I formed the impression that although in many people's opinion, and especially in his own, he appeared to be wise, in fact he was not. Then when I began to try to show him that he only thought he was wise and was not really so, my efforts were

d   resented both by him and by many of the other people present. However, I reflected as I walked away: 'Well, I am certainly wiser than this man. It is only too likely that neither of us has any knowledge to boast of; but he thinks that he knows something which he does not know, whereas I am quite conscious of my ignorance. At any rate it seems that I am wiser than he is to this small extent, that I do not think that I know what I do not know.'

After this I went on to interview a man with an even greater reputation for wisdom, and I formed the same impression again;

e   and here too I incurred the resentment of the man himself and a number of others.

From that time on I interviewed one person after another. I realized with distress and alarm that I was making myself unpopular, but I felt compelled to put the god's business first; since I was trying to find out the meaning of the oracle, I was bound to

22a   interview everyone who had a reputation for knowledge. And by Dog,[25] gentlemen (for I must be frank with you), my honest impression was thus: it seemed to me, as I pursued my investigation at the god's command, that the people with the greatest reputations were almost entirely deficient, while others who were supposed to be their inferiors were much more noteworthy for their general good sense.

I want you to think of my adventures as a cycle of labours [26] undertaken to establish the truth of the oracle once for all. After I had finished with the politicians I turned to the poets, dramatic, lyric, and all the rest, in the belief that here I should expose myself b as a comparative ignoramus.[27] I used to pick up what I thought were some of their most polished works and question them closely about the meaning of what they had written, in the hope of incidentally enlarging my own knowledge. Well, gentlemen, I hesitate to tell you the truth, but it must be told. It is hardly an exaggeration to say that any of the bystanders could have explained those poems better than their actual authors. So I soon made up my mind about the poets too: I decided that it was not wisdom c that enabled them to write their poetry, but a kind of instinct or inspiration, such as you find in seers and prophets who deliver all their sublime messages without knowing in the least what they mean.[28] It seemed clear to me that the poets were in much the same case; and I also observed that the very fact that they were poets made them think that they had a perfect understanding of all other subjects, of which they were totally ignorant. So I left that line of inquiry too with the same sense of advantage that I had felt in the case of the politicians.

Last of all I turned to the skilled craftsmen.[29] I knew quite well that I had practically no understanding myself, and I was sure that d I should find them full of impressive knowledge. In this I was not disappointed; they understood things which I did not, and to that extent they were wiser than I was. However, gentlemen, these professional experts seemed to share the same failing which I had noticed in the poets; I mean that on the strength of their technical proficiency they claimed a perfect understanding of every other subject, however important; and I felt that this error eclipsed their positive wisdom. So I made myself spokesman for the oracle, and e asked myself whether I would rather be as I was – neither wise with their wisdom nor ignorant with their ignorance – or possess both qualities as they did. I replied through myself to the oracle that it was best for me to be as I was.

Section D: The results of Socrates' interrogations: odium, poverty, wealthy youths who enjoy imitating him, and charges that he is responsible for corrupting them.

The effect of these investigations of mine, gentlemen, has been to arouse against me a great deal of hostility, and hostility of a particularly bitter and persistent kind, which has resulted in various malicious suggestions, and in having that term 'wise' applied to me. This is due to the fact that whenever I succeed in disproving another person's claim to wisdom in a given subject, the bystanders assume that I know everything about that subject myself.[30] But the truth of the matter, gentlemen, is likely to be this: that real wisdom is the property of the god, and this oracle is his way of telling us that human wisdom has little or no value. It seems to me that he is not referring literally to Socrates, but has merely taken my name as an example, as if he would say to us, 'The wisest of you men is he who has realized, like Socrates, that in respect of wisdom he is really worthless.'

That is why I still go about seeking and searching in obedience to the divine command, if I think that anyone is wise, whether citizen or stranger; and when I decide that he is not wise, I try to assist the god[31] by proving that he is not. This occupation has kept me too busy to do much either in politics or in my own affairs; in fact, my service to God has reduced me to extreme poverty.

Furthermore the young men – those with wealthy fathers and plenty of leisure – have of their own accord[32] attached themselves to me because they enjoy hearing other people cross-questioned. These often take me as their model, and go on to try to question other persons; whereupon, I suppose, they find an unlimited number of people who think that they know something, but really know little or nothing. Consequently their victims become annoyed, not with themselves but with me; and they complain that there is a pestilential busybody called Socrates who fills young people's heads with wrong ideas. If you ask them what he does, and what he teaches that has this effect, they have no answer, not knowing what to say; but as they do not want to admit their confusion, they fall back on the stock charges against any seeker after wisdom: that he teaches his pupils about things in the heavens and below the earth, and to disbelieve in gods, and to make the weaker argument defeat the stronger. They would be very loath, I fancy, to admit the truth: which is that they are being convicted of pretending to knowledge when they are entirely ignorant. They were so jealous, I suppose, for their own reputation,   *e* and also energetic and numerically strong, and spoke about me with such vigour and persuasiveness, that their harsh criticisms have for a long time now been monopolizing your ears.

Section E: Conclusion of the narrative concerned with Socrates' activities and of Socrates' reply to the 'Old Accusers'.

There you have the causes which led to the attack upon me by Meletus[33] and Anytus[34] and Lycon, Meletus being aggrieved on behalf of the poets, Anytus on behalf of the professional men and politicians, and Lycon on behalf of the orators.[35] So, as I said at   24a the beginning, I should be surprised if I were able, in the short time that I have,[36] to rid your minds of a misconception so deeply implanted.

There, gentlemen, you have the true facts, which I present to you without any concealment or suppression, great or small. I am fairly certain that this plain speaking of mine is the cause of my unpopularity; and this really goes to prove that my statements are true, and that I have described correctly the nature and the grounds of the calumny which has been brought against me. Whether you inquire into them now or later, you will find the   *b* facts as I have just described them.

Section F: The cross-examination, part I. Socrates here proceeds to lose any sympathy which he may have gained in describing his activity by giving the jury a demonstration of how it works. Meletus's lack of thought for the upbringing of young men is exposed.

So much for my defence against the charges brought by the first group of my accusers. I shall now try to defend myself against Meletus – high-principled and patriotic as he claims to be – and after that against the rest.

Let us first consider their affidavit again, as though it represented

a fresh prosecution. It runs something like this: 'Socrates is guilty of corrupting the minds of the young, and of believing in super-
c natural things of his own invention instead of the gods recognized by the State.'[37] Such is the charge; let us examine its points one by one.

Now it claims that I am guilty of corrupting the young. But I say, gentlemen, that Meletus is guilty of treating a serious matter with levity, since he summons people to stand their trial on frivolous grounds, and professes concern and keen anxiety in matters to which he has never given the slightest attention.[38] I will try to prove this to your satisfaction.

Come now, Meletus, tell me this. You regard it as supremely important, do you not, that our young people should be exposed
d to the best possible influence?

'I do.'

Very well, then; tell these gentlemen who it is that influences the young for the better. Obviously you must know, if you pay it so much attention. You have discovered the vicious influence, as you say, in myself, and you are now prosecuting me before these gentlemen; speak up and inform them who it is that has a good influence upon the young – You see, Meletus, that you are tongue-tied and cannot answer. Do you not feel that this is discreditable, and a sufficient proof in itself of what I said, that you have not paid attention to the subject? Tell me, my friend, who is it that makes the young good?

'The laws.'

e That is not what I mean, my dear sir; I am asking you to name the person whose first business it is to know the laws.

'These gentlemen here, Socrates, the members of the jury.'

Do you mean, Meletus, that they have the ability to educate the young, and to make them better?

'Certainly.'

Does this apply to all jurymen, or only to some?

'To all of them.'

Excellent! a generous supply of benefactors. Well, then, do these spectators who are present in court have an improving influence,
25a or not?

'Yes, they do.'

And what about the members of the Council?

'Yes, the Councillors too.'

But surely, Meletus, the members of the Assembly[39] do not corrupt the young? Or do all of them too exert an improving influence?

'Yes, they do.'

Then it would seem that the whole population of Athens has a refining effect upon the young, except myself; and I alone corrupt them. Is that your meaning?

'Most emphatically, yes.'

A great misfortune, indeed, you've damned me for! Well, let me put another question to you. Take the case of horses; do you believe that those who improve them make up the whole of *b* mankind, and that there is only one person who has a bad effect on them? Or is the truth just the opposite, that the ability to improve them belongs to one person or to very few persons, who are horse-trainers, whereas most people, if they have to do with horses and make use of them, do them harm? Is not this the case, Meletus, both with horses and with all other animals? Of course it is, whether you and Anytus deny it or not. It would be a singular dispensation of fortune for our young people if there were only one person who corrupted them, while all the rest had a beneficial effect. Well then, Meletus, you've given ample proof that you have *c* never bothered your head about the young; and you make it perfectly clear that you have never paid the slightest attention to the matters over which you are now indicting me.

Here is another point. Tell me seriously, Meletus, is it better to live in a good or in a bad community? Answer my question, like a good fellow; there is nothing difficult about it. Is it not true that wicked people do harm to those with whom they are in the closest contact, and that good people have a good effect?

'Quite true.'

Is there anyone who prefers to be harmed rather than benefited *d* by his associates? Answer me, please; the law commands you to answer. Is there anyone who prefers to be harmed?

'Of course not.'

Well, then, when you summon me before this court for corrupting the young and making their characters worse, do you mean that I do so intentionally or unintentionally?[40]

'I mean intentionally.'

Why, Meletus, are you at your age so much wiser than I at mine? You have discovered that bad people always have a bad effect, and good people a good effect, upon their nearest neighbours; am I so hopelessly ignorant as not even to realize that by spoiling the character of one of my companions I shall run the risk of getting some harm from him? So ignorant as to commit this grave offence intentionally, as you claim? No, I do not believe it, Meletus, and I do not suppose that anyone else does. Either I have not a bad influence, or it is unintentional; so in either case what you claim is false. And if I unintentionally have a bad influence, the correct procedure in cases of such involuntary misdemeanours is not to summon the culprit before this court, but to take him aside privately for instruction and reproof; because obviously if my eyes are opened, I shall stop doing what I do not intend to do. But you deliberately avoided my company in the past[41] and refused to enlighten me, and now you bring me before this court, which is the place appointed for those who need punishment, not for those who need enlightenment.

Section G: The cross-examination, part II. With a suspicious-sounding argument Socrates tries to show that Meletus's formal charge contradicts itself. Meletus is made to claim that Socrates believes in no gods whatever, and, after confusing Socrates with Anaxagoras, is finally made to assent to the notion that the 'supernatural things' referred to in the charge could only be believed in by one who believed in gods.

It is quite clear by now, gentlemen, that Meletus, as I said before, has never paid the slightest attention to this subject. However, I invite you to tell us, Meletus, in what sense you make out that I corrupt the minds of the young. Surely the terms of your indictment make it clear that you accuse me of teaching them to believe in new deities instead of the gods recognized by the state; isn't that the teaching of mine which you say has this demoralizing effect?

'That is precisely what I maintain.'

Then I appeal to you, Meletus, in the name of these same gods about whom we are speaking, to explain yourself a little more clearly to myself and to the jury, because I cannot make out what your point is. Is it that I teach people to believe in some gods (which implies that I myself believe in gods, and am not a complete atheist, and so not guilty on that score), but in different gods from those recognized by the state, so that your accusation rests upon the fact that they are different? Or do you assert that I believe in no gods at all, and teach others to do the same?

'Yes; I say that you disbelieve in gods altogether.'[42]

You surprise me, Meletus; what is your object in saying that? *d*
Do you suggest that I do not believe that the sun and moon are gods,[43] like other men do?

'He certainly does not, gentlemen of the jury, since he says that the sun is a stone and the moon a mass of earth.'

Do you imagine that you are prosecuting Anaxagoras, my dear Meletus? Have you so poor an opinion of these gentlemen, and do you assume them to be so illiterate as not to know that the writings of Anaxagoras of Clazomenae[44] are full of theories like these? And do you seriously suggest that it is from me that the young get these ideas, when they can buy them on occasion in the orchestra[45] for a drachma at most, and so have the laugh on *e*
Socrates if he claims them for his own, especially when they are so peculiar? Tell me honestly, Meletus, is that your opinion of me? Do I believe in no god?

'No, none at all; not in the slightest degree.'

You are not at all convincing, Meletus; not even to yourself, I suspect. In my opinion, gentlemen, this man is quite unable to restrain his insolence, and it is simply this which makes him bring this action against me – a kind of insolence or lack of restraint or youthful aggression. He seems to be devising a sort of riddle for me, saying to himself, 'Will the infallible Socrates realize that I am *27a*
contradicting myself for my own amusement, or shall I succeed in deceiving him and the rest of my audience?' It certainly seems to me that he is contradicting himself in this indictment, which might just as well run: 'Socrates is guilty of not believing in the gods, but believing in the gods.' And this is pure flippancy.

I ask you to examine with me, gentlemen, the line of reasoning which leads me to this conclusion. You, Meletus, will please answer my questions. And will the rest of you all please remember, as I requested at the beginning, not to interrupt if I conduct the *b*
discussion in my customary way?

Is there anyone in the world, Meletus, who believes in human matters, and not in human beings? Make him answer, gentlemen, and don't let him keep on making these continual objections. Is there anyone who does not believe in horses, but believes in equine matters? Or who does not believe in musicians, but believes in musical matters? No, there is not, my worthy friend. If you do not want to answer, I will supply it for you and for these gentlemen too. But the next question you must answer: Is there anyone who believes in supernatural matters and not in supernatural beings?[46]

'No.'

How good of you to give a bare answer under compulsion by the court! Well, do you assert that I believe and teach others to believe in supernatural matters? It does not matter whether they are new or old; the fact remains that I believe in them according to your statement; indeed you solemnly swore as much in your affidavit. But if I believe in supernatural matters, it follows inevitably that I also believe in supernatural beings. Is not that so? It is; I assume your assent, since you do not answer. Do we not hold that supernatural beings are either gods or the children of gods?[47] Do you agree or not?

'Certainly.'

Then if I believe in supernatural beings, as you assert, if these supernatural beings are gods in any sense, we shall reach the conclusion which I mentioned just now when I said that you were testing me with riddles for your own amusement, by stating first that I do not believe in gods, and then again that I do, since I believe in supernatural beings. If on the other hand these supernatural beings are bastard children of the gods by nymphs or other mothers, as they are reputed to be, who in the world would believe in the children of gods and not in the gods themselves? It would be as ridiculous as to believe in the young of horses or donkeys and not in horses and donkeys themselves. No, Meletus; there is no avoiding the conclusion that you brought this charge against me to try me out, or else in despair of finding a genuine offence of which to accuse me. As for your prospect of convincing any living person with even a smattering of intelligence that belief in the supernatural does not imply belief in the divine, and again that non-belief in gods does not imply non-belief in supernatural beings and heroes, it is outside all the bounds of possibility.[48]

Section H: Socrates is committed to his activities as if to his position in battle; he will not be prevailed upon to give them up. The section is important, in that Socrates puts his obligation to Apollo (based on a dubious personal interpretation of the oracle) ahead of a hypothetical command from the city that he should stop philosophizing. This section is more rhetorical at first,[49] becoming chatty later.

As a matter of fact, gentlemen, I do not feel that it requires much defence to clear myself of Meletus's accusation; what I have said already is enough. But you know very well the truth of what I said in an earlier part of my speech, that I have incurred a great deal of bitter hostility; and this is what will bring about my destruction, if anything does; not Meletus or Anytus, but the slander and jealousy of a very large section of the people. They have been fatal to a great many other innocent men, and I suppose will continue to be so; there is no likelihood that they will stop at me. But perhaps someone will say, 'Do you feel no compunction, Socrates, at having pursued an activity which puts you in danger of the death penalty?' I might fairly reply to him, 'You are mistaken, my friend, if you think that a man who is worth anything ought to spend his time weighing up the prospects of life and death. He has only one thing to consider in performing any action; that is, whether he is acting justly or unjustly, like a good man or a bad one. On your view the heroes who died at Troy would be poor creatures, especially the son of Thetis.[50] He, if you remember, made so light of danger in comparison with incurring dishonour that when his goddess mother warned him, eager as he was to kill Hector, in some such words as these, I fancy, "My son, if you avenge your comrade Patroclus's death and kill Hector, you will die yourself;

Next after Hector is thy fate prepared," [51]

– when he heard this warning, he made light of his death and danger, being much more afraid of an ignoble life and of failing to avenge his friends. "Let me die forthwith," said he, "when I have requited the villain, rather than remain here by the beaked ships to be mocked, a burden on the ground." Do you suppose that he gave a thought to death and danger?'

The truth of the matter is this, gentlemen. Where a man has

once taken up his stand, either because it seems best to him or in obedience to his orders, there I believe he is bound to remain and face the danger, taking no account of death or anything else before dishonour.

This being so, it would be shocking inconsistency on my part, gentlemen, if when the officers whom you chose to command me assigned me my position at Potidaea and Amphipolis and Delium,[52] I remained at my post like anyone else and faced death, and yet afterwards, when God appointed me, as I supposed and believed, to the duty of leading the philosophic life, examining myself and others, I were then through fear of death or of any other danger to desert my post. That would indeed be shocking, and then I might really with justice be summoned to court for not believing in the gods, and disobeying the oracle, and being afraid of death, and thinking that I am wise when I am not. For let me tell you, gentlemen, that to be afraid of death is only another form of thinking that one is wise when one is not; it is to think that one knows what one does not know. No one knows with regard to death whether it is not really the greatest blessing that can happen to a man; but people dread it as though they were certain that it is the greatest evil; and this ignorance, which thinks that it knows what it does not, must surely be ignorance most culpable. This, I take it, gentlemen, is the extent, and this the nature of my superiority over the rest of mankind; and if I were to claim to be wiser than my neighbour in any respect, it would be in this: that not possessing any real knowledge of what awaits us in Hades, I am also conscious that I do not possess it. But I do know that to do wrong and to disobey my superior, whether god or man, is bad and dishonourable; and so I shall never feel more fear or aversion for something which, for all I know, may really be a blessing than for those evils which I know to be evils.

Suppose, then, that you acquit me, and pay no attention to Anytus, who has said that either I should not have appeared before this court at all, or, since I have appeared here, I must be put to death, because if I once escaped your sons would all immediately become utterly corrupted by putting the teaching of Socrates into practice. Suppose that, in view of this, you said to me, 'Socrates, on this occasion we shall disregard Anytus and acquit you, but only on one condition: that you give up spending your time on this quest and stop philosophizing.[53] If we catch you going on in the same way, you shall be put to death.' Well, supposing, as I said, that you should offer to acquit me on these *d* terms, I should reply, 'Gentlemen, I am your very grateful and devoted servant, but I owe a greater obedience to God than to you; and so long as I draw breath and have my faculties, I shall never stop practising philosophy and exhorting you and indicating the truth for everyone that I meet. I shall go on saying, in my usual way, "My very good friend, you are an Athenian and belong to a city which is the greatest and most famous in the world for its wisdom and strength. Are you not ashamed that you give your attention to acquiring as much money as possible, and similarly with reputation and honour, and give no attention or thought to *e* truth and understanding and the perfection of your soul?" And if any of you disputes this and professes to care about these things, I shall not at once let him go or leave him; no, I shall question him and examine him and put him to the test; and if it appears that in spite of his profession he has made no real progress towards goodness, I shall reprove him for neglecting what is of supreme *30a* importance, and giving his attention to trivialities. I shall do this to everyone that I meet, young or old, foreigner or fellow-citizen; but especially to you my fellow-citizens, inasmuch as you are closer to me in kinship. This, I do assure you, is what my god commands; and it is my belief that no greater good has ever befallen you in this city than my service to my god; for I spend all my time going about trying to persuade you, young and old, to make your first and chief concern not for your bodies or for your possessions, but for the highest welfare of your souls, proclaiming *b* as I go, "Wealth does not bring goodness, but goodness brings wealth and every other blessing, both to the individual and to the state." Now if I corrupt the young by this message, the message would seem to be harmful; but if anyone says that my message is different from this he is talking nonsense. And so, gentlemen,' I would say, 'You can please yourselves whether you listen to Anytus or not, and whether you acquit me or not; you know that I am not going to alter my conduct, not even if I have to die a hundred deaths.' *c*

Section I: Socrates represents his activity as a benefaction to the city. This is presented more like an old man's story than as a piece of court oratory.

Order, please, gentlemen! Abide by my request to give me a hearing without interruption; besides, I believe that it will be to your advantage to listen. I am going to tell you something else which may provoke a clamour; but please restrain yourselves. I assure you that if I am what I claim to be, and you put me to death, you will harm yourselves more than me. Neither Meletus nor Anytus can do me any harm at all; they would not have the power, because I do not believe that the law of God permits a better man to be harmed by a worse.[54] No doubt my accuser might put me to death or have me banished or deprived of civic rights; but even if he thinks, as he probably does (and others too, I dare say), that these are great calamities, I do not think so; I believe that it is far worse to do what he is doing now, trying to put a man to death unjustly. For this reason, gentlemen, far from pleading on my own behalf, as might be supposed, I am really pleading on yours, to save you from misusing the gift of God by condemning me. If you put me to death, you will not easily find anyone to take my place. To put it bluntly (even if it sounds rather comical) God has assigned me to this city, as if to a large thoroughbred horse which because of its great size is inclined to be lazy and needs the stimulation of some stinging fly. It seems to me that God has attached me to this city to perform the office of such a fly; and all day long I never cease to settle here, there, and everywhere, rousing, persuading, reproving every one of you. You will not easily find another like me, gentlemen, and if you take my advice you will spare my life. But perhaps before long you may awake from your drowsing, and in your annoyance take Anytus's advice and finish me off thoughtlessly with a single slap; and then you could go on sleeping till the end of your days, unless God in his care for you sends someone to take my place.

If you doubt whether I am really the sort of person who would have been sent to this city as a gift from God, you can convince yourselves by looking at it in this way. Does it seem human that I should have neglected my own affairs and endured the humiliation of allowing my family to be neglected for all these years, while I busied myself all the time on your behalf, going like a father or an elder brother to see each one of you privately, and urging you to set your thoughts on goodness? If I had got any enjoyment from it, or if I had been paid for my good advice, there would have been some explanation for my conduct; but as it is you can see for yourselves that although my accusers unblushingly charge me with all sorts of other crimes, there is one thing that they have not had the impudence to pretend on any testimony, and that is that I have ever exacted or c asked a fee from anyone. The witness that I can offer to prove the truth of my statement is good enough, I think – my poverty.

Section J: Socrates' failure to participate in public affairs is attributed to the timely intervention of his supernatural sign. Euthyphro (3b) shows how the very existence of such a sign could have been held against Socrates, and he might have been better advised not to introduce it. Similarly he would have been better advised not to suggest in a fiercely democratic court that any person committed to justice could not survive if he played a full part in the political life of his city. He also reprovingly draws attention to the time when he opposed unconstitutional action favoured by the people, and recalls a similar incident when he was given orders by the notorious Thirty. Neither story could have improved his standing with the jurors very much.

It may seem curious that I should go round giving advice like this and busying myself in people's private affairs, and yet never venture publicly to address you as a whole and advise on matters of state. The reason for this is what you have often heard me say before on many other occasions: that I am subject to a divine or supernatural experience, which Meletus saw fit to travesty in his d indictment. It began in my early childhood – a sort of voice which comes to me; and when it comes it always dissuades me from what I am proposing to do, and never urges me on. It is this that debars me from entering public life, and a very good thing too, in my opinion; because you may be quite sure, gentlemen, that if I had tried long ago to engage in politics, I should long ago have lost my life, without doing any good either to you or to myself. Please do not be offended if I tell you the truth. No man on earth e who conscientiously opposes either you or any other organized

democracy, and flatly prevents a great many wrongs and illegalities from taking place in the state to which he belongs, can possibly
32a escape with his life. The true champion of justice, if he intends to survive even for a short time, must necessarily confine himself to private life and leave politics alone.

I will offer you substantial proofs of what I have said; not theories, but what you better appreciate, facts. Listen while I describe my actual experiences, so that you may know that I would never submit wrongly to any authority through fear of death, but would refuse at any cost – even that of my life. It will be a commonplace story, such as you often hear in the courts;[55] but it is true.

The only office which I have ever held in our city, gentlemen,
b was when I served on the Council. It so happened that our tribe Antiochis was presiding[56] when you decided that the ten commanders who had failed to rescue the men who were lost in the naval engagement[57] should be tried en bloc; which was illegal, as you all recognized later. On this occasion I was the only member of the executive who opposed your acting in any way unconstitutionally, and voted against the proposal; and although the public speakers were all ready to denounce and arrest me, and you were all urging
c them on at the top of your voices, I thought that it was my duty to face it out on the side of law and justice rather than support you, through fear of prison or death, in your wrong decision.

This happened while we were still under a democracy. When the oligarchy came into power, the Thirty Commissioners in their turn summoned me and four others to the Round Chamber[58] and instructed us to go and fetch Leon of Salamis from his home for execution. This was of course only one of many instances in which they issued such instructions, their object being to implicate as many people as possible in their crimes. On this occasion, however,
d I again made it clear, not by my words but by my actions, that the attention[59] I paid to death was zero (if that is not too unrefined a claim); but that I gave all my attention to avoiding doing anything unjust or unholy. Powerful as it was, that government did not terrify me into doing a wrong action; when we came out of the Round Chamber the other four went off to Salamis and arrested Leon,[60] and I went home. I should probably have been put to death for this, if the government had not fallen soon afterwards.
e There are plenty of people who will testify to these statements.

Section K: A transitional passage (somewhat dogmatic and rhetorical) leads into further consideration of the effect that Socrates has had upon young men. Socrates explains why he has always made himself freely available to them, and observes that Meletus has failed to call any of his followers – or their relatives – as witnesses to the corruption charge.

Do you suppose that I should have lived as long as I have if I had moved in the sphere of public life, and conducting myself in that sphere like an honourable man, had always upheld the cause of right, and conscientiously set this end above all other things? Not by a very long way, gentlemen; neither would any other man. You will find that throughout my life I have been consistent in any public duties that I have performed, and the same also in my personal dealings: I have never countenanced any action that was incompatible with justice on the part of any person, including those whom some people maliciously call my pupils. I have never set up as any man's teacher; but if anyone, young or old, is eager to hear me conversing and carrying out my private mission, I never grudge him the opportunity; nor do I charge a fee for talking to him, and refuse to talk without one; I am ready to answer questions for rich and poor alike, and I am equally ready if anyone prefers to listen to what I have to say and answer my questions. If any given one of these people becomes a good citizen or a bad one, I cannot with justice be held responsible, since I have never promised or imparted any teaching to anybody; and if anyone asserts that he has ever learned or heard from me privately anything which was not open to everyone else, you may be quite sure that he is not telling the truth.

But how is it that some people enjoy spending a great deal of time in my company? You have heard the reason, gentlemen; I told you quite frankly. It is because they enjoy hearing me examine those who think that they are wise when they are not; an experience which has its amusing side. This duty I have accepted, as I said, in obedience to God's commands given in oracles and dreams and in every way that any other divine dispensation has ever impressed a duty upon man.[61] This is a true statement, gentlemen, and easy to verify.

If it is a fact that I am in process of corrupting some of the

d young, and have succeeded already in corrupting others; and if it
were a fact that some of the latter, being now grown up, had
discovered that I had ever given them bad advice when they were
young, surely they ought now to be coming forward to denounce
and punish me; and if they did not like to do it themselves, you
would expect some of their families – their fathers and brothers
and other near relations – to remember it now, if their own flesh
and blood had suffered any harm from me. Certainly a great many
of them have found their way into this court, as I can see for
myself: first Crito[62] over there, my contemporary and near neigh-
e bour, the father of this young man Critobulus; and then Lysanias
of Sphettus, the father of Aeschines[63] here; and next Antiphon of
Cephisia, over there, the father of Epigenes. Then besides there are
all those whose brothers have been members of our circle: Nico-
stratus the son of Theozotides, the brother of Theodotus – but
Theodotus is dead, so he cannot appeal to his brother – and
Paralius here, the son of Demodocus; his brother was Theages.[64]
34a And here is Adimantus[65] the son of Ariston, whose brother Plato
is over there; and Aeantodorus, whose brother Apollodorus[66] is
here on this side. I can name many more besides, some of whom
Meletus most certainly ought to have produced as witnesses in the
course of his speech. If he forgot to do so then, let him do it now –
I'll make a concession; let him state whether he has any such
evidence to offer. On the contrary, gentlemen, you will find that
they are all prepared to help me – the corrupter and evil genius of
their nearest and dearest relatives, as Meletus and Anytus say. The
b actual victims of my corrupting influence might perhaps be excused
for helping me; but as for the uncorrupted, their relations of
mature age, what other reason can they have for helping me
except the just and proper one, that they know Meletus is lying
and I am telling the truth?

*Section L: Socrates excuses himself from the common practice of
making pitiful appeals to the jurors. He does so on three grounds:
that it would be dishonourable, that it would be inviting injustice,
and that in inviting an unjust decision contrary to the juryman's
oath, it would be impious. Being impious, he observes, it would be
the way of one who does not believe in the gods. Socrates' tone
has become that of a moral campaigner, lecturing the Athenians*

about their discreditable court practices. Socrates, on trial for his life, is virtually condemning the de facto procedures of the Athenian courts!

There, gentlemen: that, and perhaps a little more to the same effect, is the substance of what I can say in my defence. It may be that some one of you, remembering his own case, will be annoyed that whereas he, in standing his trial upon a less serious charge than this, made pitiful appeals to the jury with floods of tears, and had his infant children produced in court to excite the maximum of sympathy, and many of his relatives and friends as well, I on the contrary intend to do nothing of the sort, and that although I am facing (as it might appear) the utmost danger. It may be that one of you, reflecting on these facts, will harden himself against me, and being irritated by his reflections, will give his vote in anger. If one of you is so disposed – I do not expect it of you, but there is the possibility – I think that I should be quite justified in saying to him, 'My dear sir, of course I have some relatives. To quote the very words of Homer, even I am not sprung "from an oak or from a rock",[67] but from human parents, and consequently I have relatives; yes, and sons too, gentlemen, three of them,[68] one almost grown up and the other two only children; but all the same I am not going to produce them here and beseech you to acquit me.'

Why do I not intend to do anything of this kind? Not out of perversity, gentlemen, nor out of contempt for you; whether I am brave or not in the face of death has nothing to do with it; the point is that for my own credit and yours and for the credit of the state as a whole, I do not think that it is honourable for me to use any of these methods at my age and with my reputation – which may be true or it may be false, but at any rate the view is established that Socrates is different from the common run of mankind. Now if those of you who are supposed to be distinguished for wisdom or courage or any other virtue were to behave in this way, it would be a disgrace. I have often noticed that some people of this type, for all their high standing, go to extraordinary lengths when they come up for trial, which shows that they think it will be a dreadful thing to lose their lives; as though they would be immortal if you did not put them to death! In my opinion these

people bring disgrace upon our city. Any of our visitors might be
b excused for thinking that the finest specimens of Athenian manhood, whom their fellow-citizens choose in preference to themselves for archonships and other high positions,[69] are no better
than women. If you have even the smallest reputation, gentlemen,
you ought not to descend to these methods; and if we do so, you
must not give us licence. On the contrary, you must make it clear
that anyone who stages these pathetic scenes and so brings ridicule
upon our city is far more likely to be condemned than if he kept
perfectly quiet.

But apart from all question of appearances, gentlemen, I do not
c think that it is *just* for a man to appeal to the jury or to get
himself acquitted by doing so; he ought to inform them of the
facts and convince them by argument. The jury does not sit to
dispense justice as a favour, but to decide where justice lies; and
the oath which they have sworn is not to show favour at their own
discretion, but to return a just and lawful verdict. It follows that
we must not develop in you, nor you allow to grow in yourselves,
the habit of perjury; that would be impious[70] for us both. Therefore you must not expect me, gentlemen, to behave towards you in
a way which I consider neither reputable nor just nor consistent
d with my religious duty; and above all you must not expect it when
I stand charged with impiety by Meletus here. Surely it is obvious
that if I tried to persuade you and prevail upon you by my
entreaties to go against your solemn oath, I should be teaching
you contempt for religion; and by my very defence I should be
virtually accusing myself of having no religious belief. But that is
very far from the truth. I have a more sincere belief, gentlemen,
than any of my accusers; and I leave it to you and to God to judge
me in whatever way shall be best for me and for yourselves.

The verdict is 'Guilty'

*Section M: Socrates, having now been convicted by a comparatively
narrow margin of sixty votes, has to propose a penalty as an
alternative to the death penalty claimed by the prosecution. He
still adheres to some of the bolder theses of his defence speech,
something which Plato is able to use to draw the threads of his
picture of Socrates together. But the jurors would probably have*

been dismayed to see how little his attitude has changed. Socrates
argues that he deserves to be sentenced to dining at public expense
like victors at the Games. After firmly rejecting prison or exile, he
offers a fine, firstly one within his means, and secondly thirty
times that after his friends offer to help.

There are a great many reasons, gentlemen, why I am not
distressed by this result – I mean your condemnation of me – but
the chief reason is that the result was not unexpected. What does
surprise me is the number of votes cast on the two sides. I should
never have believed that it would be such a close thing; but now it
seems that if a mere thirty votes[71] had gone the other way, I
should have been acquitted. Even as it is, I feel that so far as
Meletus's part is concerned I have been acquitted; and not only
that, but anyone can see that if Anytus and Lycon had not come
forward to accuse me, Meletus would actually have lost a thousand
drachmae for not having obtained one fifth of the votes.[72]

However, we must face the fact that he demands the death
penalty. Very good. What alternative penalty shall I propose to
you, gentlemen? Obviously it must be what's deserved. Well, what
penalty do I deserve to pay or suffer, in view of what I have done?

I have never lived an ordinary quiet life. I did not care for the
things that most people care about: making money, having a
comfortable home, high military or civil rank, and all the other
activities – political appointments, secret societies, party organiza-
tions – which go on in our city; I thought that I was really too
fair-minded to survive if I went in for this sort of thing. So instead
of taking a course which would have done no good either to you
or to me, I set myself to do you individually in private what I hold
to be the greatest possible service: I tried to persuade each one of
you not to think more of practical advantages than of his mental
and moral well-being, or in general to think more of advantage
than of well-being, in the case of the state or of anything else.
What do I deserve for behaving in this way? Some reward, gentlemen, if I am bound to suggest what I really deserve; and what is
more, a reward which would be appropriate for myself. Well,
what is appropriate for a poor man who is a public benefactor and
who requires leisure for the purpose of giving you moral encourage-
ment? Nothing could be more appropriate for such a person than

free dining in the Prytaneum.[73] He deserves it much more than any victor in the races at Olympia, whether he wins with a single horse or a pair or a team of four. These people give you the semblance of success, but I give you the reality; they do not need maintenance, but I do. So if I am to suggest an appropriate penalty which is strictly in accordance with justice, I suggest free maintenance by the state.

Perhaps when I say this I may give you the impression, as I did in my remarks about exciting sympathy and making passionate appeals, that I am showing a stubborn perversity. That is not so, gentlemen; the real position is this. I am convinced that I never wrong anyone intentionally, but I cannot convince you of this, because we have had so little time for discussion. If it was your practice, as it is with other nations, to give not one day but several to the hearing of capital trials, I believe that you might have been convinced; but under present conditions it is not easy to dispose of grave allegations in a short space of time. So being convinced that I do no wrong to anybody, I can hardly be expected to wrong myself by asserting that I deserve something bad, or by proposing a corresponding penalty.[74] Why should I? For fear of suffering this penalty proposed by Meletus, when, as I said, I do not know whether it is a good thing or a bad? Do you expect me to choose something which I know very well is bad by making my counter-proposal? Imprisonment? Why should I spend my days in prison, in subjection to whichever Eleven hold office?[75] A fine, with imprisonment until it is paid? In my case the effect would be just the same, because I have no money to pay a fine. Or shall I suggest banishment? You would very likely accept the suggestion.[76]

I should have to be desperately in love with life to do that, gentlemen. I am not so blind that I cannot see that you, my fellow-citizens, have come to the end of your patience with my discussions and conversations; you have found them too irksome and irritating, and now you are trying to get rid of them. Will any other people find them easy to put up with? That is most unlikely, gentlemen. A fine life I should have if I left this country at my age and spent the rest of my days trying one city after another and being turned out every time! I know very well that wherever I go the young people will listen to my conversation just as they do here; and if I try to keep them off, they themselves will prevail upon their elders and

have me thrown out, while if I do not, the fathers and other   e
relatives will drive me out of their own accord for the sake of the
young.

Perhaps someone may say, 'But surely, Socrates, after you have
left us you can spend the rest of your life in quietly minding your
own business.' This is the hardest thing of all to make some of you
understand. If I say that this would be disobedience to God, and
that is why I cannot 'mind my own business', you will not believe
me – you'll think I'm pulling your leg.[77] If on the other hand I tell   38a
you that to let no day pass without discussing goodness and all the
other subjects about which you hear me talking and examining
both myself and others is really the very best thing that a man can
do, and that life without this sort of examination is not worth
living, you will be even less inclined to believe me. Nevertheless
that is how it is, gentlemen, as I maintain; though it is not easy to
convince you of it. Besides, I am not accustomed to think of   b
myself as deserving punishment. If I had money, I would have
suggested a fine that I could afford, because that would not have
done me any harm. As it is, I cannot, because I have none; unless
of course you like to fix the penalty at what I could pay. I suppose
I could probably afford a hundred drachmae and I suggest a fine
of that amount.[78]

One moment, gentlemen. Plato here, and Crito and Critobulus
and Apollodorus, want me to propose three thousand drachmae
on their security. Very well, I agree to this sum, and you can rely
upon these gentlemen for its payment.[79]

The penalty is death

*Section N: Socrates converses with the jurymen after being sen-
tenced by an increased majority of jurors (over two-thirds) to
death rather than a fine.*

Well, gentlemen, for the sake of a very small gain in time you   c
are going to earn the reputation – and the blame from those who
wish to disparage our city – of having put Socrates to death, 'that
wise man', because they will say I am wise even if I am not, these
people who want to find fault with you. If you had waited just a
little while, you would have had your way in the course of nature.

You can see that I am well on in life and near to death. I am
d saying this not to all of you but to those who voted for my
execution, and I have something else to say to them as well.

No doubt you think, gentlemen, that I have been condemned for
lack of the arguments which I could have used if I had thought it
right to leave nothing unsaid or undone to secure my acquittal.
But that is very far from the truth. It is not a lack of arguments
that has caused my condemnation, but a lack of effrontery and
impudence,[80] and the fact that I have refused to address you in the
way which would give you most pleasure. You would have liked
to hear me weep and wail, doing and saying all sorts of things
e which I declare to be unworthy of myself, but which you are used
to hearing from other people. But I did not think then that I ought
to stoop to servility because I was in danger, and I do not regret
now the way in which I pleaded my case; I would much rather die
as the result of this defence than live as the result of the other sort.
In a court of law, just as in warfare, neither I nor any other ought
39*a* to use his wits to escape death by any means. In battle it is often
obvious that you could escape being killed by giving up your arms
and throwing yourself upon the mercy of your pursuers; and in
every kind of danger there are plenty of devices for avoiding death
if you are unscrupulous enough to stop at nothing. But I suggest,
gentlemen, that the difficulty is not so much to escape death; the
real difficulty is to escape from wickedness, which is far more fleet
b of foot. In this present instance I, the slow old man, have been
overtaken by the slower of the two, but my accusers, who are
clever and quick, have been overtaken by the faster: by iniquity.
When I leave this court I shall go away condemned by you to
death, but they will go away convicted by Truth herself of deprav-
ity and injustice. And they accept their sentence even as I accept
mine. No doubt it was bound to be so, and I think that the result
is fair enough.

c Having said so much, I feel moved to prophesy to you who have
given your vote against me; for I am now at that point where the
gift of prophecy comes most readily to men: at the point of death.
I tell you, my executioners, that as soon as I am dead, vengeance
shall fall upon you with a punishment far more painful than your
killing of me. You have brought about my death in the belief that
through it you will be delivered from submitting the conduct of

your lives to criticism; but I say that the result will be just the opposite. You will have more critics, whom up till now I have restrained without your knowing it; and being younger they will *d* be harsher to you and will cause you more annoyance.

If you expect to stop denunciation of your wrong way of life by putting people to death, there is something amiss with your reasoning. This way of escape is neither possible nor creditable; the best and easiest way is not to stop the mouths of others, but to make yourselves as well behaved as possible. This is my last message to you who voted for my condemnation.

As for you who voted for my acquittal, I should very much like *e* to say a few words to reconcile you to this result, while the officials are busy and I am not yet on my way to the place where I must die. I ask you, gentlemen, to spare me these few moments; there is no reason why we should not exchange a few words while the law permits. I look upon you as my friends, and I want to *40a* show you the meaning of what has now happened to me.

Gentlemen of the jury[81] – for you deserve to be so called – I have had a remarkable experience. In the past the prophetic voice to which I have become accustomed has always been my constant companion, opposing me even in quite trivial things if I was going to take the wrong course. Now something has happened to me, as you can see, which might be thought and is commonly considered to be a supreme calamity; yet neither when I left home this *b* morning, nor when I was taking my place here in the court, nor at any point in any part of my speech, did the divine sign oppose me. In other discussions it has often checked me in the middle of a sentence; but this time it has never opposed me in any part of this business in anything that I have said or done. What do I suppose to be the explanation? I will tell you. I suspect that this thing that has happened to me is a blessing, and we are quite mistaken in supposing death to be an evil. I have good grounds for thinking *c* this, because my accustomed sign could not have failed to oppose me if what I was doing had not been sure to bring some good result.

We should reflect that there is much reason to hope for a good result on other grounds as well. Death is one of two things. Either it is annihilation, and the dead have no consciousness of anything; or, as we are told,[82] it is really a change: a migration of the soul

from this place to another. Now if there is no consciousness but
d only a dreamless sleep, death must be a marvellous gain. I suppose
that if anyone were told to pick out the night on which he slept so
soundly as not even to dream, and then to compare it with all the
other nights and days of his life, and then were told to say, after
due consideration, how many better and happier days and nights
than this he had spent in the course of his life – well, I think that
the Great King himself,[83] to say nothing of any private person,
e would find these days and nights easy to count in comparison with
the rest. If death is like this, then, I call it gain; because the whole
of time, if you look at it in this way, can be regarded as no more
than one single night. If on the other hand death is a removal from
here to some other place, and if what we are told is true, that all
the dead are there, what greater blessing could there be than this,
41*a* gentlemen of the jury? If on arrival in the other world, beyond the
reach of these so-called jurors here, one will find there the true
jurors who are said to preside in those courts, Minos and Rhada-
manthys and Aeacus[84] and Triptolemus[85] and all those other
demi-gods who were upright in their earthly life, would that be an
unrewarding place to settle? Put it in this way: how much would
one of you give to meet Orpheus and Musaeus, Hesiod and
Homer?[86] I am willing to die ten times over if this account is true.
b For me at least it would be a wonderful personal experience to
join them there, to meet Palamedes and Ajax the son of Telamon[87]
and any other heroes of the old days who met their death through
an unjust trial, and to compare my fortunes with theirs – it would
be rather amusing, I think – and above all I should like to spend
my time there, as here, in examining and searching people's minds,
to find out who is really wise among them, and who only thinks
that he is. What would one not give, gentlemen, to be able to
c scrutinize the leader of that great host against Troy, or Odysseus,
or Sisyphus,[88] or the thousands of other men and women whom
one could mention, their company and conversation – like the
chance to examine them – would be unimaginable happiness? At
any rate I presume that they do not put one to death there for such
conduct; because apart from the other happiness in which their
world surpasses ours, they are now immortal for the rest of time,
if what we are told is true.

You too, gentlemen of the jury, must look forward to death

with confidence, and fix your minds on this one belief, which is certain: that nothing can harm a good man either in life or after death, and his fortunes are not a matter of indifference to the gods. This present experience of mine does not result from mere earthly causes; I am quite clear that the time had come when it was better for me to die and be released from my distractions. That is why my sign never turned me back. For my own part I bear no grudge at all against those who condemned me and accused me, although it was not with this kind intention that they did so, but because they thought that they were hurting me; and that is culpable of them. However, I ask them to grant me one favour. When my sons grow up, gentlemen, if you think that they are putting money or anything else before goodness, take your revenge by plaguing them as I plagued you; and if they fancy themselves for no reason, you must scold them just as I scolded you, for neglecting the important things and thinking that they are good for something when they are good for nothing. If you do this, I shall have had justice at your hands – I *and* my children.

Well, now it is time to be off, I to die and you to live; but which of us has the happier prospect is unknown to anyone but God.

JUSTICE AND DUTY (ii)

SOCRATES IN PRISON: *CRITO*

INTRODUCTION

The *Crito* is a short but highly controversial work. This controversy is focused upon the theory set forth in the speech of the
Laws of Athens, as improvised by Socrates at the end of the work.
The basic question is quite simple: can one reconcile the relations
between individual and state recommended here with what we
hear elsewhere from Plato's Socrates?

This issue is not helped, perhaps, by the confidence with which
scholars usually assume that this is an early, and therefore 'Socratic' work of Plato. Even when the question of how Socratic any
of Plato's works really are is very much contested,[1] scholars
assume that the task must somehow be to reconcile the *Crito* with
what Socrates says in the *Apology* and elsewhere. In a sense they
are right; Socrates did stay in prison when he might very well have
escaped, and it is clear that his profound reluctance to flout the
law must have outweighed a man's natural desire to stay alive,
make provision for his family and continue to enjoy the occasional
society of his friends in exile.

Yet the difficulties in accepting as Socrates' own the 'social-
contract theory'[2] (and more particularly the apparent sacrifice of
the individual's moral independence for the rule of conventional
law) naturally lead to questioning whether this is really Socratic or
even Platonic. It has recently been proposed that Plato's nephew
and successor Speusippus wrote the work.[3] There are certainly
oddities about it which need explaining: a lack of any obvious
Socratic irony,[4] unusual religious elements,[5] the absence of the
Socratic elenchus,[6] and a lack of any obviously 'Platonic' metaphysical or psychological infrastructure. The last feature is perhaps
explicable in an early work; the first three are still more difficult
to explain on this hypothesis. It is in fact difficult to accept that it
is very early, as at 53b there appears to be an allusion to Polycrates'
Accusation of Socrates, in which he had called Socrates a 'destroyer

of the laws'.[7] A significant problem of language occurs in the central discussion of the constant need to be just.[8] Recent work on Platonic chronology has indicated that there is unusually little homogeneity of style in the *Crito*.[9] The work is often assumed to be early because it seems simple and because it is allegedly Socratic. But is it really as Socratic as assumed? Readers ought to keep this question in the forefront of their minds as they read the work.

As they do so they should also bear in mind a significant difference from other Socratic works. Elsewhere the setting is chosen in order to maximize the impact and the relevance of the philosophy, but it remains secondary; we are asked to approve the doctrine, not the events which occurred. Here, while the setting and the philosophy again go hand in hand, the philosophy evolves in order to explain the events. The chief question is whether Socrates' actions are explicable in terms of Socratic philosophy, and what we are asked to approve are the actions rather than the philosophy. It was not a question that any follower of Socrates could give a simple answer to, for while they hoped to see his conduct as consistent with his beliefs so that his philosophy would turn out to be viable, nothing suggests that the political and legal theory used to explain his behaviour was routinely associated with Socrates.

The structure of the *Crito* is fairly simple. There is (i) a scene-setting introduction where we meet a serene Socrates in prison, two days before his death, and a distraught Crito trying to arrange his escape; (ii) a speech by Crito in which he pleads with Socrates to escape now; (iii) a discussion in which Socrates goes over his habitual arguments for putting justice first; and (iv) a reply by Socrates to Crito's arguments for escaping, cast in the form of an address to Socrates by the Laws of Athens. Section iii is what seems so Socratic, for it painstakingly sets out the Socratic doctrine on the basis of which his unwillingness to escape is explained. But it assumes that the reader is familiar with this doctrine, perhaps with Plato's own account of it in the *Gorgias*. It does not follow that section iv must be Socratic; it is emphasized in section iii that what is being propounded is long-standing Socratic theory, but the theory of iv is presented as an external voice which he currently finds persuasive.

Why is this external voice introduced? Not merely to distance

Socrates from the views there expounded, nor simply to avoid Socrates having to deliver an uncharacteristic monologue in court-room fashion. It was more important that the personification of the Laws of Athens in this way lends much-needed credibility to the notion that Socrates could have personal obligations towards them and could commit injustice against them. Socrates justifies his unwillingness to escape by claiming that it would be unjust to do so. Being unjust traditionally involved being unjust to some-body.

It is beneficial here to consider how Socrates' opponents would have regarded his staying to face the death penalty. They could readily use the argument that either his friends had failed him because they realized his guilt, or that he himself had recognized that death was what he deserved according to law and had decided to pay the penalty. Supposing Socrates was innocent of the charges brought by Meletus, was he not guilty of bringing the law into disrepute by allowing himself to be convicted and put to death? Had he not committed a kind of suicide by default which reflected badly on the Athenian legal system? As Crito shows at 45e, the whole episode from trial to death would have made ordinary Athenians view Socrates and his followers in a very bad light.

Any author defending Socrates' failure to escape from prison would have had to work within narrow limits. He would have to have shown a respect in Socrates for the due processes of Athenian law without showing a respect for the verdict and sentence which he had received. Thus Plato must establish that Socrates would have been unjust in escaping, not because he owed it to his accusers and jurymen to stay, but because he owed it to the city and its legal system considered in abstract. Obligations in the eyes of the Greeks were either to living human beings, or to departed humans, or to the gods. Justice looked after the first kind, piety (often regarded as a branch of justice) the other two. It was not natural to think of injustice towards abstract institutions, only towards people. But Socrates would not be wronging people by escaping, only the law of the state. So in order that the notion of injustice may be made plausible the Laws of Athens have to be seen as themselves akin to rational animate beings.

Furthermore, men do not have any obligations of justice to all rational animate beings; there must exist some tie which imposes a duty on one or both parties. Socrates is made to view the Laws as akin to those human beings to whom the Greek has his foremost duty, his parents. It was not just his human parents who brought him up; in a sense they were only serving the Laws of the city, which prescribed how it should all be done. Socrates is therefore obliged to obey them as he would a parent, and (it is argued) had on reaching maturity agreed to respect their authority by the very act of remaining in their city. He has two alternatives: either he must persuade them to change their mind, or else he must do as they command. He must obey not because it is naturally unjust to disobey the established law, but because it is naturally unjust to disobey an agreement that has been (i) freely and honestly made, and (ii) made with good reason.[10]

The personification of the Laws, and the fact that they are cast in the role of parents with high expectations, has great emotional impact – more so for the Greeks than for us – but the theory is incredibly strained. It raises a whole series of new questions about Socrates' conduct. If injustice is the greatest of evils for the person who commits it, then the son who cherishes his parent ought to do his utmost to avoid having that parent be unjust to him. It may be argued that it is not the Laws so much as a percentage of the people of Athens who have wronged Socrates, but the argument lacks any conviction. If the Laws, not persons, were responsible for raising Socrates, then the Laws were responsible also for his downfall.

Whether these were the same laws as those under which Socrates was brought up some sixty or so years before is also an issue. The agreement made between Socrates and the Laws had been made long ago; thus the Laws can represent only the long-standing aspects of the Athenian legal system. Certainly they cannot embrace *ad hoc* decrees, or recent emendations out of sympathy with the traditional law of the city; certainly they cannot embrace legislation passed by the oligarchic regimes of 411 and 404 B.C. But even on this point Socrates' situation is unclear. He had remained in the city during the latter regime, when he might very well have followed the example of many of his fellow-Athenians and gone into exile. By staying in the city, had he made an agreement with Critias and his followers, and the dictatorial system which they were introducing?

One should not leave these questions without mentioning the character of Crito: he is a man of the same generation as Socrates, generally respected, concerned for the things which an Athenian ought to be concerned for. Thus the somewhat patriotic arguments of the Laws would have been expected to appeal to him. He is also a follower of Socrates, owing some loyalty to Socratic moral principles, but perhaps no great intellectual. This is likely to tell us something about the intended audience for this work. It is not to Athenian intellectuals that Plato addresses himself, but to the many patriotic citizens who found Socrates' failure to escape difficult to explain.

CRITO

Section A: Introduction. Tredennick described the scene as follows: 'A room in the State prison at Athens in the year 399 B.C. The time is half an hour before dawn and the room would be almost dark but for the light of a little oil lamp. There is a pallet bed against the back wall. At the head of it a small table supports the lamp; near the foot of it CRITO is sitting patiently on a stool. He is an old man, kindly, practical, simple-minded; at present he is suffering from acute emotional strain. On the bed lies SOCRATES asleep. He stirs, yawns, opens his eyes and sees CRITO.'

43a SOCRATES: Here at this hour, Crito? Surely it's still early?

CRITO: Indeed it is.

SOCRATES: About what time?

CRITO: Just before dawn.

SOCRATES: I wonder that the warder agreed to listen to you.

CRITO: He is used to me now, Socrates, because I come here so often;[11] besides, he is under some small obligation to me.[12]

SOCRATES: Have you only just come, or have you been here for long?

CRITO: Quite a while.

b SOCRATES: Then why didn't you wake me at once, instead of sitting in silence by my bed?

CRITO: I wouldn't dream of such a thing, Socrates. I only wish I were not so sleepless and depressed myself. I have been marvelling at you all along, seeing how sweetly you were sleeping; and I deliberately didn't wake you because I wanted you to have the pleasantest possible time. I have often felt throughout my life how fortunate you are in the way you handle things, but I feel it more than ever now in your present misfortune when I see how easy it is for you to take it calmly.

SOCRATES: Well, really, Crito, it would strike an odd chord for a man of my age to resent having to face death.

CRITO: Other people just as old as you are get involved in these   c
misfortunes, Socrates, but their age doesn't alleviate their resentment when they find themselves in your position.

SOCRATES: Quite true. But tell me, why have you come so early?

CRITO: Because I bring bad news, Socrates; not so bad from
your point of view, I suppose, but it will be very hard to bear
for me and your other friends, and I suspect that I shall find it
hardest of all.

SOCRATES: Why, what is this news? Has the boat come in from
Delos – the boat which ends my reprieve when it arrives?[13]   d

CRITO: It hasn't actually come in yet, but I expect that it will be
here today, judging what some people report – they have just
arrived from Sunium[14] and left it there. It's quite clear from their
account that it will be here today; and so by tomorrow, Socrates,
you will be forced to end your life.

SOCRATES: Well, Crito, I hope that it'll be for the best; if that's
what the gods want, so be it. All the same, I don't think it will
arrive today.

CRITO: What makes you believe that?   44

SOCRATES: I will try to explain. I think I am right in saying that I
have to die on the day after the boat arrives?

CRITO: Yes, that's what the authorities say.

SOCRATES: Then I don't think it will arrive on this day that is
just beginning, but on the day after. I am going by a dream that I
had this very night, only a little while ago. It looks as though you
were right not to wake me up.

CRITO: Why, what was the dream about?

SOCRATES: I thought I saw a gloriously beautiful woman dressed
in white robes, who came up to me and addressed me in these   b
words: 'Socrates,

To the pleasant land of Phthia on the third day thou shalt come.'[15]

CRITO: Your dream was a weird one, Socrates.

SOCRATES: To my mind, Crito, it was perfectly clear.

*Section B: Crito's arguments. Crito believes that Socrates should
escape because (i) he is endangering the good reputation of his
friends, (ii) he need not worry about any risks these friends may be*

running, (iii) nor should he worry about the money needed for an escape attempt, (iv) there will be good places to go to, where he can lead an enjoyable life, (v) he is acting unjustly by joining the efforts of his enemies against himself, (vi) he is acting unjustly by not striving to fulfil his obligations to his children, and (vii) it amounts to cowardice to accept this situation without resistance. Finally Crito returns to theme (i), observing that the cowardice is going to reflect badly on Socrates' friends as well as himself.

CRITO: Too clear, apparently. But look here, Socrates, it is still not too late to take my advice and escape. Your death means a double calamity for me: quite apart from losing a friend whom I can never possibly replace, I'll have this additional problem, that a great many people who don't know you and me very well will

c   think that I let you down, saying that I could have saved you if I had been willing to spend the money; and what could be more shameful than to get a name for thinking more of money than of your friends? Most people will never believe that it was you who refused to leave this place when we tried our hardest to persuade you.

SOCRATES: But my dear Crito, why should we pay so much attention to what 'most people' think? The most sensible people,[16] who have more claim to be considered, will believe that things have been done exactly as they have.

d   CRITO: As you can see for yourself, Socrates, one is obliged to bear in mind popular opinion as well. Present circumstances are quite enough to show that the capacity of ordinary people for doing one harm is not confined to petty annoyances, but has hardly any limits if you once get a bad name with them.

SOCRATES: I only wish that ordinary people had an unlimited capacity for doing harm; that would mean they had an unlimited power for doing good,[17] which would be a splendid thing. In actual fact they have neither. They cannot make a man wise or foolish;[18] they achieve whatever luck would have it.

e   CRITO: Have it that way if you like; but tell me this, Socrates. I hope that you aren't worrying about the possible effects on me and the rest of your friends, and thinking that if you escape we shall have trouble with informers for having helped you to get away, and have to forfeit all our property or pay an enormous

fine, or even incur some further punishment? If any idea like that
is troubling you, dismiss it altogether. It's surely right for us to run   45a
that risk in saving you, and even worse, if necessary. Take my
advice, and do as I bid.

SOCRATES: All that you say is very much in my mind, Crito, and
a great deal more besides.

CRITO: Please don't be afraid of these things. Actually it's quite a
moderate sum that certain people want for rescuing you from here
and getting you out of the country. And then surely you realize
how cheap these informers are to buy off; we wouldn't need much
money to settle them. You've got my money at your disposal —   b
that'll be enough, I think; but supposing that in your anxiety for
my safety you feel that you oughtn't to spend my money, there are
these foreign gentlemen staying in Athens who are quite willing to
spend theirs.[19] One of them, Simmias of Thebes, has actually
brought enough money with him for this very purpose; and Cebes
and a number of others are quite ready to do the same. So as I say,
you mustn't let any fears like this make you dispirited about
escaping; and you mustn't feel any misgivings like those you
mentioned at your trial, that you wouldn't know what to do with
yourself if you left this country. Wherever you go, there are plenty   c
of places where you will find a welcome, particularly if you choose
to go to Thessaly — I have friends there who will make much of
you and give you complete protection, so that no one in Thessaly
can interfere with you.

Besides, Socrates, I don't even feel that it is just for you to do
what you are doing, throwing away your life when you might save
it. You are doing your best to treat yourself in exactly the same
way as your enemies would, or rather did, when they wanted to
ruin you. What is more, it seems to me that you are betraying your
sons too. You have it in your power to finish bringing them up
and educating them, and instead of that you're proposing to go off   d
and desert them, and so far as you are concerned they'll be left to
get along as the whim of fortune determines. They will probably
have the kind of luck that usually comes to orphans when they
lose their parents. Either one ought not to have children at all, or
one ought to see their upbringing and education through to the
end, but it strikes me that you are taking the most irresponsible
course. You ought to make the choice of a good man and a brave

one, considering that you profess to have made goodness your
principal concern all through life. Really, I am ashamed, both on
your account and on ours your friends'; it will look as though we
had played something like a coward's part all through this affair
of yours. First there was the way you came into court when it was
quite unnecessary – that was the first act; then there was the
conduct of the defence – that was the second; and finally, to
complete the farce, we get this situation, which makes it appear
that we have let you slip out of our hands through some lack of
courage and enterprise on our part, because we didn't save you,
and you didn't save yourself, when it would have been quite
possible and practicable, if we had been any use at all.

There, Socrates; if you aren't careful, besides the harm there
will be all this disgrace for you and us to bear.[20] Come, make your
plans. Really it's past the time for that now; the decision should
have been made already. There is only one plan – the whole thing
must be carried through during this coming night. If we lose any
more time, it can't be done, it will be too late. I appeal to you,
Socrates, on every ground; take my advice and please do as I say!

*Section C: Socrates begins his reply by going over long-standing
points of Socratic philosophy. (i) One should always take expert
advice rather than majority advice, (ii) since the soul is more
important than the body, this applies particularly in matters concerned with the well-being of the soul, and (iii) one should never
under any circumstances commit an act of injustice. Points (i) and
(ii) have the effect of answering more fully Crito's complaints that
the ordinary folk will blame Socrates' friends for the disgraceful
circumstances surrounding his death: for the moment, however,
the question of where justice lies is left aside.*

SOCRATES: My dear Crito, I would greatly appreciate your
enthusiasm if it is right and proper; if not, the stronger it is, the
more of a problem it is. Therefore we should consider whether
we ought to follow your advice or not; my attitude is not un-
precedented, for it's always been my nature never to accept advice
from any of my 'friends'[21] except the argument that seems best on
reflection. I cannot abandon the arguments which I used to expound in the past[22] simply because this accident has happened to

me; their conclusions seem to me to be much as they were, and I
respect and value the same arguments now as before. So unless we   c
can find better ones on this occasion, you can be quite sure that I
shall not agree with you; not even if the power of the people conjures
up fresh hordes of bogies to terrify our childish minds, by subjecting
us to chains and executions and confiscations of our property.

Well, then, how can we consider the question most reasonably?
Suppose that we begin by reverting to your point about people's
opinions.[23] Was it always right to argue that some opinions should
be taken seriously but not others? Or was it always wrong?[24]   d
Perhaps it was right before the question of my death arose, but
now we can see clearly that we were pointlessly persisting in a
theory which was really childish nonsense. I should like very much
to inquire into this problem, Crito, with your help, and to see
whether the argument will appear in any different light to me now
that I am in this position, or whether it will remain the same; and
whether we shall dismiss it or accept it.[25]

People with something to say, I believe, have always stated
some such view as the one which I mentioned just now: that some
of the opinions which people entertain should be taken seriously,   e
and others not. Now I ask you, Crito, don't you think this is a fair
proposition? – You are safe from the prospect of dying tomorrow,
in all human probability; and you are not likely to have your   47a
judgement upset by this impending calamity.[26] Consider, then;
don't you think that it is good enough to say that one should not
value all the opinions that people hold, but only some and not
others? What do you say? Isn't that a fair statement?

CRITO: Fair enough.

SOCRATES: In other words, one should regard the sound ones
and not the flawed?

CRITO: Yes.

SOCRATES: The opinions of the wise being sound, and the
opinions of the foolish flawed?

CRITO: Naturally.

SOCRATES: To pass on, then: what do you think of the sort of
illustration that I used to employ? When a man is in training, and   b
taking it seriously, does he pay attention to all praise and criticism
and opinion indiscriminately, or only when it comes from the one
qualified person, the actual doctor or trainer?

CRITO: Only when it comes from the one qualifed person.

SOCRATES: Then he should be afraid of the criticism and welcome the praise of the one qualified person, but not those of the general public.

CRITO: Obviously.

SOCRATES: So he ought to regulate his actions and exercises and eating and drinking by the judgement of his instructor, who has expert knowledge, rather than by the opinions of all the rest put together.

CRITO: That is so.

c SOCRATES: Very well. Now if he disobeys the one man and disregards his opinion and commendations, and prefers the advice of the many who have no expert knowledge, surely he will suffer some bad effect?

CRITO: Certainly.

SOCRATES: And what is this bad effect? Where is its impact? – I mean, in what part of the disobedient person?

CRITO: His body, obviously; that is what's ruined.

SOCRATES: Very good. Well now, tell me, Crito – we don't want to go through all the examples one by one – does this apply as a general rule, and above all to the issues which we are trying now to resolve: just and unjust, honourable and dishonourable, good and bad? Ought we to be guided and intimidated by the opinion of

d the many or by that of the one – assuming that there is someone with expert knowledge? Is it true that we ought to respect and fear this person more than all the rest put together; and that if we do not follow his guidance we shall spoil and impair that part of us which, as we used to say, is improved by just conduct and ruined by unjust?²⁷ Or is this all nonsense?

CRITO: No, I think it is true, Socrates.

SOCRATES: Then consider the next step. There is a part of us which is improved by healthy actions and ruined by unhealthy ones. If we completely wreck it by taking advice contrary to that of the experts, will life be worth living when this part is once

e ruined? The part I mean is the body; do you accept this?

CRITO: Yes.

SOCRATES: Well, is life worth living with a body which is worn out and ruined?

CRITO: Certainly not.

SOCRATES: What about the part of us which is impaired by unjust actions and benefited by just ones? Is life worth living with this part ruined? Or do we believe that this part of us, whatever it may be, with which justice and injustice are concerned, is of less importance than the body?

CRITO: Certainly not.

SOCRATES: It is really more precious?

CRITO: Much more.

SOCRATES: In that case, my dear fellow, what we ought to worry about is not so much what people in general will say about us but what the expert in justice and injustice says, the single authority and with him the truth itself.[28] So in the first place your proposal is not well-founded when you claim that we must consider popular opinion about what is just and honourable and good, or the opposite. 'But all the same,' one might object, 'the people have the power to put us to death.'[29]

CRITO: That's clear enough! It would be said, Socrates; you're quite right.

SOCRATES: But so far as I can see, my dear fellow, the argument which we have just been through is quite unaffected by it. At the same time I should like you to consider whether we still agree on this point: that the really important thing is not to live, but to live well.

CRITO: Agreed.

SOCRATES: And is it still agreed or not that to live well amounts to the same thing as to live honourably and justly?

CRITO: Yes.

SOCRATES: Then in the light of this admission we must consider whether or not it is just for me to try to get away without being released by the Athenians. If it turns out to be just, we must make the attempt; if not, we must drop it. As for the considerations you raise about expense and reputation and bringing up children, I am afraid, Crito, that these are the concerns of the ordinary public, who think nothing of putting people to death, and would bring them back to life if they could,[30] with equal indifference to reason.[31] Our real task, I fancy, since the argument leads that way, is to consider one question only, the one which we raised just now: shall we be acting justly in paying money and showing gratitude to these people who are going to rescue me, and in escaping or arranging the escape ourselves, or shall we really be acting unjustly in doing all this? If it becomes clear that such conduct is unjust, I cannot help thinking that the question whether we are sure to die, or to suffer any other ill-effect for that matter, if we stand our ground and take no action, ought not to weigh with us at all in comparison with the risk of acting unjustly.

CRITO: I agree with what you say, Socrates; now consider what we are to do.

SOCRATES: Let us look at it together, Crito; and if you can
e challenge any of my arguments, do so and I will listen to you; but if you can't, be a good fellow and stop telling me over and over again that I ought to leave this place without official permission. I am very anxious to obtain your approval before I adopt the course which I have in mind; I don't want to act against your convictions. Now give your attention to the starting point of this inquiry if you
49a are happy with the way I've put it, and try to answer my questions to the best of your judgement.

CRITO: Well, I will try.

SOCRATES: Do we say that there is no way that one must ever willingly commit injustice, or does it depend upon circumstance? Is it true, as we have often agreed before, that there is no sense in which an act of injustice is good or honourable? Or have we jettisoned all our former convictions in these last few days? Can you and I at our age, Crito, have spent all these years in serious
b discussions without realizing that we were no better than a pair of children? Surely the truth is just what we have always said. Whatever the popular view is, and whether the consequence is pleasanter than this or even tougher, the fact remains that to commit injustice is in every case bad and dishonourable for the person who does it. Is that our view, or not?

CRITO: Yes, it is.

SOCRATES: Then in no circumstances must one do wrong.

CRITO: No.

SOCRATES: In that case one must not even return injustice when one is wronged, which most people regard as the natural course.

c CRITO: Apparently not.

SOCRATES: Tell me another thing, Crito: ought one to inflict injuries or not?

CRITO: Surely not, Socrates.

SOCRATES: And tell me: is it right to inflict an injury in retaliation, as most people believe, or not?

CRITO: No, never.

SOCRATES: Because, I suppose, there is no difference between injuring people and doing them an injustice?[32]

CRITO: Exactly.

SOCRATES: So one ought not to return an injustice or an injury to any person, whatever the provocation. Now be careful, Crito, that in making these single admissions you do not end by admitting *d* something contrary to your real beliefs. I know that there are and always will be few people who think like this; and consequently between those who do think so and those who do not there can be no shared deliberation; they must always feel contempt when they observe one another's decision.[33] I want even you to consider very carefully whether you share my views and agree with me, and whether we can proceed with our discussion from the established hypothesis that it is never right to commit injustice or return injustice or defend one's self against injury by retaliation; or whether you dissociate yourself from any share in this view as a basis for discussion. I have held it for a long time, and still hold *e* it;[34] but if you have formed any other opinion, say so and tell me what it is. If, on the other hand, you stand by what we have said, listen to my next point.

CRITO: Yes, I stand by it and agree with you. Go on.

SOCRATES: Well, here is my next point, or rather question. Ought one to fulfil all one's agreements, provided that they are just,[35] or break them?

CRITO: One ought to fulfil them.

SOCRATES: Then consider the logical consequence. If we leave this place without first persuading the state to let us go, are we or *50a* are we not doing an injury, and doing it to those we've least excuse for injuring? Are we or are we not abiding by our just agreements?

CRITO: I can't answer your question, Socrates; I am not clear in my mind.

Section D1: Socrates introduces the voice of the Laws of Athens, who persuade him that justice requires him to stay and face death. They claim that escaping would be unjust because (i) it would constitute a step towards their own destruction, and (ii) there is an agreement between him and the Laws, akin to that between a son and his parents and of even greater weight, requiring filial obedience on his part in return for the upbringing they have given him. Such obedience is demanded irrespective of the inconvenience and dangers which he may face. He may try to persuade them of the justice of his case, but if he fails it is his duty to obey. To what extent arguments (i) and (ii) are separable is a matter of controversy. Bostock (1990) takes the view that they are, and whereas he sees little authoritarianism in (i), because only one law clearly overrides individual freedoms, namely the law requiring court verdicts to be carried out, he sees little hope of rescuing Plato from charges of general authoritarianism in relation to (ii). As Allen (1980, p.82) notes, the Laws' language is that of a speech, which though at times majestic and authoritative, is nevertheless tempered with an intimacy and concern for their 'child'.

SOCRATES: Look at it in this way. Suppose that while we were preparing to run away from here (or however one should describe it) the Laws and communal interest of Athens were to come and confront us with this question: 'Now, Socrates, what are you proposing to do? Can you deny that by this act which you are contemplating you intend, so far as you have the power, to destroy us, the Laws, and the whole State as well?[36] Do you imagine that a city can continue to exist and not be turned upside down, if the legal judgements which are pronounced in it have no force but are nullified and destroyed by private persons?' – How shall we answer this question, Crito, and others of the same kind? There is much that could be said, especially by an orator, to protest at the abolition of this law which requires that judgements once pronounced shall be binding. Shall we say, 'Yes: the State is guilty of an injustice against me, you see, by passing a faulty judgement at my trial'?[37] Is this to be our answer, or what?
CRITO: What you have said, certainly, Socrates.
SOCRATES: Then what if the Laws say, 'Was there provision for this in the agreement between you and us, Socrates? Or did you undertake to abide by whatever judgements the State pronounced?' If we expressed surprise at such language, they would probably say: 'Don't be surprised at what we say, Socrates, but answer our

questions; after all, you are accustomed to the method of question and answer. Come now, what charge do you bring against us and *d* the State, that you are trying to destroy us? Did we not give you life in the first place?[38] Was it not through us that your father married your mother and brought you into this world? Tell us, have you any complaint against those of us Laws that deal with marriage?'[39] 'No, none,' I should say. 'Well, have you any against the Laws which deal with children's upbringing and education, such as you had yourself? Are you not grateful to those of us Laws which were put in control of this, for requiring your father to give you an education in music and gymnastics?'[40] 'Yes', I should say. *e* 'Very good. Then since you have been born and brought up and educated, can you deny, in the first place, that you were our child and slave, both you and your ancestors? And if this is so, do you imagine that your rights and ours are on a par, and that whatever we try to do to you, you are justified in retaliating? Though you did not have equality of rights with your father, or master if you had one, to enable you to retaliate, and you were not allowed to answer back when you were scolded nor to hit back when you *51a* were beaten, nor to do a great many other things of the same kind, will you be permitted to do it to your country and its Laws, so that if we try to put you to death in the belief that it is just to do so, you on your part will try your hardest to destroy your country and us its Laws in return? And will you, the true devotee of goodness, claim that you are justified in doing so? Are you so wise as to have forgotten that compared with your mother and father and all the rest of your ancestors your country is something far more precious, more venerable, more sacred, and held in greater *b* honour both among gods and among all reasonable men? Do you not realize that you are even more bound to respect and placate the anger of your country than your father's anger? That you must either persuade your country or do whatever it orders, and patiently submit to any punishment that it imposes, whether it be flogging or imprisonment? And if it leads you out to war, to be wounded or killed, you must comply, and it is just that this should be so – you must not give way or retreat or abandon your position. Both in war and in the lawcourts and everywhere else you must do whatever your city and your country commands, or *c* else persuade it that justice is on your side; but violence against mother or father is an unholy act,[41] and it is a far greater sin against your country.' – What shall we say to this, Crito? That what the Laws say is true, or not?

CRITO: Yes, I think so.

Section D2: The Laws go on to explain that Socrates has freely validated their agreement with him by remaining in the city – and doing so more consistently than other individuals.

SOCRATES: 'Consider, then, Socrates,' the Laws would probably continue, 'whether it is also true for us to claim that what you are now trying to do to us is not just. Although we have brought you into the world and reared you and educated you, and given you and all your fellow-citizens a share in all the good things at our
d   disposal, nevertheless by the very fact of granting our permission we openly proclaim this principle: that any Athenian, on attaining to manhood[42] and seeing for himself the political organization of the State and us its Laws, is permitted, if he is not satisfied with us, to take his property and go away wherever he likes. If anyone of you chooses to go to one of our colonies, supposing that he should not be satisfied with us and the State, or to emigrate to any other country, not one of us Laws hinders or prevents him from
e   going away wherever he likes, without any loss of property. On the other hand, if any one of you stands his ground when he can see how we administer justice and the rest of our public organiza-tion, we hold that by so doing he has in fact undertaken to do anything that we tell him;[43] and we maintain that anyone who disobeys is guilty of doing wrong on three separate counts: first because we brought him into this world, and secondly because we reared him; and thirdly because, after promising obedience, he is neither obeying us nor persuading us to change our decision if we
52a are at fault in any way; and although we set a choice before him and do not issue savage commands, giving him the choice of either persuading us or doing what we say,[44] he is actually doing neither. These are the charges, Socrates, to which we say that you too will be liable if you do what you are contemplating; and you'll not be the least culpable of the Athenians, but one of the most guilty.' If I said, 'Why do you say that?' they would no doubt pounce upon me with perfect justice and point out that there are very few

people in Athens who have entered into this agreement with them
as explicitly as I have. They would say, 'Socrates, we have substan-   b
tial evidence that you are satisfied with us and with the State.
Compared with all other Athenians, you would not have been so
exceptionally much in residence if it had not been exceptionally
pleasing to you. You have never left the city to attend a festival –
except once to the Isthmus [45] – nor for any other purpose except on
some military expedition;[46] you have never travelled abroad as
other people do, and you have never felt the impulse to acquaint
yourself with another country or other laws; you have been   c
content with us and with our city. So deliberately have you chosen
us, and undertaken to observe us in all your activities as a citizen,
that you have actually fathered children in it because the city suits
you.[47] Furthermore, even at the time of your trial you could have
proposed the penalty of banishment, if you had chosen to do so;
that is, you could have done then with the sanction of the State
what you are now trying to do without it.[48] But whereas at that
time you made a fine show of your indifference if you had to die,
and in fact preferred death, as you said, to banishment, now you
show no respect for your earlier professions, and no regard for us,
the Laws, whom you are trying to destroy; you are behaving like   d
the lowest slave, trying to run away in spite of the contracts and
undertakings by which you agreed to act as a member of our
State. Now first answer this question: Are we or are we not
speaking the truth when we say that you have undertaken, in deed
and not in word,[49] to play the role of citizen in obedience to us?'
What are we to say to that, Crito? Are we not bound to admit it?
CRITO: We must, Socrates.
SOCRATES: 'It is a fact, then,' they would say, 'that you are
breaking covenants and undertakings made with us, although you   e
made them under no compulsion or misunderstanding, and were
not compelled to decide in a limited time;[50] you had seventy
years [51] in which you could have left the country, if you were not
satisfied with us or felt that the agreements were unjust. You did
not choose Sparta or Crete – your favourite models of good
government [52] – or any other Greek or foreign state; you could not   53a
have absented yourself from the city less if you had been lame or
blind or decrepit in some other way. It is quite obvious that you
outstrip all other Athenians in your satisfaction with this city –

and for us its Laws, for who could be pleased with a city without its laws? And now, after all this, are you not going to stand by your agreement? Yes, you are, Socrates, if you will take our advice; and then you will at least escape being laughed at for leaving the city.

Section D3: Socrates will achieve nothing by escaping: the stigma of a law-breaker will attach to him wherever he goes, it will make a mockery of his past moral views, and it will not help his sons. It will also put him in a difficult position when he faces the judges of the Underworld.

'Just consider, what good will you do yourself or your friends if you breach this agreement and fall short in one of these require-
b ments. It is fairly obvious that the risk of being banished and either losing their citizenship or having their property confiscated will extend to your friends as well. As for yourself, if you go to one of the neighbouring states, such as Thebes or Megara which are both well governed, you will enter them as an enemy to their constitution, and all good patriots will eye you with suspicion as a destroyer of laws. You will confirm the opinion of the jurors, so that they'll seem to have given a correct verdict – for any destroyer
c of laws might very well be supposed to have a destructive influence upon young and foolish human beings.[53] Do you intend, then, to avoid well-governed states and the most disciplined people? And if you do, will life be worth living? Or will you approach these people and have the impudence to converse with them? What subjects will you discuss, Socrates? The same as here, when you said that goodness and justice, institutions and laws, are the most precious possessions of mankind? Do you not think that Socrates
d and everything about him will appear in a disreputable light? You certainly ought to think so. But perhaps you will retire from this part of the world and go to Crito's friends in Thessaly? There you'll find disorder and indiscipline,[54] and no doubt they would enjoy hearing the amusing story of how you managed to run away from prison by arraying yourself in some costume – putting on a shepherd's smock or some other conventional runaway's disguise, and altering your personal appearance. And will no one comment on the fact that an old man of your age, probably with only a

short time left to live, should dare to cling so greedily to life, at the e
price of violating the most stringent laws? Perhaps not, if you
avoid irritating anyone. Otherwise, Socrates, you'll be the object
of a good many humiliating comments. So you will live as the
toady and slave of all the populace, literally 'roistering in
Thessaly',[55] as though you had left this country for Thessaly to
attend a banquet there; and where will your discussions about
justice and other good qualities be then, we should like to know? 54a

'But of course you want to live for your children's sake, so that
you may be able to bring them up and educate them. Indeed! by
first taking them off to Thessaly and making foreigners of them,
so that they'll have that to enjoy too? Or if that is not your
intention, supposing that they are brought up here, will they be
better cared for and educated because of your being alive, even
without you there?[56] Yes, your friends will take care of them. But
will they look after your children if you go away to Thessaly, and
not if you go off to the next world? Surely if those who profess to
be your friends are worth anything, you must believe that they b
would care for them.

'No, Socrates; be advised by us who raised you – do not think
more of your children or of your life or of anything else than you
think of what is just; so that when you enter the next world you
may have all this to plead in your defence before the authorities
there.[57] Neither in this world does doing this appear to be any
better, or more just, or more holy – not to you nor to any of your
family – nor will it be better for you when you reach the next
world. As it is, you will leave this place, when you do, as the
victim of a wrong done not by us, the Laws, but by your fellow- c
men.[58] But if you leave in that dishonourable way, returning
injustice for injustice and injury for injury,[59] breaking your agreements and covenants with us, and injuring those whom you least
ought to injure – yourself, your friends, your country, and us –
then you will have to face *our* anger while you live, and in that
place beyond when our brothers, the Laws of Hades, know that
you have done your best to destroy even us, they will not receive
you with a kindly welcome. Do not take Crito's advice in prefer- d
ence to ours.'

That, my dear friend Crito, I do assure you, is what I seem to
hear them saying, just as a mystic seems to hear the strains of

pipes;[60] and the sound of their arguments rings so loudly in my head that I cannot hear the other side. I warn you that, as my opinion stands at present, it will be useless to urge a different view. However, if you think that you will do any good by it, speak up.

CRITO: No, Socrates, I have nothing to say.

SOCRATES: Then give it up, Crito, and let us follow this course, since God leads the way.

WISDOM AND THE SOUL

SOCRATES ABOUT TO DIE: *PHAEDO*

INTRODUCTION

The *Phaedo*, being a mature work of Plato, is also considerably larger than the three works so far encountered, yet it is tied together by an unusual unity of subject-matter. The obvious way to view the work is as Plato's attempt to persuade us that the soul is immortal, using four distinct arguments, dealing with two objections, and fusing his own ideas with various traditional elements to produce an attractive myth near the end. A final reason for believing that the soul is immortal is the amazingly optimistic attitude of a seemingly inspired man as he prepares to die.

There are dangers, however, in seeing the work purely as an attempted proof of this one Platonic belief. To those readers who do not share Plato's concepts of soul and of its desired objects of knowledge, concepts upon which the arguments are founded, the whole work might in that case be found irritating and pointless, a logical exercise based on unacceptable premises. Yet if they are able to enter fully into its compelling drama – if they can be induced to puzzle over the attitudes of its amazing tragic hero as he moves ever nearer to the inevitable end of his earthly sojourn – then they may be able to bridge the gulf between our world and Plato's and to see how pressing the various issues had become.

This work is addressed to Plato's fellow-philosophers rather than to the ordinary people of Athens. The story is told to a puzzled Pythagorean in a Peloponnesian town; most of the arguments within that story are addressed to the Pythagoreans Simmias and Cebes from Thebes. These are people who very much want Socrates to be correct, yet are honest enough to express their fears that he may not be. They are not worldly men, and are themselves devoted to the pursuits of the mind rather than to those of the body. They, if anyone, can understand the way Socrates' mind worked; they, if anyone, can share in the strange mixture of pleasure and grief which was felt by his friends on the day of his death, and the release from such conflicts of emotion which philosophy (and its consummation in death) could bring.

In a sense the work is about the process of the soul's withdrawal and release rather than about its immortality. One might consider why this work is called *Phaedo*: Platonic dialogues are not ordinarily named after the narrator, yet Phaedo plays only a small part in the conversation which he narrates. Why is it his dialogue? Dialogues tend to be named after the participant who seems to possess, in an ordinary, everyday way, the quality or skill or whatever which the dialogue makes its principal theme. Phaedo of Elis had himself been released in a way analogous to the release of the philosopher's soul, for Phaedo had been captured, enslaved, and pressed into service in a brothel.[1] He had used his philosophic contacts to have his freedom purchased, and seems to have remained a follower of Socrates, making his own contributions to Socratic literature. Phaedo had been rescued from the pursuits and distractions of the flesh in a very concrete manner.

Another case of such a release had been the release of Theseus and his followers, and of Athens as a whole, from the perils of the Minotaur's labyrinth and Minoan Crete. His story is briefly recalled at 58a–b. The Minotaur itself, half man and half bull, can be seen as a symbol for the ways of the flesh and for sexual pleasures in particular. Considerable ingenuity has recently been spent in spelling out the possible significance of this background story for the dialogue as a whole.[2] The underworld that Socrates later envisages is itself a labyrinth. At the end of the work Socrates' outward self can glare like a bull about to charge (117b), but his inner self is without aggression. Has he slain *his* minotaur? Certainly he would hope to have delivered us from a rather different bogey – the fear of death that lurks in the recesses of our minds (77e).

PLEASURE AND RELEASE

The main release theme concerns the philosopher's release from the preoccupation with the body – having constantly to satisfy its needs, only to find them recurring a short while later. In the background lies the notion that earthly pleasures are just the satisfaction of needs, and pains the growth of these needs or the needs themselves. There can be no satisfaction without the initial need, so pleasure and pain are linked, often observably linked (59a, 60b–c); and assuming that the strength of the pleasure is in proportion to the strength of the need that has been felt,[3] it is futile to pursue a balance of earthly pleasure over pain. The philosopher must free himself from this purposeless alternation of pain and pleasure, illustrated by the example of Penelope's weaving (84a) – undoing by night what she had woven in the day.[4] The philosopher pursues this freedom during this life in so far as it is possible for a man, and indeed much of the message of the *Phaedo* is for us who live this life, suggesting how best we might fulfil our intellectual goals here and now. It is not merely the immortality of the soul which would lead us to follow the writer's advice.

However, Plato must have been aware that without some life after death Socrates' own goals in life could look just as vain as that of the profligate who nurtures nagging desires merely for the sake of the pleasures of their satisfaction. At least the profligate has led an active life; what has the philosopher been achieving?[5] Why struggle to acquire knowledge and virtue, if these are both terminated as a result of one's earthly conduct: conduct which one had undertaken in the name of knowledge and virtue? Furthermore, Socrates had been committed to the doctrine that just and honourable conduct was also good conduct, i.e. advantageous, and advantageous not just for society but for the individual as well. Assuming that Socrates' death was honourable, can it also have been *advantageous* for Socrates to die if there was no after-life? He might still achieve freedom from pains which would soon plague him, but that is merely an absence of disadvantage. Socrates had to be dying *for some purpose* if the conduct leading to his death were to be seen as (i) good, hence (ii) honourable, hence (iii) just.

DESIRING DEATH AND SUICIDE

So we meet in the *Phaedo* a further Platonic treatment of the notion that conduct leading to one's own death can be just, honourable and good. But this has to be carefully distinguished from ordinary suicide, to which Plato felt unable to give his approval. And to convince his friends, Socrates will give a new defence speech, answering Simmias's charge that he is recklessly complying with those who would separate him not only from fine friends but also from fine masters in this world (63b ff.)

We may pause briefly to consider the issue of the ban on suicide. Cebes finds some difficulty in two premises to which Socrates subscribes: (A) that the philosopher desires to be released from this world, and (B) that he should not take his own life. If it is also granted (A₂) that death is good for him, why ought he not to pursue death? Here Bostock has an interesting discussion (1986, pp.16–20), but one which leads to the notion that, for Plato, an element of altruism enters into such conduct. Genuinely altruistic action, such as Christianity approves, seems not to be part of Greek ethics, and caution is required.

To help bring out some difficulty in reconciling A₂ with B, Bostock supplies the additional premise that (C) if somebody ought to follow a given course of action, then that course of action must be good for him. This seems a Socratic enough premise, effectively identifying what is morally correct with what is advantageous. But if it is right, then not taking one's life will also be good for one, and there is apparently a contradiction with A₂. Bostock thus demands some reason, besides self-interest, why the philosopher does not take his own life. It is not enough, he argues, that God bans it, for God must himself be basing his decisions on moral grounds.⁶ If God bans suicide for the sake of other men, fearing for instance that there would be no philosophers left, then it is for the sake of other men that it is ultimately avoided.

The point which should not have been admitted, however, is that C and B together are in contradiction with A₂. C and B establish that it is in the philosopher's interests not to take his life. A establishes that it is in his interests to be dead. That it is good to *be dead* does not entail that it is good to *become dead* by any means, even unjust or impious ones. To incur divine displeasure may challenge the very serenity which he thinks he will enjoy on death. He acts in his own interests by waiting for another means of death, just as a slave who is promised freedom tomorrow acts against his own interest if he annoys his master by running away today. So he waits for self-interested reasons, not for altruistic ones, even though his master may have the interests of the rest of his household at heart when he bans premature escape.[7]

THE SECOND APOLOGY

Socrates is virtually accused of being far too ready to desert both good friends and good divine masters. He cannot argue that he will not be upsetting his friends or that it is in *their* interests for him to die; and he does not choose to argue that his conduct is pleasing or helpful to the gods either. He argues, in fact, that it is in *his own* interests. He expects to have a further existence in which he will again have fine friends and fine gods for his masters, and that death, as separation from the body and its needs, will merely be the natural culmination of everything which he had been pursuing in this life too. Thus it will be only a slight step further along the path which he was already travelling. At the end of the work we meet an excellent illustration of the slightness of this step as Socrates fades gently out of this life, the soul leaving the body from the feet upward. As Christopher Gill (1973) has pointed out, this is not an illustration of the normal effects of hemlock poisoning, but a piece of idealistic fiction illustrating the main message of the dialogue. Socrates is released, and released without violence because he had practically released himself already.

THE SOUL

In order to appreciate why Socrates sees death as the natural goal of his life's work one must appreciate what it was that he thought survived death. The Greek term *psyche*, usually though not invari- ably translated 'soul', did not represent a fixed concept. It is reasonable to suppose that the average Greek in Plato's day would have had a rough idea what he meant by it, something like the inner person, one's intellectual and emotional self; but there would have been plenty of questions about it which he would never have tried to answer. The concepts of soul proposed by Greek

philosophers vary considerably, but all of them see it as principally responsible either for motion (including growth), or for sensation, etc., or for both. It could be distinguished from the body
either by its being non-material or by its being a finer, more
mobile type of matter. But in general it was contrasted with our
bodies and with body in general.

The idea of an inner self which survived death, a continuing
person who might experience good or bad fortune in another
world, was deeply implanted in the Greek consciousness. It was
there in Homer in the form of the 'shades', which experienced a
dark existence in the underworld kingdom of Hades. It was there
in the Orphic poems, which had special influence on the more
religious minds of the classical period. It was there in the expectations of those about to die in Greek tragedies. The term *psyche*
was not always used for this entity, but was fluid enough to be so
used. It was natural for Socrates and his friends, acutely conscious
as they were of their mental endeavours, to presume that such an
entity existed, in much the same way as it is easy for us to assume
that we have a mind. Sometimes, in fact, the term can most easily
be translated as 'mind', though this has been avoided here in the
interests of consistency. Sometimes it tends to be identified with
the person – with the continuing entity which underlies all changes
to our physical and mental being through growth, injury, learning
or character degeneration.[8]

Thus at the end of the work Socrates indicates that he is to be
identified with his soul; his former body is no longer Socrates
(115c). Death is viewed as the moment of separation of soul from
body, after which the body begins to decay and the soul continues
its existence, complete with memory, thought, and powers of
communication, though without the organs of sense. It goes on
experiencing the society of other souls, and is able to suffer
emotional trauma though not physical pain and inner contentment
though not physical pleasure.

There are a number of issues concerning the soul which the
dialogue does not, perhaps cannot, clarify. Since late antiquity
Platonists have debated whether Plato intended that the whole
soul should be seen as immortal, whether only the rational part
was to have that status, or whether some third possibility should
apply. In fact the work makes no explicit division of the soul into

'parts' (such as are found in *Republic* 4), but much of the discussion is carried on as if the entire human soul were *in its true nature* capable of functioning as a totally unified rational being which retained both motivation and feelings.

Obviously Plato wanted to promise us a genuinely attractive life hereafter, and this had to involve a range of activities: the promise of a life of perpetual mental calculations would not be any comfort to the majority of men. On the other hand for Socrates' case to work, what *he* met in the other life had to be such as to free him from the more immediate influences of sense-perception and from the demands of desires associated with our life in the body. Does that mean that he should have no emotions at all in that world? Does it mean that he should have nothing *akin* to sensation: no awareness of the present, no interaction (philosophic or not) with other disembodied souls, no power to reflect on sensations remembered from this life? That would mean that we have two competing versions of the nature of the soul's immortality in the one dialogue, one traditional, generously postulating the continuity of a wide range of faculties, and one philosophical, postulating the continuity of mind alone. The latter is what Socrates promises himself, and the former is what he offers the ordinary reader.[9]

This cannot be right. The *Apology* shows that Socrates' philosophy was no 'practice of death', if death is merely detached contemplation. Nor is he content to discover without the satisfaction which results from discovery. He hopes for something akin to hearing by which he will 'listen to' famous men of old (*Apology* 41a–c). And he can scarcely continue to be the same person without the memory of what he experienced in this life or the ability to experience new surroundings there. He does not need to leave behind all these functions of the soul; what he must leave behind is the direct influence of the body, and the sensations to the extent that their intensity and their preoccupation with physical reality interferes with his mental processes – processes which will lead to the cognition of a higher reality. The philosopher has to give up no more than a soul must inevitably give up if it leaves its body to lead a discarnate life.

Once this is appreciated there are fewer problems with Plato's theory regarding the future of the common man's soul. The common man, we are told, has much greater difficulty leaving the body behind (81c–e); his soul has to be purged of the body's effects. He has not managed to draw together all the threads of the soul, some of them deeply involved with the body, and to unify them as Socrates requires (67c, 70a, 80e, 83a). Whether his soul is really capable of overcoming the divisions induced by the body is unclear, but there seems little doubt that he will not spend much time in philosophy in the other world even after purification. Physically the body is no longer with him, but through memory and through habit its influence can still be felt. Wedded as it was to sensation and without the ability to lift its mind towards the 'Ideas', one can imagine that it will find Hades a dark world indeed. Among these souls the philosopher will stand out as fully in control of all available faculties, like Homer's Teiresias among the other dead (*Meno* 100a).[10]

POPULAR AND SOCRATIC MORALITY

The *Meno* had used the contrast between Teiresias and other dead souls to contrast virtue based upon *understanding* the right course with ordinary virtue which relies upon intuition or guesswork. Clearly Socrates had always hoped for the former type, but the latter was all that men were normally able to achieve. The *Meno* was probably the first dialogue to distinguish between the philosopher's virtue and ordinary virtue, but it leaves much of the detail of the distinction to our imagination. The *Phaedo* again takes up this theme at 82a–b and, more interestingly, at 68b–69d. The philosophers are actually said to be particularly brave and particularly temperate even according to popular criteria, facing death cheerfully and not being excited by physical desires. By contrast other people are brave only because they fear other things more and temperate only because they fear that profligacy will later deprive them of other pleasures for which their desire is greater. These people have neither mastered fear nor mastered desire. They may be choosing the same course of action as the philosopher, and doing exactly what they ought to be doing, but their motivation is not much different from that of the coward and the profligate. They too think in terms of avoidance of pain and pursuit of pleasure.

How then does the philosopher differ? A fearfully obscure passage of text (69a–b) has concealed the details from us. Ordinary virtue seems to be compared with a system of barter in which goods of a similar kind are exchanged for one another. The philosopher's virtue, however, introduces wisdom (*phronesis*, that particular kind of 'knowledge' that was conceived of as an appropriate guide to behaviour) as the equivalent of a system of currency. He will brave dangers and sacrifice pleasures in order to obtain wisdom. So far, so good. It seems that the philosopher is going to be aiming at wisdom rather than at a balance of pleasure over pain. But a system of currency is not an end in itself; money is valued because it can be used to purchase other things, and if the analogy is to hold, then wisdom must in turn become a purchasing agent, selecting what it is right for the individual to experience. This has not escaped Plato's notice, for he speaks of buying as well as selling, and it seems that what are to be 'bought' with wisdom are again pleasures and fears. We select our pleasures and our fears with a view to wisdom; we use our wisdom to select our pleasures and fears – to perform for us a hedonistic calculus.

At first sight this will not do. The philosopher will seem to be operating with the same hedonistic motives that the common people have employed. Indeed from 69b5–6 it might seem that it is less the hedonistic motivation that Socrates objects to, but the fact that wisdom is not overseeing the process. On reflection, however, where wisdom controls the process, it will do so only in such a way as to encourage the acquisition of further wisdom. All pleasure-seeking and pain-avoiding has wisdom as an aim; the converse does not have to be true. Pleasures may not have been given up, but they have become subordinated to the search for wisdom, as one would expect in the case of the philosopher (who is literally a 'wisdom-lover'). Hence it is possible for Socrates to represent true temperance, justice and courage as cleansing operations that sweep away hedonistic motivation, and wisdom as the cleansing agent.

There will of course be scepticism as to how far Socrates has painted a picture of virtue which should be admired. There seems to be a rigorous pursuit of the philosopher's own interests and of the particular activity which brings him satisfaction (pleasure, even!). Even within Plato's Academy Eudoxus was to take the view that all creatures, including philosophers, pursued pleasure and avoided pain.[11] Bostock feels that Socrates' self-seeking, ascetic 'virtue' is a recipe for injustice (1986, p.34), but this overlooks the fact that wisdom will control conduct, and wisdom can never (almost by definition) behave in a manner which is to the detriment of its possessor, nor (by the Socratic equation of what is good with what is honourable) disgraceful.

ARGUMENTS FOR IMMORTALITY: AN OUTLINE

With the very first argument for immortality we are plunged into the world of the Greek physicists' principles, which will operate in the background to a surprising extent. Socrates was not usually known for his interest in physics, but he can scarcely avoid the subject here bearing in mind that the Greeks had so far tackled the nature of the soul in the context of the study of the natural world. No other path is available here. Socrates, we must remember, is arguing primarily with two Pythagoreans, whose school's contribution to physics was much admired by Plato and commemorated in his *Timaeus*. The tale is being told in Phlius to another Pythagorean. They have to be convinced that the laws which apply to physical realities (and to their favourite mathematical entities too),[12] if applied to soul, will make it such as to survive death and survive it permanently. The need to tackle the problem within the context of the workings of the whole universe will also make it necessary for Plato to reveal the Ideas, his own contribution to the universal picture. Consequently many of these arguments have implications for Plato's metaphysics, though we ought not to suppose that the chief message depends on the reader's familiarity with this theory. I have chosen to save my discussion of the Theory of Ideas for a postscript, though some help also will be offered in the notes.

The physicists had rejected the notions of outright coming-to-be and passing away, regarding all generation and destruction as no more than a modification of eternal underlying substance: either (i) substances able to take on various opposite qualities (e.g. soul in live condition and soul in dead condition), or (ii) substances which could produce opposite effects by changes of their mixture, as in Empedocles (e.g. soul combined with body, soul separated from body). The first argument (70c ff.) is designed to show that, according to these principles, that which is living will come from that which is non-living (dead), and that which is non-living from that which is living.

Next we proceed to the argument from recollection (72e ff.) which in fact suggests that the inner person or soul exists *prior to* this life, but to show this much would be a big psychological step towards convincing the reader of an after-life too. The theory had apparently been set out already in the *Meno* (81a ff.), and it remains part of the machinery utilized by the *Phaedrus* some years later. The *Meno* had shown Socrates eliciting the correct answers on a problem of geometry from a slave who knew no geometry. Some dim 'memory' is allegedly awakened within the slave, ensuring that he forms correct opinions; eventually those opinions can be transformed into knowledge proper. The *Phaedo* is particularly keen to show that such recollected knowledge includes knowledge of the Platonic Ideas, those standards of absolute justice, beauty, equality, etc., with which the philosopher must concern himself if we heed the *Phaedo*. It is in fact important to Plato to suggest that these alleged objects of Socrates' inquiry (whether or not he knew it) were the objects with which the soul would have come into contact in its disembodied life, thus giving the philosopher the expectation of meeting them in his next disembodied life too. Plato believes that we had some dim awareness of the Ideas when we first recognized their instances through the senses, but only the philosopher can convert this dim awareness into true understanding. The recollection argument suggests the existence of a stock of disembodied souls, repeatedly drawn upon as new living creatures are generated. The argument from opposites is then utilized once more in order to establish that this stock will need to be replenished by the souls which had been living earlier lives in the body (77d).

Thereafter the principle of a stock of souls seems to be accepted, but their recycling does not mean that individual souls must retain their identity after death. Presocratic theories of cycles of generation involved the *breaking down* of matter for subsequent redevelopment, or at least its breaking down as far as atoms (for Leucippus and Democritus). Why should the soul, often thought of as being related to breath, not be dissipated at death (77d–e), only forming new souls when some process draws together bunches of dissipated soul-stuff? An argument is now brought forward in order to show that such dissipation is improbable.

The similarity argument is central to the *Phaedo*, and probably given less attention than it should receive, perhaps because it is an inductive argument and not therefore compelling. The argument examines the characteristic features of (A) Bodies and (B) Platonic Ideas.

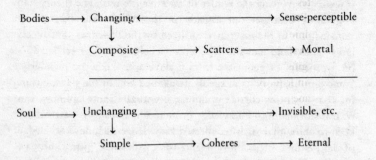

Our body is found to be sense-perceptible and mortal like other bodies; but our soul is invisible, creating the impression that it may be immortal. It does, however, resemble the changing as well as the unchanging, depending on whether or not it is in contact with the body (79d); the case is by no means simple, but one might expect it to be unchanging *in its own right*. This creates a presumption in favour of immortality, but that is all. If not immortal, it would be expected to be nearly so (80b).

During the argument Plato avoided saying that only the composite can be sense-perceptible, though he clearly wanted this to be so. To us there may seem to be no obvious connection. But to somebody brought up in the environment of Presocratic theories of sensation there would have been an automatic connection. Empedocles (see *Meno* 76c–d) and the atomists had explained sight, etc., in terms of effluxes emanating from bodies, and actually consisting of the parts of those bodies. Without parts, there could be no sensation. The idea that the soul's invisibility made it simple rather than compound harmonizes well with the physics with which Socrates and Plato had been familiar.

Because this argument had only created a presumption in favour of immortality, and because Socrates is dealing with the qualities of the soul without first trying to discover what it really is, Plato's job is not done. The objections raised by Simmias and Cebes may remind one that it was not Plato's purpose merely to induce in us a true belief, for true beliefs are transient (*Meno* 97b–98b); he wanted to teach us, and teaching required a superior kind of argument, one which appealed to the very nature of the subject under discussion. The reaction of the company, and indeed of Echecrates (88c–e), to the objections of Simmias and Cebes are supposed to be typical of those who have been persuaded to accept mere opinions. The reaction of Socrates, however, is that of one who knows.

He begins by appealing for confidence in argument, confidence that it can lead us to the truth if we use it correctly: far too often at this time arguments were seen as pointers rather than proofs, as evidence which could readily be manipulated and was no more objective than a human witness. Simmias's suggestion that the soul might be like a harmony, and vanish when the object which it harmonizes is broken, is dismissed on two counts (91c ff.): (i) this theory is incompatible with the Theory of Recollection, which Simmias takes to be proven, and (ii) the soul itself is susceptible to being more or less harmonious, unlike a harmony. Cebes' objection that the soul may be longer-lasting than the body but still end up perishing is what requires the last, and most impressive, argument for immortality.

The final argument explains why 'Socrates' (Plato surely) had come to try to explain the world in terms of Ideas being present to objects, some essentially, some accidentally. That this explanation has come after (i) a fascination for Presocratic physics, and (ii) an admiration for the Anaxagorean idea that the world is governed by an Intelligence, is no accident. The Ideas may be introduced to the bodies (etc.) which are to participate in them by some kind of vector (for want of a better term)[13] which entails their presence (albeit not a material presence), much as warmth is introduced to a body by the vector 'fire' in Presocratic physics. The Ideas are Plato's supreme realities, much as the physical qualities (hot, cold, wet, dry, etc.) are the supreme realities of the Presocratic world. As fire, as vector of heat, cannot become cold, so three, as vector of 'odd', cannot become even, and so, apparently, soul, as vector of life, cannot become dead. Yet fire does not have to go on to another existence; it can be quenched and cease to be fire. Cannot soul too *either* withdraw *or* be quenched? This option is closed by what is for us virtually an appeal to our intuitions: if what is deathless (i.e. cannot become dead) can be destroyed, how can there be anything which is not destroyed?[14] Nobody resists now; all the company are as convinced as a man can be over such a topic.

Socrates now goes on to give his account of the universe, an account into which are built not merely an elaborate underworld bearing some strange relation to Greek tradition, but also an upper world where superior souls can eventually dwell upon the true surface of the earth – that upper world of superior entities for which the philosopher is always striving. This leads into an eschatological 'myth' in which Plato details the fates of various types of soul as they are rewarded or punished in the after-life. It is not surprising in this work where Pythagoreans are continually addressed that the myth is so closely bound up with an account of the geography of the *physical* universe, and that this geography does its best to incorporate many of the features of the 'Orphic' underworld. Nor is it surprising that Plato is once again trying to illustrate his conception of the workings of the psychical or metaphysical world via his picture of the physical world, for physics has never been left far behind.

Both the geography and the eschatology are designed to ring true, yet to seem strange and remote, just as Socrates himself is designed to seem remote but knowledgeable as he gets closer to death. The work builds up to a considerable climax, when a man whom we have come so much to admire has to drink his hemlock, die, and be healed (118a). It is an emotional moment, but in the end it is an optimistic one too. The virtuous man, it seems, is duly rewarded.

PHAEDO

In a remote Peloponnesian township Echecrates catches up on the details of Socrates' death. At last a traveller had arrived who could tell them – Phaedo of Elis, a follower of Socrates who had been with him on his final day.

ECHECRATES: Were you there with Socrates yourself, Phaedo, the day when he drank the poison, or did you hear about it from somebody else?

PHAEDO: I was there myself, Echecrates.

ECHECRATES: Then what did the Master say before he died, and how did he meet his end? I should very much like to hear. None of the people in Phlius go to Athens much in these days, and it is a long time since we had a visitor from there who could give us any definite information, except that he was executed by drinking hemlock; nobody could tell us anything more than that.

PHAEDO: Then haven't you even heard how his trial went?

ECHECRATES: Yes, someone told us about that; and we were surprised because there was obviously a long interval between it and the execution. How was that, Phaedo?

PHAEDO: A fortunate coincidence, Echecrates. It so happened that on the day before the trial they had just finished garlanding the stern of the ship which Athens sends to Delos.

ECHECRATES: What ship is that?

PHAEDO: The Athenians say it's the one in which Theseus sailed away to Crete with the seven youths and seven maidens, and saved their lives and his own as well. The story says that the Athenians made a vow to Apollo that if these young people's lives were saved they would send a solemn mission to Delos every year; and ever since then they have kept their vow to the god, right down to the present day. They have a law that as soon as this mission begins the city must be kept pure, and no public executions may take

place until the ship has reached Delos and returned again; which sometimes takes a long time, if they meet winds which hold it
c back. The mission is considered to begin as soon as the priest of Apollo has garlanded the stern of the ship; and this happened, as I say, on the day before the trial. That's why Socrates spent such a long time in prison between his trial and execution.

ECHECRATES: What about the actual circumstances of his death, Phaedo? What was said and done, and which of the man's companions were with him? Or did the authorities refuse them admission, making him pass away without a friend at his side?

d PHAEDO: Oh no; some of them were there – quite a number, in fact.

ECHECRATES: Please be kind enough to give us a really detailed account – unless you are pressed for time.

PHAEDO: No, I have the time, and I'll try to describe it for you. Nothing gives me more pleasure than recalling the memory of Socrates, either by talking myself or by listening to someone else.

ECHECRATES: Well, Phaedo, you'll find that your audience feels just the same about it. Now try to describe every detail as carefully as you can.

e PHAEDO: In the first place, my own feelings at the time were quite extraordinary. It never occurred to me to feel sorry for him, as you might have expected me to feel at the deathbed of a very close friend. The man actually seemed quite happy, Echecrates, both in his manner and in what he said; he met his death so fearlessly and nobly. I could not help feeling that even on his way to the other world he would have divine protection, and that when he arrived there too all would be well with him, if that could ever be said of
59a anybody.[15] So I felt no sorrow at all, as you might have expected on such an occasion of mourning; and at the same time I felt no pleasure at being occupied in our usual philosophical discussions – that was the form that our conversation took – I experienced a quite weird sensation, a sort of curious blend of pleasure and pain combined, as my mind took it in that in a little while my friend was going to die. All of us who were there were afflicted in much the same way, alternating between laughter and tears; one of us in particular, Apollodorus – you know the man and what he's like,
b don't you?[16]

ECHECRATES: Of course I do.

PHAEDO: Well, he quite lost control of himself; and I and the others were very much upset.

ECHECRATES: Who were actually there, Phaedo?

PHAEDO: Why, of the Athenians there were this man Apollodorus, and Critobulus and his father,[17] and then there were Hermogenes and Epigenes and Aeschines and Antisthenes.[18] Oh yes, and Ctesippus of Paeanis,[19] and Menexenus,[20] and some other local people. I believe that Plato was ill.[21]

ECHECRATES: Were there any visitors from outside?

PHAEDO: Yes: Simmias of Thebes, with Cebes and Phaedondas; and Euclides and Terpsion from Megara.[22]   c

ECHECRATES: Oh, weren't Aristippus and Cleombrotus there?

PHAEDO: No, they were in Aegina, apparently.

ECHECRATES: Was there anybody else?

PHAEDO: I think that's about all.

ECHECRATES: Well, what path did the discussion take?

PHAEDO: I will try to tell you all about it from the very beginning. We had all made it our regular practice, even in the period before, to visit Socrates every day; we used to meet at daybreak by the court-house where the trial was held, because it was close to the prison. We always spent some time in conversation while we waited for the door to open, which was never very early; and when it did open, we used to go in to see Socrates, and spend the best part of the day with him. On this particular day we met earlier than usual, because when we left the prison on the evening before, we heard that the boat had just arrived back from Delos; so we urged one another to meet at the usual place as early as possible. When we arrived, the porter, instead of letting us in as usual, told us to wait and not to come in until he gave us the word. 'The Eleven[23] are taking off Socrates' chains,' he said, 'and warning him that he is to die today.' After a short interval he came back and told us to go in.

When we went inside we found Socrates just released from his   60a
chains, and Xanthippe[24] – you know her! – sitting by him with the little boy on her knee. As soon as Xanthippe saw us she burst out into the kind of thing women generally say: 'Oh, Socrates, this is the last time that you and your friends will be able to talk together!' Socrates looked at Crito. 'Crito,' he said, 'someone had better take her home.' Some of Crito's servants led her away crying hysterically.   b

Socrates sat up on the bed and drew up his leg and massaged it, saying as he did so, 'What a queer thing it is, my friends, this sensation which is popularly called pleasure! It is remarkable how closely it is connected with its apparent opposite, pain.[25] They will never come to a man both at once, but if you pursue one of them and catch it, you are virtually compelled always to have the other as well; they are like two bodies attached to the same head. I am sure that if Aesop had thought of it he would have made up a fable about them, something like this: God wanted to stop their continual quarrelling,[26] and when he found that it was impossible, he fastened their heads together; so wherever one of them appears, the other is sure to follow after. That's exactly what seems to be happening to me. Because I had a pain in my leg from the fetter, the pleasure seems to have come as a consequence of it.'

Here Cebes broke in and said, 'Oh yes, Socrates, I am glad you reminded me. Evenus[27] asked me a day or two ago, as others have done before, about the lyrics which you have been composing lately by adapting Aesop's fables and the prelude to Apollo; he wanted to know what induced you to write them now after you had gone to prison, when you had never done anything of the kind before. If you would like me to be able to answer Evenus when he asks me again – as I am sure he will – tell me what I am to say.'

'Tell him the truth,' said Socrates, 'I did not compose them to rival either him or his poetry – which I knew would not be easy; I did it in the attempt to discover the meaning of certain dreams, and to clear my conscience, in case this was the art which I had been told to practise. It's like this, you see. In the course of my life I have often had the same dream, appearing in different forms at different times, but always saying the same thing: "Socrates, practise and cultivate the arts."[28] In the past I used to think that it was impelling and exhorting me to do what I was actually doing; I mean that the dream, like a spectator encouraging a runner in a race, was urging me on to do what I was doing already, that is, practising the arts; because philosophy is the greatest of the arts, and I was practising it. But when my trial had taken place, and this god's festival was delaying my execution,[29] I decided that, in case it should be this popular form of art that the dream intended me to practise, I ought to compose and not disobey; I reasoned that it would be safer not to take my departure before I had

cleared my conscience by writing poetry in obedience to the   *b*
dream. I began with some verses in honour of the god whose
festival it was. When I had finished my hymn, I reflected that a
poet, if he is to be worthy of the name, ought to work on stories,
not discourses; and I was no story-writer. So it was the stories that
I knew and had handy which I versified – Aesop's, the first ones
that occurred to me. You can tell Evenus this, Cebes, and bid him
farewell from me, and tell him, if he's wise, to follow me as
quickly as he can. I shall be going today, it seems; those are my   *c*
country's orders.'

Section A: The philosopher avoids suicide but welcomes death.[30]

'What a piece of advice for Evenus, Socrates!' said Simmias. 'I
have had a good deal to do with him before now, and from what I
know of him he will not be at all ready to obey you.'

'Why?' he asked. 'Isn't Evenus a philosopher?'

'So I believe,' said Simmias.

'Well then, he will be quite willing, just like anyone else worthy
of his role in philosophy. However, he will hardly do himself
violence, because they say that it is not legitimate.' As he spoke he
lowered his feet to the ground, and sat like this for the rest of the   *d*
discussion.

Cebes now asked him, 'Socrates, what do you mean by saying
that it is not legitimate to do one's self violence, although a
philosopher will be willing to follow a friend who dies?'

'Why, Cebes, have you and Simmias never heard about these
things while you have been with Philolaus?'[31]

'Nothing definite, Socrates.'

'Well, even my information is only based on hearsay; but I don't
mind at all telling you what I have heard. I suppose that for one who   *e*
is soon to leave this world there is no more suitable occupation than
inquiring into our views about the future life, and trying to imagine
what it is like. What else can one do in the time before sunset?'

'Tell me then, Socrates, what are the grounds for saying that
suicide is not legitimate? I have heard it described as wrong before
now (as you suggested) both by Philolaus, when he was staying
with us, and by others as well; but I have never yet heard any
definite explanation for it.'

62a   'Well, you must not lose heart,' he said; 'perhaps you are about to hear one. However, no doubt you will think it amazing that this[32] should be the one straightforward moral question, and that it should never happen in the case of life and death (as it does in all other cases) that sometimes and for some people death is better than life;[33] and it probably seems amazing to you that it should be unholy for any to whom death would be an advantage[34] to benefit themselves, but that they should have to await the services of someone else.'

Cebes laughed gently and said, 'Aye, that it does,' slipping into his own dialect.

b   'Yes,' went on Socrates, 'put in that way it would seem unreasonable – but no, perhaps it has good reason. The hidden message[35] about it from mystics who say that we men are put in a sort of lock-up,[36] from which one must not release oneself or run away, seems to me to be a lofty belief and difficult to understand. All the same, Cebes, I believe that this much is true: that we men are in the care of the gods, one of their possessions. Don't you think so?'

'Yes, I do,' said Cebes.

c   'Then take your own case; if one of your possessions were to destroy itself without intimation from you that you wanted it to die, wouldn't you be angry with it and punish it, if you had any means of doing so?'

'Certainly.'

'So if you look at it in this way I suppose it is not unreasonable to say that we must not put an end to ourselves until God sends some necessary circumstance like the one which we are facing now.'

'That seems likely, I admit,' said Cebes. 'But what you were saying just now, that philosophers would be willing to die without qualms – that seems illogical, Socrates, assuming that we were right in saying a moment ago that God is our keeper and we are his possessions. If our service here is directed by the gods, who are the very best of directors, it is inexplicable that the very wisest of men should not be grieved at quitting it; because he surely cannot expect to provide for himself any better when he is free. On the other hand a stupid person might get the idea that it would be to his advantage to escape from his master; he might not reason it out that one should not escape from a good master, but remain

with him as long as possible; and so he might run away unreflect-
ingly. A sensible man would surely wish to remain always with his
superior. If you look at it this way, Socrates, the reasonable thing
is just the opposite of what we said just now – it's natural for the
wise to be grieved when they die, and for fools to be happy.'

When Socrates had listened to this he seemed to me to be
delighted with Cebes' persistence, and looking round at us he said,   63a
'You know, Cebes is always tracking down arguments, and he is
not at all willing to accept every statement at first hearing.'

Simmias said, 'Well, but, Socrates, I actually think that this time
there is something in what he says. Why should a really wise man
want to desert masters who are better than himself, and to get rid
of them so lightly? I think Cebes is aiming his criticism at you,
because of the extent to which you make light of leaving not just
us, but the gods too, who as you admit are good masters.'

'What you and Cebes say is perfectly fair,' said Socrates. 'You   b
mean, I suppose, that I must make a court-style defence against
this charge.'

*Section B: The new defence speech. Socrates replies to the charge
that he is leaving this world far too readily, deserting a world in
which he has kindly gods for his masters. He explains why the
philosopher should be happy at the prospect of death. The philosopher desires to understand the Ideas of things, and is hindered by
the distractions of the body. Death will be the culmination of a
life's work in search of wisdom – on which alone morality can be
founded.*

'Exactly,' said Simmias.

'Very well then; let me try to make a more convincing defence
to you than I made at my trial. If I did not expect to enter the
company, first, of other wise and good gods,[37] and secondly of
men now dead who are better than those who are in this world
now, it is true that it would be unjust for me not to grieve at
death. As it is, you can be assured that I expect to find myself
among good men; while I would not particularly insist on this, I   c
assure you that I could commit myself upon the next point if I
could upon anything:[38] that I shall find there divine masters who
are supremely good. That is why I am not so much distressed as I

might be, and why I have a firm hope that there is something in store for those who have died, and (as we have been told since antiquity) something much better for the good than for the wicked.'

'Why is this, Socrates?' asked Simmias. 'Do you mean to leave us with your ideas locked in your own mind, or will you communi-

d cate them to us too? I think that we also have a claim on this benefit; besides, it will serve as your defence, if we are satisfied with what you say.'

'Very well, I will try,' he replied. 'But before I begin, Crito here seems to have been wanting to say something for some time; let us find out what it is.'

'Only this, Socrates,' said Crito, 'that the man who is to give you the poison has been asking me for an equally long time to tell you to talk as little as possible; he says that as you talk more it increases your heat, and that you ought not to do anything to

e affect the action of the poison.[39] Otherwise it is sometimes necessary to take a second dose, or even a third.'

'Leave him to his own devices,' said Socrates. 'Let him for his part make ready to administer it twice or three times if necessary.'

'I virtually knew your answer,' said Crito, 'but he's been bothering me for ages.'

'Never mind him,' said Socrates. 'Now for you, my jury, I want to explain to you how natural it seems to me that a man who has really devoted his life to philosophy should be confident in the

64a face of death, and hopeful of winning the greatest of prizes in the next world after death. I will try to make clear to you, Simmias and Cebes, how this can be so.

'Ordinary people seem not to realize that those who really apply themselves in the right way to philosophy are directly and of their own accord preparing themselves for dying and death. If this is true, and they have actually been looking forward to death all their lives, it would of course be absurd to be troubled when the thing comes for which they have so long been preparing and looking forward.'

Simmias laughed and said, 'Upon my word, Socrates, you have

b made me laugh, though I was not at all in the mood for it. I am sure that if they heard what you said, most people would think – and our fellow-countrymen would heartily agree – that it was a very good hit at the philosophers to say that they are half dead already, and that normal people like themselves are quite aware that death would serve the philosophers right.'

'And they would be quite correct, Simmias; except in thinking that they are "quite aware". They are not at all aware in what sense true philosophers are half dead, or in what sense they deserve death, or what sort of death they deserve. But let us *c* dismiss them and talk among ourselves. Do we believe that there is such a thing as death?'

'Most certainly,' said Simmias in reply.

'Is it simply the release of the soul from the body? Is death nothing more or less than this, the separate condition of the body by itself when it is released from the soul, and the separate condition by itself of the soul when released from the body? Is death anything else than this?'

'No, just that.'[40]

'Well then, Simmias, see whether you agree with me; I fancy that this will help us to find out the answer to our problem. Do *d* you think that it's a philosopher's business to concern himself with what people call pleasures [41] – food and drink, for instance?'

'Certainly not, Socrates,' said Simmias.

'What about those of sex?'

'Not in the least.'

'And what about the other ways in which we devote attention to our bodies? Do you think that a philosopher attaches any importance to them? I mean things like providing himself with smart clothes and shoes and other bodily ornaments; do you think that he values them or despises them – in so far as there is no real necessity for him to go in for that sort of thing?'   *e*

'I think the true philosopher despises them,' he said.

'Then it is your opinion in general that a man of this kind is not preoccupied with the body, but keeps his attention directed as much as he can away from it and towards the soul?'

'Yes, it is.'

'So it is clear first of all in the case of physical pleasures that the philosopher frees his soul from association with the body (so far *65a* as is possible) in a way that other men don't?'

'It seems so.'

'And most people think, do they not, Simmias, that a man who takes neither pleasure nor part in these things does not deserve to live, and that anyone who thinks nothing of pleasures connected with the body has one foot in the grave?'

'That is perfectly true.'

'Now take the acquisition of wisdom; is the body a hindrance or not, if one takes it into partnership to share an investigation? b What I mean is this: is there any certainty in human sight and hearing, or is it true, as the poets[42] are always dinning into our ears, that we neither hear nor see anything accurately? Yet if these senses are not clear and accurate, the rest[43] can hardly be so, because they are all inferior to the first two. Don't you agree?'

'Certainly.'

'Then when is it that the soul attains to truth? When it tries to investigate anything with the help of the body, it is obviously liable to be led astray.'

c 'Quite so.'

'Is it not in the course of reasoning, if at all, that the soul gets a clear view of reality?'

'Yes.'

'Surely the soul can reason best when it is free of all distractions such as hearing or sight or pain or pleasure of any kind – that is, when it leaves the body to its own devices,[44] becomes as isolated as possible, and strives for reality while avoiding as much physical contact and association as it can.'

'That is so.'

'Then here again the philosopher's soul is most disdainful of the d body, shunning it and seeking to isolate itself.'

'It seems so.'

'Here are some more questions, Simmias. Do we recognize such a thing as justice itself?'[45]

'Indeed we do.'

'And beauty itself and goodness too?'

'Of course.'

'Have you ever seen any of these things with your eyes?'

'Certainly not,' said he.

'Well, have you ever apprehended them with any other bodily sense? By "them" I mean them all, including tallness or health or strength in themselves, the real nature of any given thing – what it e actually is. Is it through the body that we get our truest view of them? Isn't it true that in any inquiry you are likely to attain more nearly to knowledge of your object in proportion to the care and accuracy with which you have prepared yourself to understand that object in itself?'

'Certainly.'

'Don't you think that the person who is most likely to achieve this flawlessly is the one who approaches each object, as far as possible, with the unaided intellect, without taking account of any sense of sight[46] in his thinking, or dragging any other sense into his reckoning – the man who pursues the truth by applying his pure and unadulterated thought to the pure and unadulterated object, cutting himself off as much as possible from his eyes and ears and virtually all the rest of his body, as an impediment which, if present, prevents the soul from attaining to the truth and clear thinking? Is not this the person, Simmias, who will reach the goal of reality, if anybody can?'

'What you say is absolutely true, Socrates,' said Simmias.

'All these considerations,' said Socrates, 'must surely prompt serious philosophers to review the position in some such way as this. "It looks as if it's a side-track, to divert us – and reason along with us – in our investigation.[47] So long as we keep to the body and our soul is contaminated with this imperfection, there is no chance of our ever attaining satisfactorily to our object, which we assert to be Truth. In the first place, the body provides us with innumerable distractions in the pursuit of its necessary sustenance, and any diseases which attack us hinder our quest for reality. Besides, the body fills us with loves and desires and fears and all sorts of fancies and a great deal of nonsense, with the result that we literally never get an opportunity to think at all about anything. Wars and revolutions and battles, you see, are due simply and solely to the body and its desires. All wars are undertaken for the acquisition of wealth; and the reason why we have to acquire wealth is the body, because we are slaves in its service. That is why, on all these accounts, we have so little time for philosophy. Worst of all, if we do obtain any leisure from the body's claims and turn to some line of inquiry, the body intrudes once more into our investigations, interrupting, disturbing, distracting, and preventing us from getting a glimpse of the truth. We are in fact convinced that if we are ever to have pure knowledge of anything, we must

66a

b

c

d

e

get rid of the body and contemplate things in isolation with the soul in isolation. It's likely, to judge from our argument, that the wisdom which we desire and upon which we profess to have set our hearts will be attainable only when we are dead, and not in our lifetime. If no pure knowledge is possible in the company of the body, then either it is totally impossible to acquire knowledge, or it is only possible after death, because it is only then that the soul will be isolated and independent of the body. It seems that so long as we are alive, we shall keep as close as possible to knowledge if we avoid as much as we can all contact and association with the body, except when they are absolutely necessary; and instead of allowing ourselves to become infected with its nature, purify ourselves from it until God himself gives us deliverance. In this way, by keeping ourselves uncontaminated by the follies of the body, we shall probably reach the company of others like ourselves [48] and gain direct knowledge of all that is pure and uncontaminated – that is, presumably, of Truth. For one who is not pure himself to attain to the realm of purity would no doubt be a breach of the divine order." Something to this effect, Simmias, is what I imagine all real lovers of learning must say to one another and believe themselves; don't you agree with me?'

'Most emphatically, Socrates.'

'Very well, then,' said Socrates; 'if this is true, there is good reason for anyone who reaches the end of this journey which lies before me to hope that there, if anywhere, he will attain the object to which all our efforts have been directed in life gone by. So this journey which is now ordained for me carries a happy prospect for any other man also who believes that his mind has been made ready – and pure, so to speak.'

'It does indeed,' said Simmias.

'And doesn't this "purification", as we saw some time ago in our discussion, consist in separating the soul as much as possible from the body, and accustoming it to withdraw from its dispersal throughout the body and concentrate itself in isolation? And to have its dwelling, so far as it can, both now and in the future, alone by itself, freed from the chains [49] of the body. Does not that follow?'

'Yes, it does,' said Simmias.

'Is not what we call death a freeing and separation of soul from body?'

'Certainly,' he said.

'And the desire to free the soul is found chiefly, or rather only, in the true philosopher; in fact the philosopher's occupation consists precisely in the freeing and separation of soul from body. Isn't that so?'

'Apparently.'

'Well then, as I said at the beginning, if a man has trained himself throughout his life to live in a state as close as possible to death, would it not be ridiculous for him to be distressed when death comes to him?'

'It would, of course.'

'Then it is a fact, Simmias, that true philosophers make dying their profession, and that to them of all men death is least alarming. Look at it in this way. If they are thoroughly dissatisfied with the body, and long to have their souls in isolation, when this happens would it not be entirely unreasonable to panic and be annoyed? Would they not naturally be glad to set out for the place where there is a prospect of attaining the object of their lifelong desire, which is wisdom, and of escaping from an association of which they disapproved? Surely there are many who have chosen of their own free will to follow dead beloveds [50] [and wives and sons] to the next world, in the hope of seeing and meeting there the persons whom they loved. If this is so, will a true lover of wisdom who has firmly grasped this same conviction – that he will never attain to wisdom worthy of the name elsewhere than in the next world – will he be grieved at dying? Will he not be glad to make that journey? We must suppose so, my comrade; that is, if he is a genuine "philosopher";[51] because then he will be of the firm belief that he will never find wisdom in all its purity in any other place. If this is so, would it not be quite unreasonable (as I said just now) for such a man to be afraid of death?'

'It would, indeed.'

'So if you see anyone distressed at the prospect of dying,' said Socrates, 'it will be proof enough that he is a lover not of wisdom but of the body (this same man would presumably be a lover of money) and of prestige, one or the other, or both.'[52]

'Yes, you are quite right.'

'Doesn't it follow, Simmias,' he went on, 'that the virtue which we call courage belongs primarily to those of philosophic disposition?'[53]

'Yes, no doubt it does,' he said.

'Take temperance, too, as it is understood even in the popular sense – not being carried away by the desires, but preserving a decent indifference towards them: is not this appropriate only to those who regard the body with the greatest indifference and spend their lives in philosophy?'

d   'Certainly,' he said.

'If you care to consider courage and temperance as practised by other people,' said Socrates, 'you will find them illogical.'[54]

'How so, Socrates?'

'You know, don't you, that everyone except the philosopher regards death as a great evil?'

'Yes, indeed.'

'Isn't it true that when a brave man faces death he does so through fear of something worse?'

'Yes, it is true.'

'So in everyone except the philosopher courage is due to fear and dread; although it is illogical that fear and cowardice should make a man brave.'

e   'Quite so.'

'What about self-controlled people? Is it not, in just the same way, a sort of self-indulgence that makes them temperate? We may say that this is impossible, but all the same those who practise this simple form of temperance are in much the same case as that which I have just described. They are afraid of losing other pleasures which they desire, so they refrain from one kind because they cannot resist the other. Although they define self-indulgence

69a as the condition of being ruled by pleasure, it is really because they cannot resist some pleasures that they succeed in resisting others; which amounts to what I said just now – that they control themselves, in a sense, by self-indulgence.'

'Yes, that seems to be true.'

'Wonderful, Simmias. No, I am afraid that, from the moral standpoint, it is not the right method to exchange one denomination of pleasure or pain or fear for another, like coins of different values. I suspect there is only one currency for which all these things should be exchanged, and that is wisdom. When they are

b   sold for wisdom and purchased with it,[55] – that's when they really amount to courage and self-control and justice[56] or, in a word, true virtue, when pleasures, fears, and all such things are added or subtracted with wisdom's help; whereas when they're exchanged in isolation from wisdom, I suspect that the resulting 'virtue' is a mere illusion, slavish in fact, with nothing sound or honest about it. The real thing, whether self-control or justice or courage, is in c fact a kind of purification from all this kind of motivation, and wisdom itself is a sort of cleansing agent. Perhaps these people who have established religious initiations are not so far from the mark, and all the time there has been a hidden meaning beneath their claim that he who enters the next world uninitiated and unenlightened shall lie in the mire, but he who arrives there purified and enlightened shall dwell among the gods. You know how those involved in initiations say:

"Many bear the emblem, but the devotees are few."[57]

Well, in my opinion these devotees are simply those who have d lived the philosophic life in the right way; a company which, all through my life, I have done my best in every way to join, leaving nothing undone which I could do to attain this end. Whether I was right in this ambition, and whether we have achieved anything, we shall know for certain (God willing) when we reach the other world; and that, I imagine, will be fairly soon.

'This is the defence which I offer you, Simmias and Cebes, to show that it is natural for me to leave you and my earthly rulers without any feeling of grief or bitterness, since I believe that I shall e find there, no less than here, good rulers and good friends. If I am any more convincing in my defence to you than I was to my Athenian jury, I shall be satisfied.'

Section C: The challenge of Cebes and the Argument from Oppo-sites. Socrates tries to establish the principle that opposites emerge from opposites, and consequently that the dead come from the living and the living from the dead. There are a number of problems, including ones of definition. The trickiest is what is actually meant by opposites, and indeed whether Plato consistently adheres to a single concept of an opposite. The principal opposites used to explain the Presocratic universe had been such physical pairs as wet/dry, light/dark, hot/cold. Plato tends to convert these to wetter/drier, etc. (cf. Philebus 25c–d), and he is concerned with the kind of process by which a given thing becomes wetter than it was previously rather than wetter than some other thing. Obviously what becomes wetter must have been drier before. The claim is that whatever substrate acquires a new predicate does so by acquiring (more of) a given quality than it previously had, and that, where the predicate has an opposite, it would previously have had (more of) the opposite quality. But Plato wants his rule to hold where there is no scale of (e.g.) temperature or humidity: becoming awake involves coming from a state of sleep, and becoming asleep involves departing from the waking state. So does not being dead involve coming from a state of life? And does not becoming alive involve coming from a state of death? One must also ask what it is that Plato can possibly think of as able to be alive and dead. Not souls, one might assume, for they are never dead, just embodied or disembodied; and how can it be argued that bodies become living which were previously dead? Is it previously dead people who become living people? The shadow of Heraclitus, who seems to have believed in a natural harmonious balance between opposite powers and opposite processes (and that this balance is the source of the preservation of the universe), is present throughout this section.[58]

When Socrates had finished, Cebes made his reply. 'The rest of your statement, Socrates,' he said, 'seems excellent to me; but what you said about the soul leaves the average person with grave misgivings that when it's released from the body it may no longer exist anywhere, but be dispersed and destroyed on the very day that the man himself dies, as soon as it is freed from the body; that as it emerges it may be dissipated like breath or smoke, and vanish away, so that it will nowhere amount to anything.[59] Of course if it still existed as a complete unity in itself, released from all the evils which you have just described, there would be a strong and glorious hope, Socrates, that what you say is true. But I fancy that it requires no little faith and assurance to believe that the soul exists after death and retains some active force and intelligence.'

'Quite true, Cebes,' said Socrates. 'But what are we to do about it? Is it your wish that we should go on speculating about the subject, to see whether this view is likely to be true or not?'

'For my part,' said Cebes, 'I should be very glad to hear what you think about it.'

'At any rate,' said Socrates, 'I hardly think that anyone who heard us now – even a comic poet – would say that I am playing about[60] and discoursing on subjects which do not concern me. So if that is how you feel, we had better continue our inquiry. Let us approach it from this point of view: do the souls of the departed exist in the other world or not?

'There is an old legend, which we've been recalling,[61] to the effect that they do exist there, after leaving here; and that they return again to this world and come into being from the dead.[62] If this is so – that the living come into being again from the dead – does it not follow that our souls would exist in the other world? They could not come into being again if they did not exist; and it will be sufficient proof that my contention is true if it really becomes apparent that the living come from the dead, and from nowhere else.[63] But if this is not so, we shall need some other argument.'

'Quite so,' said Cebes.

'If you want to understand the question more readily,' said Socrates, 'consider it with reference not only to human beings but to all animals and plants. Let us see whether in general everything that *comes to be so* of anything *comes to be* in this way and no other – opposites from opposites, wherever there is an opposite;[64] as for instance beauty is opposite to ugliness and right to wrong, and there are countless other examples. Let us consider whether it is a necessary law that everything which has an opposite is brought about from that opposite and from no other source: for example, when a thing becomes bigger, it must, I suppose, have been smaller first before it became bigger?'

'Yes.'

'And similarly if it becomes smaller, it must be bigger first, and become smaller afterwards?'

'That is so,' said Cebes.

'And the weaker comes from the stronger, and the faster from the slower?'

'Certainly.'

'What about this: if a thing becomes worse, is it not from being better, and if more just, from being more unjust?'

'Of course.'

'Are we satisfied, then,' said Socrates, 'that all opposites are brought about in this way – from opposites?'[65]

'Perfectly.'

'Here is another question. Do not these examples present another feature, that between each pair of opposites there are two processes of generation, one from the first to the second, and another from the second to the first? Between a larger and a smaller object are there not the processes of increase and decrease, and do we not describe them in this way as increasing and decreasing?'

'Yes,' said Cebes.

'Is it not the same with separating and combining, cooling and heating, and all the rest of them? Even if we sometimes do not use the actual terms, must it not in fact hold good universally that they come one from the other, and that there is a process from each which brings about the other?'

'Certainly,' said Cebes.

'Well then,' said Socrates, 'is there an opposite to living, as sleeping is opposite to waking?'

'Certainly.'

'What?'

'Being dead.'[66]

'So if they are opposites, they come from one another, and have their two processes of generation between the two of them?'

'Of course.'

'Very well, then,' said Socrates, 'I will state one pair of opposites which I mentioned just now; the opposites themselves and the processes between them; and you shall state the other. My opposites are sleeping and waking, and I say that waking comes from sleeping and sleeping from waking, and that the processes between them are going to sleep and waking up. Does that satisfy you,' he asked, 'or not?'

'Perfectly.'

'Now you tell me in the same way,' he went on, 'about life and death. Do you not admit that death is the opposite of life?'

'I do.'

'And that they come from one another?'

'Yes.'

'Then what comes from the living?'

'The dead.'

'And what,' asked Socrates, 'comes from the dead?'

'I must admit,' he said, 'that it is the living.'

'So it is from the dead, Cebes, that living things and people come?'

'Evidently.'

'Then our souls do exist in the other world?'[67]

'So it seems.'

'And one of the two processes in this case is really quite certain – dying is certain enough, isn't it?'

'Yes, it is,' said Cebes.

'What shall we do, then? Shall we omit the complementary process, and leave a defect here in the law of nature? Or must we supply an opposite process to that of dying?'

'Surely we must supply it,' he said.

'And what is it?'

'Coming to life again.'[68]

'Then if there is such a thing as coming to life again,' said Socrates, 'it must be a process from death to life?'

'Quite so.'

'So we agree upon this too: that the living have come from the dead no less than the dead from the living.[69] But I think we decided that if this was so, it was a sufficient proof that the souls of the dead must exist in some place from which they are reborn.'

'It seems to me, Socrates,' he said, 'that this follows necessarily from our agreement.'

'I think there is another way too, Cebes, in which you can see that we were not wrong in our agreement.[70] If there were not a constant correspondence in the process of generation between the two sets of opposites, going round in a sort of cycle; if generation were a straight path to the opposite extreme without any return to the starting-point or any deflection, do you realize that in the end everything would have the same quality and reach the same state, and change would cease altogether?'

'What do you mean?'

'Nothing difficult to understand,' replied Socrates. 'For example, if "falling asleep" existed, and "waking up" did not balance it by making something come out of sleep, you must realize that in the end everything would make Endymion[71] look foolish; he would be nowhere, because the whole world would be in the same state – asleep. And if everything were combined and nothing separated, we should soon have Anaxagoras's "all things together".[72] In just the same way, my dear Cebes, if everything that has some share of life were to die, and if after death the dead remained in that form and did not come to life again, would it not be quite inevitable that in the end everything should be dead and nothing alive? If

d living things came from other living things,[73] and the living things died, what possible means could prevent their number from being exhausted by death?'

'None that I can see, Socrates,' said Cebes. 'What you say seems to be perfectly true.'

'Yes, Cebes,' he said, 'if anything is true, I believe that this is, and we were not mistaken in our agreement upon it; coming to life again is a fact, and it is a fact that the living come from the dead,

e and a fact that the souls of the dead exist.'

Section D: The Theory of Recollection is introduced as further evidence that our souls have an existence before this earthly life. Cebes no doubt thinks of the theory as supporting the Orphic doctrines to which the previous argument had tried to give credence. That some learning is in fact the recollection of knowledge familiar from a previous existence is 'proved' in this dialogue by the fact that men appear to have clear concepts of (e.g.) equality itself, untainted by the imperfections of any earthly pair of equals. The difference between earthly equals and actual equality is established by the way in which the former may look unequal from a particular viewpoint, but no viewpoint could give the Idea of equality an unequal appearance. It is granted that earthly equals bring to mind the concept of actual equality, yet cannot strictly teach us that concept, since there is at least one predicate applicable to the concept at odds with a predicate of the earthly instances. Plato's purpose here seems to go beyond the desire to prove the soul pre-exists the body. There is a discussion of the mechanics of recollection processes in general, which, being not strictly necessary for the argument, must have had its own independent importance for Plato in the context of this work.[74] There is also considerable attention to the difference between the particulars of this world and the Platonic Ideas, and more effort devoted to picturing the Ideas as a worthy object of the philosopher's knowledge which can only be properly experienced in isolation from the body.

'Besides, Socrates,' rejoined Cebes, 'there is that theory which you have often mentioned to us[75] – that what we call learning[76] is really just recollection. If that is true, then surely what we recollect now we must have learned at some time before; which is impossible unless our souls existed somewhere before they entered this human shape. So in that way too it seems likely that the soul is immortal.' 73a

'How did the proof of that theory go, Cebes?' broke in Simmias. 'Remind me, because at the moment I can't quite remember.'[77]

'One very good argument,' said Cebes, 'is that when people are asked questions, if the question is put in the right way they can answer everything correctly, which they could not possibly do unless they were in possession of knowledge and a correct explanation.[78] Then again, if you confront people with a diagram[79] or b anything like that, the way in which they react provides the clearest proof that the theory is correct.'

'And if you don't find that convincing, Simmias,' said Socrates, 'see whether this appeals to you. I suppose that you find it hard to understand how what we call learning can be recollection?'

'Not at all,' said Simmias. 'All that I want is to be helped to do what we are talking about – to recollect. I can practically remember enough to satisfy me already, from the way Cebes set about explaining it; but I should be none the less glad to hear how you meant to explain it.'

'I look at it in this way,' said Socrates. 'We are agreed, I c suppose, that if a person is to be reminded of anything, he must first know it at some time or other?'

'Quite so.'

'Are we also agreed in calling it recollection when knowledge comes in a particular way? I will explain it rather like this. Suppose that a person on seeing or hearing or otherwise noticing one thing not only becomes conscious of that thing but also thinks of something else which is an object of a different sort of knowledge; are we not justifed in saying that he was reminded of the object which he thought of?' d

'What do you mean?'

'Let me give you an example. It's a different thing, I suppose you will agree, to know a man and to know a lyre.'

'Yes, certainly.'

'Well, you know what happens to lovers when they see a lyre or a piece of clothing or any other private property of the lad they love; when they recognize the lyre, their minds conjure up a picture of the lad who owns it. That is recollection. In the same way the sight of Simmias often reminds one of Cebes; and of course there are thousands of other examples.'

'Yes, of course there are thousands,' said Simmias.

e   'So by recollection we mean the sort of experience which I have just described, especially when it happens with reference to things which we had not taken a look at for such a long time that we had forgotten them.'

'Quite so.'

'Well, then, is it possible for a person who sees a picture of a horse or a musical instrument to be reminded of a person, or for someone who sees a picture of Simmias to be reminded of Cebes?'

'Perfectly.'

'And is it possible for someone who sees a portrait of Simmias to be reminded of Simmias himself?'

74a   'Yes, it is.'

'Does it not follow from all this that recollection may be caused either by similar or by dissimilar objects?'[80]

'Yes, it does.'

'When you are reminded by similarity, surely you must also be conscious whether the similarity is perfect or only partial.'

'Yes, you must.'

'Here is a further step,' said Socrates.[81] 'We admit, I suppose, that there is such a thing as equality – not the equality of stick to stick and stone to stone, and so on, but something beyond all that and distinct from it – absolute equality. Are we to admit this or not?'

b   'Yes indeed,' said Simmias, 'most emphatically.'[82]

'And do we know what it is?'

'Certainly.'

'Where did we get our knowledge? Was it not as a result of the particular examples that we mentioned just now – from seeing equal sticks or stones or other equal objects – that the notion of equality came to mind, although it is something quite distinct from them?[83] Look at it in this way. Is it not true that equal stones and sticks, the very same ones, sometimes appear equal to one and unequal to another?'[84]

'Certainly.'

'Well, now, have you ever thought that what were actually c
equal[85] were unequal, or that equality was inequality?'[86]

'No, never, Socrates.'

'Then these equal things are not the same as actual equality.'

'Not in the least, as I see it, Socrates.'

'And yet it is these equal things that have actively brought to
mind your knowledge of absolute equality, although they are
distinct from it?'

'Perfectly true.'

'Whether it is similar to them or dissimilar?'

'Certainly.'

'It makes no difference,' said Socrates. 'So long as the sight of
one thing suggests another to you, it must be a cause of recollec- d
tion, whether the two things are alike or not.'[87]

'Quite so.'

'Well, now,' he said, 'what do we find in the case of the equal
sticks and other things of which we were speaking just now: do
they seem to us to be equal in the sense of actual equality, or do
they fall short of it in so far as they only approximate to equality?
Or don't they fall short at all?'[88]

'They do,' said Simmias, 'a long way.'

'Suppose that when you see something you say to yourself,
"This thing which I can see is intended to be like something else,
but it falls short and cannot be really like it, only a poor imitation"; e
don't you agree with me that anyone who is conscious of this must
in fact have previous knowledge of that thing which he says the
other inadequately resembles?'

'Certainly he must.'

'Well then, is our own experience of equal things and actual
equality like this?'

'Exactly.'

'Then we must have had some previous knowledge of equality
before the time when we first realized, on seeing equal things, that 75a
they were striving after equality, but fell short of it.'

'That is so.'

'And at the same time we are agreed also upon this point, that
this notion of deficiency[89] did not and could not have occurred to
us except by sight or touch or one of the other senses. I am
treating all senses as being all the same.'

'They are the same, Socrates, for the purpose of our argument.'

'So it must be as a result of the senses that we obtained the
b notion that all sensible equals are striving to realize actual equality
but falling short of it.[90] Is that correct?'

'Yes, it is.'

'So before we began to see and hear and otherwise perceive
equals[91] we must somewhere have acquired the knowledge of
equality as it really is; otherwise we could never have realized, by
using it as a standard for comparison, that all equal objects of
sense are desirous of being like it, but are only imperfect copies.'[92]

'That is the logical conclusion, Socrates.'

'Did we not begin to see and hear and utilize our other senses
from the moment of birth?'[93]

'Certainly.'

c 'But we admitted that we must have obtained our knowledge of
equality before we obtained them.'

'Yes.'

'So we must have obtained it before birth.'

'So it seems.'

'Then if we obtained it before our birth, and kept hold of it
when we were born,[94] we had knowledge, both before and at the
moment of birth, not only of what's actually equal, or greater or
smaller,[95] but of all such things. Our present argument applies no
d more to equality itself than it does to beauty itself, or goodness,
justice, holiness – all those qualities, I maintain, which we designate
in our question-and-answer discussions by the term "itself". So
we would have had to obtain knowledge of all these things before
our birth.'

'That is so.'

'And unless we invariably forget it after obtaining it, we must
always be born knowing and continue to know all through our
lives; because "to know" means simply to retain the knowledge
which one has acquired, and not to lose it. Is not what we call
"forgetting" simply the loss of knowledge, Simmias?'

e 'Most certainly, Socrates.'

'And if it is true that we acquired our knowledge before our
birth, and lost it at the moment of birth, but afterwards by
pertinent exercise of our senses, recover the knowledge which we
had once before, I suppose that what we call learning will be the

recovery of our own knowledge; and surely we should be right in calling this recollection.'

'Quite so.'

'Yes, because we saw that it is possible for the perception of an 76a object by sight or hearing or any of the other senses to suggest to the percipient another associated object which he has forgotten (whether there is any similarity or not). So, as I maintain, there are two alternatives: either we are all born with knowledge of these standards, and retain it throughout our lives; or else, when we speak of people learning, they are simply recollecting what they knew before; in other words, learning is recollection.'

'Yes, that must be so, Socrates.'

'Which do you choose, then, Simmias? That we are born with knowledge, or that we recollect after we are born the things of b which we possessed knowledge before we were born?'

'I don't know which to choose on the spur of the moment, Socrates.'

'Well, here is another choice for you to make. What do you think about this? Can a person who knows a subject thoroughly explain what he knows?'[96]

'Most certainly he can.'

'Do you think that everyone can explain these questions about which we have just been talking?'

'I should like to think so,' said Simmias, 'but I am very much afraid that by this time tomorrow there will be no one on this earth who can give a worthwhile explanation.'[97]

'So you don't think, Simmias, that everyone has knowledge c about them?'

'Far from it.'

'Then they just recollect what they once learned.'

'That must be the right answer.'

'When do our souls acquire this knowledge? It cannot be after the beginning of our mortal life.'

'No, of course not.'

'Then it must be before.'

'Yes.'

'Then our souls had a previous existence, Simmias, before they took on this human shape – they were independent of our bodies and had intelligence.'[98]

'Unless perhaps it is at the moment of birth that we acquire knowledge of these things, Socrates; there is still that time available.'

d   'No doubt, my dear fellow, but just tell me, what other time is there to lose it in? We have just agreed that we do not possess it when we are born. Do we lose it at the same moment that we acquire it? Or can you suggest any other time?'

'No, of course not, Socrates; I didn't realize what nonsense I was talking.'[99]

'Well, how do we stand now, Simmias? If all these things which we're for ever talking about, a Beauty, a Goodness, and all such entities, really exist – if it is to them that we refer all the objects of our physical perception as copies to their patterns, as we rediscover

e   our own former knowledge of them – does it not follow that our souls too must exist even before our birth, whereas if they do not exist, our discussion would seem to be a waste of time? Is this the position, that it is just as inevitable that our souls exist before our birth as it is that these realities exist, and that without the one there's not the other?'[100]

'I find it very compelling, Socrates,' said Simmias, 'that there should be this same inevitability. It suits me very well that your

77a   argument should have recourse to the thesis that our soul's existence before our birth is a similar case to the existence of these realities of yours. I cannot imagine anything more self-evident than the fact that Beauty and Goodness and all the rest that you mentioned just now exist in the fullest possible sense. In my opinion the proof is quite satisfactory.'

Section E: The combination of the recollection argument with the opposites argument becomes a proof for the existence of an afterlife. If the argument from opposites were adequate, then the recollection argument would not strictly be needed, but the latter seems to have commanded more conviction, and it also suggested something relevant to Plato's purpose about what 'being dead' might be like. Once the recollection argument gives additional credence to the notion of a stock of disembodied and intelligent souls waiting to be born, we need no more convincing that the soul can live apart from the body (so that at the very least being apart from the body cannot in itself kill off the soul), and we should

*be faced with the problem of explaining the origin of those disem-
bodied souls if it were not from previous soul–body combinations.*

'What about Cebes?' said Socrates. 'We must convince Cebes
too.'

'To the best of my belief he is satisfied,' replied Simmias. 'It's
true that he's the most determined of persons in refusing to be
convinced by argument, but I should think that he needs nothing
more to satisfy him that our souls existed before birth. As for their
still existing after we are dead, even I don't feel that that has been
proved, Socrates; the problem that Cebes mentioned still applies –   *b*
the ordinary man's fear that the soul may be disintegrated at the
very moment of his death, and that this may be the end of its
existence. Supposing that there *is* some other source from which it
is constituted at birth, and that it exists before it enters a human
body: after it has entered one, is there any reason why, at the
moment of release, it should not come to an end and be destroyed
itself?'

'Quite right, Simmias,' said Cebes. 'It seems that we've managed
to prove about half of what we wanted – that the soul existed   *c*
before birth – but now we need also to prove that it will exist after
death no less than before birth, if our proof is to be complete.'

'It has been proved already, Simmias and Cebes,' said Socrates,
'if you're prepared to combine this last argument with the one
about which we agreed before, that every living thing comes from
the dead. If (i) the soul exists before birth, and if (ii) when it's   *d*
born into life, it can only be born from death or the dead state,
surely it must also exist after death, bearing in mind that it has to
be born again. So the point which you mention has been proved
already. Even so I believe that you and Simmias would like to
hammer out the issue still more, and that you're afraid, as children
are, that when the soul emerges from the body the wind may
really puff it away and scatter it – especially when it's a person's   *e*
luck to die with a gale blowing rather than in a calm!'[101]

Cebes laughed. 'Suppose that we are afraid, Socrates,' he said,
'and try to convince us. Or not so much that it's our true selves
who are afraid – perhaps there's a kind of child with this kind of
fear hidden in us too. Try to persuade him not to be afraid of
death as though it were a bogey.'

'What you should do,' said Socrates, 'is to pronounce an enchantment over him every day until you have charmed his fears away.'

78a   'But, Socrates,' said Simmias, 'where shall we find an enchanter who understands these spells, now that you are leaving us?'[102]

'Greece is a large country, Cebes,' he replied, 'which must have good men in it; and there are many foreign races too. You must ransack all of them in your search for this enchanter, without sparing money or trouble; because you could not spend your money more opportunely on any other object. And you must search also by your own united efforts; because you may not easily find anyone better fitted for the task than yourselves.'

'We will see to that,' said Cebes. 'But let's get back to the point b where we left off, if you don't mind.'

'Of course not; why should I?'

'Splendid,' said Cebes.

Section F: The Argument from Affinity. The unseen soul, particularly when it avoids the company of the body, is more like the unchanging and indestructible Ideas than the visible, changing, perishable entities we are familiar with.[103] According to the epistemology of the Meno, *to which the* Phaedo *is general closely related, one cannot hope to know* what sort *a thing is until one has discovered* what it is. *Here Socrates argues from one property of the soul to another, but not from what it actually is. He will later be able to show the lack of total conviction which flows from this kind of argument, and discuss more fully what the soul is in the course of his reply to the doubts that still linger.*

'We ought, I think,' said Socrates, 'to ask ourselves this: What sort of thing is it that would naturally suffer the fate of being dispersed? What sort of thing should we be afraid of this happening to, and what should we not? When we have answered this, we should next consider to which class the soul belongs; and then we shall know whether to feel confidence or fear about the fate of our souls.'

'Quite true.'

c   'Would you not expect a compound or a naturally composite object to be liable to break up where it was put together? And ought not anything which is really incomposite to be the one thing of all others which is not affected in this way?'[104]

'That seems to be the case,' said Cebes.

'Is it not extremely probable that what is always constant and invariable is incomposite, and what is inconstant and variable is composite?'

'That is how it seems to me.'

'Then let us return to the same examples which we were discussing before. Does that actual nature of things – their true _d_ being which we try to describe in our discussions[105] – remain always constant and invariable, or not? Does equality itself or beauty itself or any other thing as it is in itself ever admit change of any kind? Or does each one of these entities, being uniform and self-contained, remain always constant and invariable, never admitting any alteration in any respect or in any sense?'

'They must be constant and invariable, Socrates,' said Cebes.

'Well, what about the many instances of beauty – such as men, horses, clothes, and so on – or of equality, or any other things _e_ which have the same name as those others?[106] Are they constant, or are they, on the contrary, scarcely ever in the same relation in any sense either to themselves or to one another?'

'You're right again about them, Socrates; they are never free from variation.'

'And these latter things you can touch or see or perceive by your other senses, but those constant entities you cannot possibly appre- _79a_ hend except by the workings of the mind; such things are invisible to our sight.'

'That is perfectly true,' said Cebes.

'So you think that we should assume two classes of things that may be such-and-such, one visible and the other invisible?'

'Yes, we should.'

'The invisible being invariable, and the visible never being the same?'

'Yes, let's assume that too.'

'Well, now,' said Socrates, 'are we not part body, part soul?' _b_

'Certainly.'

'Then to which class do we say that the body would have the closer resemblance and relation?'

'That's obvious to anybody – to the visible.'

'And the soul, is it visible or invisible?'

'Invisible to men, at any rate, Socrates,' he said.

'But surely we have been speaking of things visible or invisible to our human nature. Do you think that we had some other nature in view?'

'No, human nature.'

'What do we say about the soul, then? Is it visible or invisible?'[107]

'Not visible.'

'Invisible, then?'

c   'Yes.'

'So soul is more like the invisible, and body more like the visible?'

'Inevitably, Socrates.'

'Did we not say some time ago that when the soul uses the instrumentality of the body for any inquiry, whether through sight or hearing or any other sense (because using the body means using the senses), it is drawn away by the body into the realm of the variable, and loses its way and becomes confused and dizzy, as though it were tipsy, through contact with that kind of thing?'

'Certainly.'

d   'But when it investigates by itself, it passes into the realm of the pure and everlasting and deathless and changeless; and being of a kindred nature, when it is once independent and free from interference, consorts with it always and strays no longer, but remains constant and invariable when busied with them, through contact with things of a similar nature. And this condition of the soul we call Wisdom.'

'An excellent description, and perfectly true, Socrates.'

'Very well, then; in the light of all that we have said, both now and before, to which class do you think that the soul bears the closer resemblance and relation?'

e   'I think, Socrates,' said Cebes, 'that even the most slow-witted person, approaching the subject in this way, would agree that the soul is in every possible way more like the invariable than the variable.'

'And the body?'

'Like the other.'

'Look at it in this way too. When soul and body share the same place, nature teaches the one to serve and be subject, the other to rule and govern. In this relation, which do you think resembles the

80a

divine and which is like what's mortal?[108] Don't you think that it is the nature of the divine to rule and direct, and that of the mortal to be subject and serve?'

'I do.'

'Then which does the soul resemble?'

'Obviously, Socrates, soul resembles the divine, and body the mortal.'

'Now, Cebes,' he said, 'see whether this is our conclusion from all that we have said. The soul is most like that which is divine, immortal, intelligible, uniform, indissoluble, and ever self-consistent and invariable, whereas body is most like that which is human, mortal, multiform, unintelligible, dissoluble, and never self-consistent. Can we adduce any conflicting argument, my dear Cebes, to show that this is not so?'

'No, we cannot.'

'Very well, then; in that case is it not natural for body to disintegrate rapidly, but for soul to be quite or very nearly indissoluble?'[109]

'Certainly.'

'Of course you know that when a person dies, although it is natural for the visible and physical part of him, which lies here in the visible world and which we call his corpse, to decay and fall to pieces and be dissipated, none of this happens to it immediately; it remains as it was for quite some time, particularly so if death takes place when the body is in attractive condition and the weather is also fine. Indeed, when the body is dried and embalmed, as in Egypt,[110] it remains almost intact for an incredible time; and even if the rest of the body decays, some parts of it – the bones and sinews and anything else like them – are practically everlasting. That is so, is it not?'

'Yes.'

'But the soul, the invisible part, which goes away to a place that is, like itself, glorious, pure, and invisible – the true Hades or unseen world[111] – into the presence of the good and wise God (where, if God so wills, my soul must shortly go) – will it, if its very nature is such as I have described, be blown to bits and destroyed at the moment of its release from the body, as most people claim? Far from it, my dear Simmias and Cebes.

*Section G: Reflections after the similarity argument concerning the
fate of those souls which have and which have not separated
themselves from bodily concerns.*

'The truth is much more like this: if at its release the soul is
pure and does not drag along with it any trace of the body,
because it has never willingly associated with it in life; if it has
shunned it and isolated itself because that is what it always
practises – I mean doing philosophy in the right way and really
getting used to facing death calmly: wouldn't you call this "practising death"?'

81a

'Most decidedly.'

'Very well; if this is its condition, then it departs to the place
where things are like itself – invisible, divine, immortal and
wise;[112] where, on its arrival, happiness awaits it, and release from
uncertainty and folly, from fears and gnawing desires, and all
other human evils; and where (as they say of the initiates in the
Mysteries) it really spends the rest of time with divine beings. Shall
we adopt this view, Cebes, or some other?'

'This one, by all means,' said Cebes.

b

'But, I suppose, if at the time of its release the soul is tainted
and impure, because it has always associated with the body and
cared for it and loved it, and has been so beguiled by the body and
its passions and pleasures that nothing seems real to it but those
physical things which can be touched and seen and eaten and
drunk and used for sexual enjoyment, making it accustomed to
hate and fear and avoid what is invisible and obscure to our eyes,
but intelligible and comprehensible by philosophy – if the soul is

c

in this state, do you think that it will be released just by itself, uncontaminated?'

'Not in the least,' he said.

'On the contrary, it will, I imagine, be permeated by the corporeal, which fellowship and intercourse with the body will have
ingrained in its very nature through constant association and long
practice.'

'Certainly.'

'And we must suppose, my dear fellow, that the corporeal is
heavy, oppressive, earthly and visible. So the soul which is tainted
by its presence is weighed down and dragged back into the visible

world, through fear (as they say) of Hades or the invisible, and hovers about tombs and graveyards. The shadowy apparitions *d* which have actually been seen there are the ghosts of those souls which have not got clear away, but still retain some portion of the visible; which is why they can be seen.'[113]

'That seems likely enough, Socrates.'

'Yes, it does, Cebes. Of course these are not the souls of the good, but of inferior people, and they are compelled to wander about these places as a punishment for their bad conduct in the past. They continue wandering until at last, through craving for the corporeal, which unceasingly pursues them, they are impris- *e* oned once more in a body. And as you might expect, they are attached to the same sort of character or nature which they have developed during life.'[114]

'What sort do you mean, Socrates?'

'Well, those who have cultivated gluttony or assault[115] or drunkenness, instead of taking pains to avoid them, are likely to assume the form of donkeys and other perverse animals; don't you think *82a* so?'

'Yes, that is very likely.'

'And those who have deliberately preferred a life of injustice, suppression, and robbery with violence become wolves and hawks and kites; unless we can suggest any other more likely animals.'

'No, the ones which you mention are exactly right.'

'So it is easy to imagine into what sort of animals all the other kinds of soul will go, in accordance with their conduct during life.'

'Yes, certainly.'

'I suppose that the happiest people, and those who reach the best destination, are the ones who have cultivated the goodness of an ordinary citizen, so-called 'temperance' and 'justice', which is *b* acquired by habit and practice, without the help of philosophy and reason.'[116]

'How are these the happiest?'

'Because they will probably pass into some other kind of social and disciplined creature like bees, wasps and ants; or even back into the human race again, becoming decent citizens.'

'Very likely.'

'But no soul which has not practised philosophy, and is not absolutely pure when it leaves the body, may attain to the divine *c* nature; that is only for the lover of learning. This is the reason, my dear Simmias and Cebes, why true philosophers abstain from all bodily desires and withstand them and do not yield to them. It is not because they are afraid of financial loss or poverty, like the average man who thinks of money first; nor because they shrink from dishonour and a bad reputation, like lovers of prestige and authority.'[117]

'No, those would be unworthy motives, Socrates,' said Cebes.

d   'They would indeed,' he agreed. 'And so, Cebes, those who care about their souls and do not devote themselves to the body dissociate themselves firmly from these others and refuse to accompany them on their haphazard journey; they believe that it is wrong to oppose philosophy with her offer of liberation and purification, so they turn and follow her wherever she leads.'

'What do you mean, Socrates?'

'I will explain,' he said. 'Every seeker after wisdom knows that

e   up to the time when philosophy takes it over his soul is a helpless prisoner, chained hand and foot in the body, compelled to view reality not directly but only through its prison bars, and wallowing in utter ignorance. And philosophy can see the ingenuity of the imprisonment, which is brought about by the prisoner's own

83a   active desire, which makes him first accessory to his own confinement. Well, philosophy takes over the soul in this condition and by gentle persuasion tries to set it free. She points out that observation by means of the eyes and ears and all the other senses abounds with deception, and she urges the soul to refrain from using them unless it is necessary to do so, and encourages it to collect and concentrate itself in isolation, trusting nothing but its

b   own isolated judgement upon realities considered in isolation, and attributing no truth to any other thing which it views through another medium in some other thing;[118] such objects, she knows, are sensible and visible but what she herself sees is intelligible and invisible. Now the soul of the true philosopher feels that it must not reject this opportunity for release, and so it abstains as far as possible from pleasures and desires and griefs, because it reflects that the result of giving way to pleasure, fear, pain, or desire is not

c   as might be supposed the trivial misfortune of becoming ill or wasting money through self-indulgence, but the last and worst calamity of all, which the sufferer does not take into account.'

'What is that, Socrates?' asked Cebes.

'When anyone's soul feels a keen pleasure or pain it cannot help supposing that whatever causes the most violent emotion is the plainest and truest reality; which it is not. It is chiefly visible things that have this effect, isn't it?'

'Quite so.'

'Is it not on this sort of occasion that soul passes most completely *d* into the bondage of body?'

'How is that?'

'Because every pleasure or pain has a sort of rivet with which it fastens the soul to the body and pins it down and makes it corporeal, accepting as true whatever the body certifies. The result of agreeing with the body and finding pleasure in the same things is, I imagine, that it cannot help coming to share its character and its diet, so that it can never get clean away to the unseen world, but is always saturated with the body when it sets out, and so soon falls back again into another body, where it takes root and *e* grows. Consequently it has no share of fellowship with the pure and uniform and divine.'

'Yes, that is perfectly true, Socrates,' said Cebes.

'It is for these reasons, Cebes, that true philosophers exhibit self-control and courage; not for the reasons that most people do.[119] Or do you think it's for the same reasons?'

'No, certainly not,'   84a

'No, indeed. A philosopher's soul will take the view which I have described. It will not first expect to be set free by philosophy, and then allow pleasure and pain to reduce it once more to bondage, thus condemning itself to an endless task, like Penelope,[120] when she worked to undo her own weaving; no, this soul brings calm to the seas of desire[121] by following Reason and abiding always in her company, and by contemplating the true and divine and unambiguous, and drawing inspiration from it; because *b* such a soul believes that this is the right way to live while life endures, and that after death it reaches a place which is kindred and similar to its own nature, and there is rid for ever of human ills. After such a training, my dear Simmias and Cebes, the soul can have no grounds for fearing that on its separation from the body it will be blown away and scattered by the winds, and so disappear into thin air, and cease to exist altogether.'

Section H: The objections of Simmias and Cebes. Simmias feels that Socrates' theory of the soul's immortality is inconsistent with an attractive Pythagorean doctrine which views the soul as an attunement, for an instrument's harmony – its condition of being 'tuned' – is gone as soon as the instrument is broken. Cebes feels that Socrates has proved that the soul is more enduring than the body, but not that it is completely impervious to the forces of destruction. In this section we are expected to ponder a great deal over what the soul really is like, and what sort of relationship it should have with the body – whether, for instance, it 'harmonizes' the body, whether it arranges for its perpetual renewal, and whether it can in fact be worn out by such tasks.

c   There was silence for some time after Socrates had said this. He himself, to judge from his appearance, was still pondering the account which he had just given, and so were most of us; but Simmias and Cebes went on talking in a low voice. When Socrates noticed them, he said, 'Why, surely you don't feel my account inadequate? Of course it is still open to a number of doubts and objections, if you want to examine it in detail. If it is something else that you two are considering, never mind; but if you feel any difficulty about our discussion, don't hesitate to put forward your own views, and point out any way in which you think that my

d   account could be improved; and by all means make use of my services too, if you think I can help at all to solve the difficulty.'

'Very well, Socrates,' said Simmias, 'I will be quite open with you. We have both been feeling difficulties for some time, and each of us has been urging the other to ask questions. We are anxious to have your answers, but we did not like to trouble you, for fear of upsetting you in your present misfortune.'

When Socrates heard this he laughed gently and said, 'I am surprised at you, Simmias. I shall certainly find it difficult to

e   convince the outside world that I do not regard my present lot as a misfortune if I cannot even convince you, and you are afraid that I am more irritable now than I used to be. Evidently you think that I have less insight into the future than a swan; because when these birds feel that the time has come for them to die, they sing more

85a   loudly and sweetly than they have sung in all their lives before, for joy that they are going away into the presence of the god whose servants they are. It is quite wrong for human beings to make out that the swans sing their last song as an expression of grief at their approaching end;[122] people who say this are misled by their own fear of death, and fail to reflect that no bird sings when it is hungry or cold or distressed in any other way; not even the nightingale or swallow or hoopoe, whose songs are supposed to be a lament. In my opinion neither they nor the swans sing because they are sad. I believe that the swans, belonging as they do to b Apollo, have prophetic powers and sing because they know the good things that await them in the unseen world; and they are happier on that day than they have ever been before. Now I consider that I am in the same service as the swans, and dedicated to the same god; and that I am no worse endowed with prophetic powers by my master than they are, and no more disconsolate at leaving this life. So far as that fear of yours is concerned, you may say and ask whatever you like, for as long as the eleven officers of the Athenians permit.'[123]

'Thank you,' said Simmias. 'I will tell you my problem first and then Cebes shall tell you where he finds your theory unacceptable. c I think, just as you do, Socrates, that although it is very difficult if not impossible in this life to achieve certainty about these questions, at the same time it is utterly feeble not to use every effort in testing the available theories, or to leave off before we have considered them in every way, and come to the end of our resources. It is our duty to do one of two things: either to ascertain the facts, whether by seeking instruction or by personal discovery; or, if this is impossible, to select the best and most dependable theory that human intelligence can supply, and use it as a raft to d ride the seas of life – that is, assuming that we cannot make our journey with greater confidence and security by the surer means of a divine revelation. And so now, after what you have said, I shall not let any diffidence prevent me from asking my question, and so make me blame myself afterwards for not having spoken my mind now. The fact is, Socrates, that on thinking it over, and discussing it with Cebes here, I feel your explanation not altogether adequate.'

'Your feeling is very likely right, my comrade,' said Socrates, e 'but tell me where you think the inadequacies are.'

Section H (i): The attunement theory. Given that one accepts that there is something constantly 'in' the living body which brings it life, unity and perception, one is confronted with the following choice: either it will be some part of the individual distinct from the parts of the body, something which arrives when the body is in a condition apt for life and departs thereafter (whether intact and intelligent or not); or it will be some relation between the rest of the parts of the individual. Simmias understands the present theory as being of the latter type, and the 'attunement' (or 'harmony') as the lyre's state of being ready to play – with all its parts standing in the correct relation to one another and the strings at the correct tension. Thus the soul would be the body's state of being ready to live, with all its parts adequately 'attuned'. This type of theory offers an obvious challenge, since it does not allow the soul to be an independent entity of the type which Socrates advocates, thus threatening the moral theory of the Phaedo *as well as the theory of the soul's immortality. The origin of the theory may be complex. That the soul is some kind of appropriate mixture of the physical forces hot, cold, wet and dry (86b) was a natural view for the Greek medical theorists to hold. Yet harmonic theory was particularly dear to the Pythagoreans, and the Pythagorean Echecrates (88d) had long adhered to a soul-harmony theory – in spite of the Pythagorean belief in an after-life. They did not have to understand the 'harmony' as Simmias does, and indeed the soul which Plato employs in the* Timaeus *is very much a harmony without in any sense being an 'attunement' of bodily elements. Since for Pythagoreans mathematical entities were the primary reality, it makes sense that the lyre's harmony should have been an external and independent force attracted almost magically into the material lyre as soon as it was ready to be played. In criticizing the doctrine at* De Anima *407b27–28, Aristotle implies that the theory was a popular one, without specifying any particular advocates of it.*

'What I mean is this,' said Simmias. 'You might say the same thing about tuning the strings of a musical instrument: that the attunement is something invisible and incorporeal and splendid and divine, and located in the tuned instrument, while the instrument itself and its strings are material and corporeal and composite and earthly and closely related to what is mortal. Now suppose

86a

that the instrument is broken, or its strings cut or snapped. According to your theory the attunement must still exist – it cannot have been destroyed; because it would be inconceivable that when the strings are broken the instrument and the strings themselves, which have a mortal nature, should still exist, and the attunement, which shares the nature and characteristics of the *b* divine and immortal, should exist no longer, having predeceased its mortal counterpart. You would say that the attunement must still exist somewhere just as it was; and that the wood and strings will rot away before anything happens to it. I say this, Socrates, because, as I think you yourself are aware, this is very much the kind of thing that we take the soul to be;[124] the body is held together at a certain tension between the extremes of hot and cold, and dry and wet, and so on, and our soul is a balance or attunement of these same extremes, when they are combined in *c* just the right proportion. Well, if the soul is really an adjustment, obviously as soon as the tension of our body is lowered or increased beyond the proper point, the soul must be destroyed, divine though it is; just like any other attunement, either in music or in any product of the arts and crafts, although in each case the physical remains last considerably longer until they are burnt up or rot away. Find us an answer to this argument, if someone *d* insists that the soul, being a balance of physical constituents, is the first thing to be destroyed by what we call death.'

Section H (ii): Cebes' problem. Cebes accepts the notion that the soul is an independent part of the individual, and a long-lasting part at that. He rightly points out that something long-lasting does not have to be imperishable. And he raises the crucial issue that the same body may not after all last a man's lifetime since parts are constantly expended and replaced, so that the more enduring soul could last longer without lasting beyond death.

Socrates opened his eyes very wide – a favourite trick of his – and smiled. 'Really,' he said, 'Simmias's criticism is quite justified, so if any of you are more resourceful than I am, you had better answer him; it seems to me that he is not handling the argument at all badly. However, before we have the answer, I think we should hear what criticisms Cebes has to make in his turn, so that we may *e* have time to decide what to say; when we have heard him, we can either agree with them if they seem to have hit the right note somewhere, or if not, we can then take on the defence of my account. Come on, Cebes,' he said, 'tell us what has been troubling you.'

'Very well,' said Cebes. 'It seems to me that the argument is just where it was; I mean that it is open to the same criticism that we made before. The proof that our soul existed before it took on this present shape is perfectly satisfying – convincing even, if that's not too strong a word for you; I am not changing my position about that. But as for its still existing somewhere after we are dead, I think that the proof fails at this point. Mind you, I don't agree that soul is not stronger and more durable than body, as implied by Simmias's objection; it seems to me to be far superior in all those ways. "Then why," your theory might inquire, "are you still sceptical, when you can see that after a man dies even the weaker part of him continues to exist? Don't you think the more durable part of him must logically survive as long?" Well, here is my answer; I want you to consider whether there is anything in what I say – because like Simmias I must have recourse to an illustration.

'Suppose that an elderly tailor has just died. Your theory would be just like saying that the man is not dead, but still exists somewhere safe and sound; and offering as proof the fact that the cloak which he had made for himself and was wearing has not perished but is still intact. If anyone was sceptical, I suppose you would ask him which is likely to last longer, a man or a cloak which is being regularly used and worn; and when he replied that the former was far more likely, you would imagine that you had proved conclusively that the man is safe and sound, since the less enduring object has not perished. But surely this is not so, Simmias – because I want your opinion too; anyone would dismiss such a view as silly. The tailor makes and wears out any number of cloaks, but although he outlives all the others, presumably he perishes before the last one; and this does not mean that a man is lowlier or more frail than a cloak. I believe that this analogy could apply to the relation of soul to body; and I think that it would be reasonable to say of them in the same way that soul is a long-lived thing, whereas body is relatively feeble and short-lived. But while one might admit that each soul wears out a number of bodies, especially if it lives a great many years – because although the body is continually changing and disintegrating all through life, the soul never stops patching up what is worn away[125] – even so, when the soul dies, it would still have to be in possession of its final garment, and must perish before it in this case only; and it's when the soul has perished that the body at last reveals its natural frailty and quickly rots away. If you accept this view there is no justification yet for any confidence that after death our souls still exist somewhere. Suppose that one conceded even more to the exponent of your case, granting not only that our souls existed before our birth, but also that some of them may still exist when we die, and go on existing, and be born and die again several times (soul having such natural vitality that it persists through successive incarnations); unless in granting this he made the further concession that the soul suffers no ill-effects in its various rebirths, and so does not, at one of its "deaths", perish altogether; if he had to admit that nobody knows which of these "deaths" or separations from the body may prove fatal to the soul (because such insight is impossible for any of us) – on these terms, Socrates, no one has the right to face death with any but a fool's confidence, unless he can prove that the soul is absolutely immortal and indestructible. Otherwise everyone must always feel apprehension at the approach of death for fear that in this particular separation from the body his soul may be finally and utterly destroyed.'

Well, when we had heard them state their objections, we all felt very much depressed, as we told one another later. We had been quite convinced by the earlier part of the discussion, and now we felt that they had upset our convictions and destroyed our confidence not only in what had been said already, but also in anything that was to follow later, fearing that either we were incompetent judges, or these matters themselves are inherently obscure.[126]

Section I: Interlude, with comment from Echecrates.

ECHECRATES: You certainly have my full sympathy, Phaedo. After hearing your account I find myself faced with the same misgiving. How can we believe in anything after that? Socrates' argument was very convincing, and now it's fallen into discredit. That theory that our soul is some sort of attunement has an extraordinary attraction for me, now as much as ever, and your account of it reminded me that I myself had come to the same conclusion. What I really need now is another proof, right from the beginning, to convince me that when a man dies his soul does not die with him. Tell me, please, how did Socrates pick up the trail again? And did he show any sign of regret, like the rest of you, or did he come quietly to the rescue of the argument? And did he rescue it effectively or not? Tell us every detail as accurately as you can.

PHAEDO: I can assure you, Echecrates, that though Socrates often astonished me, I never admired him more than on this particular occasion. That he should have been ready with an answer was, I suppose, nothing unusual; but what impressed me was first, the pleasant, kindly, appreciative way in which he received the young men's thoughts, then his quick recognition of how the turn of the discussion had affected us; and lastly the skill with which he healed our wounds, rallied our scattered forces, and encouraged us to join him in pursuing the inquiry.

ECHECRATES: How did he do that?

Section J: Reasons for not mistrusting argument. The section is notable in that it brings the narrator into the story, thereby adding a personal touch and maintaining the focus upon the reactions of Socrates' ordinary followers.

PHAEDO: I will tell you. I happened to be sitting to the right of his bed, on a footstool, and he was much higher than I was. So he laid his hand on my head and gathered up the hair on my neck – he never missed a chance of teasing me about my hair – and said, 'Tomorrow, I suppose, Phaedo, you will cut off this beautiful crop.'

'I expect so, Socrates,' I said.

'Not if you take my advice.'

'Why not?' I asked.

'Because I shall cut off mine today, and you ought to do the same,' said Socrates, 'that is, if our argument dies and and we fail to bring it back to life again. What is more, if I were you, and let the truth escape me, I should make a vow like the Argives[127] never to let my hair grow again until I had defeated the argument of Simmias and Cebes in a return battle.'

'But', I objected, 'not even Heracles can take on two at once.'[128]

'You had better call upon me to be your Iolaus,' he said, 'while the daylight lasts.'[129]

'Very well,' I said, 'but I am Iolaus appealing to Heracles, not Heracles to Iolaus.'

'The effect will be just the same,' he said. 'But first there is one danger that we must guard against.'

'What sort of danger?' I asked.

'Of becoming "misologic",' he said, 'in the sense that people *d* become misanthropic. No greater misfortune could happen to anyone than that of developing a dislike for argument. "Misology" and misanthropy arise in just the same way. Misanthropy is induced by believing in somebody quite uncritically. You assume that a person is absolutely truthful and sincere and reliable, and a little later you find that he is shoddy and unreliable. Then the same thing happens again. After repeated disappointments at the hands of the very people who might be supposed to be your nearest and most intimate friends, constant irritation finally makes *e* you dislike everybody and suppose that there is no sincerity to be found anywhere. Have you never noticed this happening?'

'Indeed, I have.'

'Don't you feel that it is reprehensible? Isn't it obvious that such a person is trying to manage human relationships without a basic knowledge of humans? Otherwise he would surely recognize the truth: that there are not many very good or very bad people, but *90a* the great majority are something between the two.'

'How do you mean?' I asked.

'On the analogy of very large or small objects,' he said. 'Can you think of anything more unusual than coming across a very large or small man, or dog, or any other creature? Or one which is very swift or slow, ugly or beautiful, white or black? Have you never realized that extreme instances are few and rare, while intermediate ones are many and plentiful?'

'Certainly.'

'So you think that if there were a competition in wickedness, *b* very few would distinguish themselves even there?'

'Probably.'

'Yes, it is probable,' said Socrates. 'However, you've led me into a digression. The resemblance between arguments and human beings lies not in what I said just now, but in what I said before: that when one believes that an argument is true without possessing skill in logic, and then a little later decides rightly or wrongly that it is false, and the same thing happens again and again – you know

c how it is, especially with those who spend their time in arguing both sides;[130] they end by believing that they are wiser than anyone else, because they alone have discovered that there is nothing stable or dependable either in things or in arguments, and that everything fluctuates just like the Euripus,[131] and never stays at one point for any time.'

'That is perfectly true,' I said.

'Well, then, Phaedo,' he said, 'supposing that there is a kind of argument which is true and valid and capable of having its truth

d ascertained, if anyone nevertheless, through his experience of these arguments which seem to the same people to be sometimes true and sometimes false, attached no responsibility to himself and his lack of skill, but was finally content, in exasperation, to shift the blame from himself to arguments, and spend the rest of his life loathing and decrying them, and so missed the chance of knowing the truth about reality; would it not be a pitiable thing?'

'It would indeed be pitiable,' I said.

'Very well,' he said, 'that is the first thing that we must guard

e against; we must not let it enter our minds that there may be no health in argument. On the contrary we should recognize that we ourselves are still intellectual invalids, but that we must brace ourselves and do our best to become healthy – you and the others with a view to the rest of your lives too, but in my case in view of

91a my death itself; because at the moment I might easily handle this argument like a competitor instead of a philosopher. You know how, in an argument, people who have no real education care nothing for the facts of the case, and are only anxious to get their point of view accepted by the audience? Well, I feel that at this present moment I am nearly as bad as they are, apart from this: that my anxiety will be not to convince my audience (except incidentally) but to produce the strongest possible conviction in

b myself. This is how I weigh the position, my dear fellow – see how out for profit I am! If my theory is really true, it's best to believe it; while even if death is extinction, at any rate during this time before my death I shall be less likely to distress my companions by giving way to self-pity; and this ignorance of mine will not live on with me (that would be a bad thing) [132] but will shortly come to an end.

'That, my dear Simmias and Cebes, is the spirit in which I am prepared to approach the argument. As for you, if you will take my advice you will think very little of Socrates, and much more of the truth. If you think that anything I say is true, you must agree with me; if not, oppose it with every argument that you have. You must not allow me, in my enthusiasm, to deceive both myself and you, and, like a bee, to leave my sting behind when I fly away.

Section K: Socrates replies to Simmias's theory that the soul may be a kind of attunement. The theory is (i) incompatible with the Theory of Recollection, (ii) inadequate in so far as there are degrees of attunement but not of soul,[133] (iii) inconsistent with the fact that our souls can be well or badly 'tuned' themselves, and (iv) inconsistent with the soul's role as leader of the body.

'Well, we must go ahead,' he continued. 'First remind me of what you said, if you find my memory inaccurate. Simmias's doubts, I believe, are based on the fear that, though the soul is more divine and a nobler thing than the body, it may nevertheless be destroyed first, as being a kind of attunement. Cebes, on the other hand, appeared to agree with me that soul is more enduring than body, but to maintain that no one can be sure that, after repeatedly wearing out a great many bodies, it does not at last perish itself, leaving the last body behind; and he thinks that death may be precisely this, the destruction of the soul, because the body never stops perishing all the time. Am I right, Simmias and Cebes, in thinking that these are the objections which we have to investigate?'

They agreed that this was so.

'Well, then,' he said, 'do you reject all our previous arguments, or only some of them?'

'Only some of them,' they said.

'What is your opinion of that argument by which we claimed that learning is recollection, and that, if this is so, our souls must have existed somewhere else before they were confined in the body?'

'Speaking for myself,' said Cebes, 'I found it remarkably convincing at the time, and I stick to it still as I do to no other theory.'

'Yes, indeed,' said Simmias, 'it is just the same with me; I should be very much surprised if I ever changed my opinion about that.'

'But you will have to change it, my Theban friend,' said Socrates, 'if your belief still stands that an attunement is a composite thing, and that the soul is an attunement composed of our physical elements at a given tension. I imagine that you would not accept

b   even from yourself the assertion that a composite attunement existed before the elements of which it was to be composed. Or would you?'

'Not for a moment, Socrates.'

'Don't you see that that is just what it amounts to when you say that the soul exists before it enters the human form or body, and also that it is composed of elements which do not yet exist? Surely an attunement is not at all like the object of your comparison. The

c   instrument and the strings and their untuned sounds come first; the attunement is the last of all to be constituted and the first to be destroyed. How will this account harmonize with the other?'

'Not at all,' said Simmias.

'And yet,' said Socrates, 'if any account ought to be harmonious, it should be an account of attunement!'

'Yes, it should,' said Simmias.

'Well,' said Socrates, 'this one does not harmonize with your view. Make up your mind which theory you prefer: that learning is recollection, or that soul is an attunement.'

'The former, without any hesitation, Socrates,' he said. 'The

d   other appealed to me, without any proof to support it, because it came with a certain likelihood and attractiveness; which is why it appeals to most people. But I realize that theories which rest their proof upon likelihood are impostors, and unless you are on your guard, they deceive you properly, both in geometry and everywhere else. On the other hand, the theory of recollection and learning derives from a hypothesis which is worthy of acceptance.[134] It was surely stated that the theory that our soul exists even before it enters the body has the same status as its grasp of that reality of

e   which we say "as it is itself";[135] a view which I have, to the best of my belief, fully and rightly accepted. It seems therefore that I must not accept, either from myself or from anyone else, the assertion that soul is an attunement.'

'There is this way of looking at it too, Simmias,' said Socrates. 'Do you think that an attunement, or any other composite thing, should 93a be in a condition different from that of its component elements?'

'No, I do not.'

'And it should not act, or be acted upon, I presume, differently from them?'

He agreed.

'So an attunement should not control its elements, but should follow their lead?'

He assented.

'There is no question of its conflicting with them, either in movement or in sound or in any other way?'[136]

'None at all.'

'Very well, then; is it not the nature of every attunement to be an attunement in so far as it is tuned?'

'I don't understand.'

'Surely,' said Socrates, 'if it is tuned more, that is, in a greater degree (supposing this to be possible), it must be more of an b attunement; and if it is tuned less, that is, in a lesser degree, it must be less of an attunement.'

'Quite so.'

'And is this the case with the soul – that one soul is, even minutely, more or less of a soul than another?'

'Not in the least.'

'Now please give me your closest attention,' said Socrates. 'Do we say that one kind of soul possesses intelligence and goodness, and is good, and that another possesses ignorance and wickedness, and is bad? And is this true?'   c

'Yes, it is true.'

'Then how will a person who holds that the soul is an attunement account for the presence in it of goodness and badness? Will he describe them as yet another attunement or lack of it? Will he say that the good soul is in tune, and not only is an attunement itself, but contains another, whereas the bad soul is out of tune and does not contain another attunement?'

'I really could not say,' replied Simmias; 'but obviously anyone who held that view would have to say something of the sort.'

d   'But we have already agreed,' said Socrates, 'that no soul can be more or less of a soul than another; and this is tantamount to agreeing that it can be no more or less of an attunement, nor can it be an attunement in a greater or lesser degree.[137] Is that not so?'

'Certainly.'

'And that what is neither more nor less of an attunement is neither more nor less in tune. Is that so?'

'Yes.'

'Does that which is neither more nor less in tune contain a greater or smaller proportion of attunement, or an equal one?'

'An equal one.'

'Then since no soul is any more or less than just a soul, it is
e   neither more nor less in tune.'

'That is so.'

'Under this condition it cannot contain a greater proportion of discord or attunement.'

'Certainly not.'

'And again under this condition, can one soul contain a greater proportion of badness or goodness than another, assuming that badness is discord and goodness attunement?'

'No, it cannot.'

94a   'Or rather, I suppose, Simmias, by strict reasoning no soul will contain any share of badness, if it is an attunement; because surely since attunement is absolutely attunement and nothing else, it can never contain any share of discord.'

'No, indeed.'

'Nor can the soul, since it is absolutely soul, contain a share of badness.'

'Not in the light of what we have said.'

'So on this theory every soul of every living creature will be equally good — assuming that it is the nature of all souls to be equally souls and nothing else.'

'I think that follows, Socrates.'

'Do you also think that this view is right? Would the argument
b   ever have come to this if our hypothesis, that the soul is an attunement, had been correct?'

'Not the least chance of it.'

'Well,' said Socrates, 'do you hold that it is any other part of a man than the soul that governs him, especially if it is a wise one?'

'No, I do not.'

'Does it yield to the feelings of the body, or oppose them? I mean, for instance, that when a person is feverish and thirsty it impels him the other way, not to drink; and when he is hungry, not to eat; and there are thousands of other ways in which we see the soul opposing the physical instincts.[138] Is that not so?'

'Certainly.'

'Did we not also agree a little while ago that if it is an attunement it can never sound a note that conflicts with the tension or relaxation or vibration or any other condition of its constituents, but must always follow them and never direct them?'

'Yes, we did, of course.'

'Well, surely we can see now that the soul works in just the opposite way. It directs all the elements of which it is said to consist, opposing them in almost everything all through life, and exercising every form of control; sometimes by severe and unpleasant methods like those of physical training and medicine, and sometimes by milder ones; sometimes threatening, sometimes warning; and conversing with the desires and passions and fears as though it were quite separate and distinct from them. It is just like Homer's description in the *Odyssey* where he says that Odysseus

Then beat his breast, and thus reproved his heart.
"Endure, my heart; still worse hast thou endured."[139]

Do you suppose that when he wrote that he thought that the soul was an attunement, liable to be swayed by physical feelings? Surely he regarded it as capable of leading and controlling them; as something much too divine to rank as an attunement.'

'That is certainly how it seems to me, Socrates.'

'Good. In that case there is no justification for our saying that soul is a kind of attunement. We should neither agree with Homer[140] nor be consistent ourselves.'

'That is so.'

Section L: Socrates begins his response to Cebes.

'Well now,' said Socrates, 'we seem to have placated the Theban Harmonia[141] with moderate success. But what about Cadmus, Cebes? How shall we placate him, and what argument shall we use?'

'I think that you will find a way,' said Cebes. 'This argument which you brought forward against the attunement theory far surpassed all my expectations. When Simmias was explaining his difficulties I wondered very much whether anyone would be able to do anything with his argument; so I was quite astonished that it could not stand up against your very first attack. I should not be surprised if Cadmus's argument met the same fate.'

'My dear fellow,' said Socrates, 'don't tempt fate, or some jinx will turn around the argument that's on its way. However, that's God's affair; it is our task to come to close quarters in the Homeric manner and test the substance of what you say.

'What you require, in a nutshell, is this. You consider that, unless the confidence of a philosopher, who at the point of dying believes that after death he will be better off for having lived and died in philosophy rather than in any other pursuit, is to be a blind and foolish confidence, the soul must be proved to be indestructible and immortal. To show that it has great vitality and a godlike nature, and even that it existed before we were born [142] – all this, you say, may very well indicate not that the soul is immortal, but merely that it is long-lived, and pre-existed somewhere for a prodigious period of time, enjoying a great measure of knowledge and activity. But all this did not make it any the more immortal, indeed its very entrance into the human body was, like a disease, the beginning of its destruction; it lives this life in increasing weariness, and finally perishes in what we call death. You also say that, to our individual fears, it makes no difference whether it enters the body once or often; anyone who does not know and cannot prove that the soul is immortal must be afraid, unless he is a fool.

'That, I believe, is the substance of your objection, Cebes. I am deliberately reviewing it more than once, in order than nothing may escape us, and that you may add to it or subtract from it anything that you wish.'

Cebes said: 'But at the present moment there is no need for me to add or subtract anything; that is precisely my point of view.'

After spending some time in reflection, Socrates said, 'What you require is no light undertaking, Cebes. It involves a full treatment of the reasons for generation and destruction. If you like, I will describe my own experiences in this connection; and then, if you find anything helpful in my account, you can use it to reassure yourself about your own objections.'

'Yes, indeed,' said Cebes, 'I should like that very much.'

Section M: Socrates' progress in the philosophy of reasons or causes.[143] *Note that from the beginning he has been looking for the causes or explanations of coming-to-be, passing away, or being in existence: not just things coming-to-be, etc., but also the coming-to-be, etc. of those attributes which come to apply to them. He sought such causes first in the various theories of the Presocratic philosophers, but this gave rise to a new set of problems for him. The theory of Anaxagoras that intelligence governs the world awakens in him the outline of a different approach, by which physical things would be shown to conform with the requirements of intelligence, but Anaxagoras himself gives no lead in the application of such a method.*

'Then listen, and I will tell you. When I was young, Cebes, I had an extraordinary passion for that branch of learning which is called natural science; I thought it would be marvellous to know the reasons [144] for which each thing comes and ceases and continues to be.[145] I was constantly veering to and fro, puzzling primarily *b* over this sort of question: "Is it when heat and cold produce fermentation, as some have said, that living creatures are bred?[146] Is it with the blood that we become aware, or with the air or the fire that is in us?[147] Or is it none of these, but the brain that supplies our senses of hearing and sight and smell; and from these that memory and opinion arise, and from memory and opinion, when established, that knowledge comes?"[148] Then again I would consider how these things are destroyed, and study celestial and terrestrial phenomena, until at last I came to the conclusion that I *c* was uniquely unfitted for this form of inquiry. I will give you a sufficient indication of what I mean. I had understood some things plainly before, in my own and other people's estimation; but now I was so befogged by these speculations that I unlearned even what I had thought I knew, especially about the reason for growth in human beings. Previously I had thought it obvious to anybody that it was due to eating and drinking; that when, from the food which we consume, flesh is added to flesh and bone to bone, and when in *d* the same way the other parts of the body are augmented by their appropriate particles, the bulk which was small is now large; and in this way the small man becomes a big one.[149] That is what I used to believe; reasonably, don't you think?'

'I do,' said Cebes.

'Consider a little further. I had been content to think, when I saw a tall man standing beside a short one, that he was taller by a head;[150] and similarly in the case of horses. And it seemed to me even more obvious that ten is more than eight because it contains two more; and that two feet is bigger than one because it exceeds it by half its own length.'

'And what do you believe about them now?' asked Cebes.

'Why, upon my word, that I am very far from supposing that I know the explanation of any of these things. I cannot even convince myself that when you add one to one either the first or the second one becomes two, or they both become two by the addition of the one to the other. I find it hard to believe that, although when they were separate each of them was one and they were not two, now that they have come together the reason for their becoming two is simply the union explained by their juxtaposition. Nor can I believe now, when you divide one, that this time the reason for its becoming two is the division; because this reason for its becoming two is the opposite of the former one: then it was because they were brought close together and added one to the other, but now it is because they are taken apart and separated one from the other.[151] Nor can I now persuade myself that I understand how it is that things become one; nor, in short, why anything else comes or ceases or continues to be, according to this method of inquiry. So I reject it altogether, and muddle out a haphazard method of my own.

'However, I once heard someone reading from some book – of Anaxagoras, he claimed – and asserting that it is Intelligence that organizes things and is the reason for everything.[152] This explanation pleased me. Somehow it seemed right that Intelligence should be the reason for everything; and I reflected that if this is so, in the course of its arrangement Intelligence sets everything in order and arranges each individual thing in the way that is best for it. Therefore if anyone wished to discover the reason why any given thing came, continued, or ceased to be, he must find out how it

was best for that thing to be, or to act or be acted upon in any *d*
way. On this view there was only one thing for a man to consider,
with regard both to himself and to anything else, namely the best
and highest good; although this would necessarily imply knowing
what is less good, since both were covered by the same knowledge.

'When I weighed this up, I assumed to my delight that here I
had found an authority on causation who was after my own heart
– Anaxagoras. I assumed that he would begin by informing us
whether the earth is flat or round[153] and would then proceed to *e*
explain in detail the reason why it had to be with reference to
what's better – i.e. that it was better that it should be like this. So
if he asserted that the earth was in the centre, he would explain in
detail that it was better for it to be there; and if he made this clear,
I was prepared to give up hankering after any other kind of *98a*
reason. I was prepared also to learn about the sun and moon and
the other heavenly bodies in this way, about their relative velocities
and their orbits and all the other phenomena connected with them
– how it is better for each one of them to act or be acted upon as
it is. It never entered my head that a man who asserted that the
ordering of things is due to Intelligence would offer any other
explanation for them than that it is best for them to be as they are.
I thought that by assigning a reason to each phenomenon separately *b*
and to the universe as a whole he would make perfectly clear what
is best for each and what is the universal good. I would not have
parted with my hopes for a great sum of money. I lost no time in
procuring the books,[154] and began to read them as quickly as I
possibly could, so that I might know as soon as possible about
what's best and what's inferior.

'It was a wonderful hope, my friend, but it was quickly dashed.
As I read on I discovered a man who made no use of his
Intelligence[155] and assigned to it no responsibility for the order of
the world, but adduced reasons like air and ether and water and *c*
many other oddities. It seemed to me that he was just about as
inconsistent as if someone were to say: "The reason for everything
that Socrates does is intelligence", and then, in trying to account
for my several actions, said first that the reason why I am sitting
here now is that my body is composed of bones and sinews, and
that the bones are rigid and separated at the joints, but the sinews
are capable of contraction and relaxation, and form an envelope *d*

for the bones with the help of the flesh and skin, the latter holding all together; and since the bones move freely in their joints, the sinews by relaxing and contracting enable me somehow to bend my limbs; and that is the reason for my sitting here in a bent position. Or again, if he tried to account in the same way for my conversing with you, adducing reasons such as sound and air and

e hearing and a thousand others, and never troubled to mention the real reasons; which are that since Athens has thought it better to condemn me, therefore I for my part have thought it better to sit here, and more right to stay and submit to whatever penalty she orders – because, by Dog! I fancy that these sinews and bones

99a would have been in the neighbourhood of Megara or Boeotia [156] long ago (impelled by a conviction of what is best!) if I did not think that it was more just and honourable to submit to whatever penalty my country orders rather than take to my heels and run away. But to call things like that reasons is too peculiar. If it were said that without such bones and sinews and all the rest of them I should not be able to do what I think is right, it would be true; but to say that it is because of them that I do what I am doing, and not through choice of what is best – although my actions are

b controlled by intelligence – would be a very lax and inaccurate form of expression. Fancy being unable to distinguish between the reason for a thing, and the condition without which the reason couldn't be operative! [157] It is this latter, as it seems to me, that most people, groping in the dark, call a reason – attaching to it a name to which it has no right. That is why one person surrounds the earth with a vortex, and so keeps it in place by means of the heavens; and another props it up on a pedestal of air, as though it

c were a wide platter. [158] As for a power which keeps things ever in the best position, they neither search for it nor believe that it has any remarkable force; they imagine that they will some day find a more mighty and immortal and all-sustaining Atlas; [159] and they do not think that anything is really bound and held together because goodness requires it. For my part, I should be delighted to learn about the workings of such a reason from anyone at all, but since I've been denied it, and have been unable either to discover it myself or to learn about it from another, I've worked out my own

d secondary approach to the problem of causation. Would you like me to give you a demonstration of it, Cebes?'

'I should like it very much indeed.'

'Well, after this,' said Socrates, 'when I was worn out with my investigations into reality, it occurred to me that I must guard against the same sort of risk which people run when they watch and study an eclipse of the sun; some of them, you see, injure their eyes, unless they study its reflection in water or some other medium.[160] I conceived of something like this happening to myself, and I was afraid that by observing objects with my eyes and trying to comprehend them with each of my other senses I might blind my soul altogether. So I decided that I must have recourse to theories, and use them in trying to discover the truth about things. Perhaps my illustration is not quite apt; because I do not entirely agree that an inquiry by means of theory employs 'images' any more than one which confines itself to facts.[161] But however that may be, I started off in this way; and in every case I first lay down[162] the theory which I judge to be least vulnerable; and then whatever seems to agree with it – with regard either to reasons or to anything else – I assume to be true, and whatever does not I assume to be untrue. But I should like to express my meaning more clearly; because at present I don't think that you understand.'

'No, indeed I don't,' said Cebes, 'not a bit.'

Section N: Socrates explains his new theory. Particulars are what they are by participation in the Idea, and receive their descriptions from the name of that Idea. We are now entering some of the most difficult and most discussed theory of Plato's middle period. Yet Plato seems to find much of what he says perfectly obvious; Socrates thinks his method is unadventurously safe, and the interlocutors, with Echecrates too, are depicted as eager to agree on much of what we should hesitate over. While not denying that Plato would have had a more technical theory, traces of which emerge here through his choice of language, we should be wary of importing unnecessary technicalities into our understanding of texts such as this.

'Well,' said Socrates, 'what I mean is this, and there is nothing new about it; I have always said it, in fact I have never stopped saying it, especially in the discussion that's just gone by. As I am going to try to explain to you the type of reason I've worked out myself, I propose to make a fresh start from those principles of mine which are always cropping up;[163] that is, I am assuming the existence of Beauty in itself and Goodness and Largeness and all the rest of them. If you grant my assumption and admit that they exist, I hope with their help to explain causation to you, and to find a proof that the soul is immortal.'

c 'Certainly I grant it,' said Cebes; 'you need lose no time in drawing your conclusion.'

'Then consider the next step, and see whether you share my opinion. It seems to me that whatever else is beautiful apart from Beauty itself is beautiful because it partakes[164] of that Beauty, and for no other reason. Do you accept this kind of reason?'

'Yes, I do.'

'Well, now', said he, 'I cannot understand these other ingenious theories of causation. If someone tells me that the reason why a d given object is beautiful is that it has a gorgeous colour or shape or any other such attribute, I disregard all these other explanations – I find them all confusing – and I cling simply and straightforwardly, naively perhaps, to the explanation that the one thing that makes that object beautiful is the presence in it or association with it (in whatever way the relation comes about)[165] of that other Beauty. I do not go so far as to insist upon the precise detail; only upon the fact that it is by Beauty that beautiful things are beautiful. This, I feel, is the safest answer for me or for anyone else to give, e and I believe that while I hold fast to this I cannot fall; it is safe for me or for anyone else to answer that it is by Beauty that beautiful things are beautiful. Don't you agree?'

'Yes, I do.'

'Then is it also by largeness that large things are large and larger things larger, and by smallness that smaller things are smaller?'

'Yes.'

'So you too, like myself, wouldn't accept the statement that one man is taller than another "by a head" and that the shorter man is 101a shorter by the same; you would protest that the only view which you yourself can hold is that whatever is taller than something else is so simply by tallness – that is, because of tallness; and that what is shorter is so simply by shortness, that is, because of shortness.

You would be afraid, I suppose, that if you said that one man is taller than another by a head, you would be faced with a counter-argument: first that the taller should be taller and the shorter shorter by the same thing, and secondly that the taller person should be taller by a head, which is a short thing, and that it would be a miracle that a man should be made tall by something short. Isn't that so?'[166] b

Cebes laughed and said, 'Yes, it is.'

'Then you would be afraid to say that ten is more than eight "by two", or that two is the reason for its excess over eight, instead of saying that it is more than eight by, or because of, being a larger number; and you would be afraid to say that a length of two feet is greater than one foot by a half, instead of saying that it is greater by its larger size? There's the same danger here too.'

'Quite so.'

'Suppose next that we add one to one; you would surely avoid saying that the reason for our getting two is the addition; nor, if c we divided a unit, the division. You would loudly proclaim that you know of no other way in which any given attribute can come to be except by sharing the essential nature of the thing it has a share of; and that in the cases which I have mentioned you recognize no other reason for something coming to be two than its sharing in duality; and whatever is to become two must share in this, and whatever is to become one must share in unity. You would dismiss these divisions and additions and other such ingenu-ity, leaving them for persons wiser than yourself to use in their explanations, while you, being nervous of your own shadow, as d the saying is, and of your inexperience, would hold fast to the security of your hypothesis and make your answers accordingly. If anyone should question[167] the hypothesis itself, you would ignore him and refuse to answer until you could consider whether its consequences were mutually consistent or not. And when you had to substantiate the hypothesis itself, you would proceed in the same way, assuming whatever more basic hypothesis[168] commended itself most to you, until you reached one which was satisfactory. e You would not mix the two things together by discussing both the starting-point and its consequences, like one of these masters of contradictions[169] – that is, if you wanted to discover any part of the truth. They presumably have no thought or concern whatever for that, because their cleverness enables them to be well satisfied with the way they muddle everything up; but you, I imagine, if you are a philosopher, will follow the course which I describe.'

'You are perfectly right,' said Simmias and Cebes together.

ECHECRATES: And with good reason, Phaedo! It seems to me that Socrates made his meaning extraordinarily clear to even a limited intelligence.

PHAEDO: That was certainly the feeling of all of us who were present, Echecrates.

ECHECRATES: No doubt, because it's just the same with us who were not present and are hearing it now for the first time. But how did the discussion go on?

PHAEDO: I think that when Socrates had got this accepted, and it was agreed that the various Forms[170] exist, and that the reason why other things are called after the Forms is that they share in them, he next went on to ask: 'If you hold this view, I suppose that when you say that Simmias is taller than Socrates but shorter than Phaedo, you mean that at that moment there are in Simmias both tallness and shortness?'

'Yes, I do.'

'But do you agree that the statement "Simmias is bigger than Socrates" is not, as expressed, an accurate reflection of the facts?[171] Surely it's not in Simmias's own nature to be bigger – it's because of the height which he incidentally possesses; and conversely the reason why he is bigger than Socrates is not because Socrates is Socrates, but because Socrates has the attribute of shortness in comparison with Simmias's height.'

'True.'

'And again, Simmias's being smaller than Phaedo is due not to the fact that Phaedo is Phaedo, but to the fact that Phaedo has the attribute of tallness in comparison with Simmias's shortness.'

'Quite so.'

'So that is how Simmias comes to be described as both short and tall, because he's intermediate between the two of them, and lets his shortness be surpassed by the tallness of the one while he displays a tallness that surpasses the shortness of the other.' And with a smile he added, 'I seem to be talking like a technical treatise; but all the same, surely, the situation is as I say?'

Simmias agreed.

Section O: Socrates begins by making a distinction akin to that between the accidental and essential properties of an entity – between those properties which it can lose without ceasing to be the thing that it is, and others which are essential for it to remain what it is. After this he establishes that certain things necessarily imply the participation in one of a pair of opposite qualities, and cannot take on the opposing quality. Anything which has, as an essential quality, the property P which has an opposite Q, cannot take on Q-ness but must be destroyed or retire rather than become Q. The passage is a tantalizing one for those studying Plato's metaphysics because it is difficult to understand without postulating immanent form as something distinct from both Ideas and particulars, and yet no terminology peculiar to immanent form has been established.

'I am saying all this because I'd like you to share my own point of view. It seems to me not only that tallness itself absolutely declines to be short as well as tall, but also that the tallness "in"[172] us never admits smallness and declines to be surpassed. It does one of two things: either it gives way and withdraws as its opposite shortness approaches, or it has already ceased to exist by the time that the other arrives. It cannot stand its ground and receive the quality of shortness in the same way as I myself have done. If it did, it would become different from what it was before, whereas I have not lost my identity by acquiring the quality of shortness; I am the same man, only short; but my tallness could not endure to be short instead of tall. In the same way the shortness that is "in" us declines ever to become or be tall; nor will any other quality, while still remaining what it was, at the same time become or be the opposite quality; in such a situation it either withdraws or ceases to exist.'

'I agree with you entirely,' said Cebes.

At this point one of the company – I can't remember distinctly who it was – said 'Look here! Didn't we agree, earlier in the discussion,[173] on the exact opposite of what you are saying now: that the bigger comes from the smaller and the smaller from the bigger, and that it is precisely from their opposites that opposites come? Now the view seems to be that this is impossible.'

Socrates had listened with his head turned towards the speaker. 'How brave of you to refresh my memory,' he said, 'but you don't realize the difference between what we are saying now and what we said then. Then we were saying that opposite things come from opposite things; now we are saying that the opposite itself[174] can never become opposite to itself – neither the opposite which is in us nor that which is in Nature.[175] Then, my friend, we were speaking about objects which possess opposite qualities, and calling them by the names of the latter, but now we are speaking about the qualities themselves, from whose presence in them the objects which are called after them derive their names.[176] We maintain

c that the opposites themselves would absolutely refuse to tolerate coming into being from one another.' As he spoke he looked at Cebes. 'I suppose that nothing in what he said worried you too, Cebes?'

'No, not this time,' said Cebes, 'though I don't deny that a good many other things do.'

'So we are agreed upon this as a general principle: that an opposite can never be opposite to itself.'

'Absolutely.'

'Then consider this point too, and see whether you agree about it too. Do you admit that there are such things as heat and cold?'

'Yes, I do.'

'Do you think they are the same as snow and fire?'[177]

d 'Certainly not.'

'Heat is quite distinct from fire, and cold from snow?'

'Yes.'

'But I suppose you agree, in the light of what we said before, that snow, being what it is, can never admit heat and still remain snow, just as it was before, only with the addition of heat. It must either withdraw at the approach of heat, or cease to exist.'

'Quite so.'

'Again, fire must either retire or cease to exist at the approach of cold. It will never have the courage to admit cold and still remain fire, just as it was, only with the addition of cold.'

e 'That is true.'

'So we find, in certain cases like these, that the name of the Form is eternally applicable not only to the Form itself, but also to something else, which is not the Form but invariably possesses its distinguishing characteristic. But perhaps another example will make my meaning clearer. Oddness must always be entitled to this name "odd" by which I am now calling it; isn't that so?'[178]

'Certainly.'

'This is the question: is it unique in this respect, or is there something else, not identical with oddness, to which we are bound always to apply not only its own name but that of odd as well, because by its very nature it never loses its oddness? What I mean applies to the number three; there are plenty of other examples, but take the case of three. Don't you think that it must always be described not only by its own name but by that of odd, although odd and three are not the same thing? It is the very nature of three and five and all the alternate integers that every one of them is invariably odd, although it is not identical with oddness. Similarly two and four and all the rest of the other series are not identical with even, but each one of them always is even. Do you go along with this, or not?'

'Of course I do.'

'Then pay careful attention to the point which I want to make, which is this. It seems clear that the opposites themselves do not admit one another; but it also looks as though any things which, though not themselves opposites, always possess an opposite quality, similarly do not take on the opposite Idea to that which is in them, but on its approach either cease to exist or retire before it. Surely we must assert that three will sooner cease to exist or suffer any other fate than submit to become even while it is still three?'[179]

'Certainly,' said Cebes.

'And yet Two and Three are not opposites.'

'So it is not only the opposite Forms that cannot face one another's approach;[180] there are other things too which cannot face the approach of opposites.'

'That is quite true.'

'Shall we try, if we can, to specify what sort of things these are?'

'By all means.'

'Well, then, Cebes, would this describe them – that they are things which compel whatever they get a hold on to assume not only their own Idea, but invariably also some other Idea which is an opposite?'[181]

'What do you mean?'

'Just what we were saying a minute ago. You realize, I suppose, that when the Idea of Three gets a hold on any group of objects, it compels them to be odd as well as three.'

'Certainly.'

'Then I maintain that into such a group the opposite Idea to the character [182] which has this effect can never enter.'

'No, it cannot.'

'And it was the Form of Odd that had this effect?'

'Yes.'

'And the opposite of this is the Form of Even?'

'Yes.'

e   'So the Form of Even will never enter into three.'

'No, never.'

'In other words, three is incompatible with evenness.'

'Quite.'

'So the number three is uneven.'

'Yes.'

'I proposed just now to describe what sort of things they are which, although they are not themselves directly opposed to a given opposite, nevertheless do not admit it; as in the present example, three, although not the opposite of even, nevertheless does not admit it, because three is always accompanied by the opposite of even; and similarly with two and odd, or fire and cold, 105a   and hosts of others. Well, see whether you accept this definition: Not only does an opposite not admit its opposite, but if anything is accompanied by a Form which *has* an opposite, and *meets* that opposite, then the thing which is accompanied never admits the opposite of the Form by which it is accompanied. Let me refresh your memory; there is no harm in hearing a thing several times. Five will not admit the Form of Even, nor will ten, which is double five, admit the Form of Odd. Twin has an opposite of its own, but b   at the same time it will not admit the Form of Odd. Nor will one and a half, or other fractions such as a half or three-quarters and so on, admit the form of Whole, assuming that you follow me and agree.'

'I follow and agree perfectly,' said Cebes.

'Then run over the same ground with me from the beginning; and don't answer in the exact terms of the question, but follow my example. I say this because besides the "safe answer" that I described at first, as the result of this discussion I now see another means of safety. Suppose, for instance, that you ask me what must become present in a body to make it hot, I shall not return the safe but simplistic answer that it is heat, but a more sophisticated one, based on the results of our disussion – namely that it is fire. And if you ask what must become present in a body to make it diseased, I shall say not disease but fever. Similarly if you ask what must become present in a number to make it odd, I shall say not oddness but unity; and so on. See whether you have a sufficient grasp now of what I want from you.'

'Quite sufficient.'

Section P: Socrates argues that the soul is such a thing which always brings a quality to that which it occupies, and cannot itself be coupled with the opposite quality. It must retire or perish.

'Then tell me, what must be present in a body to make it alive?'
'Soul.'
'Is this always so?'
'Of course.'
'So whenever soul takes possession of a body, it always brings living with it?'
'Yes, it does.'
'Is there an opposite to living, or not?'
'Yes, there is.'
'What?'
'Dying.'
'Does it follow, then, from our earlier agreement, that soul will never admit the opposite of that which accompanies it?'
'Most definitely,' said Cebes.
'Well, now, what name did we apply just now to that which does not admit the Form of even?'
'Uneven.'
'And what do we call that which does not admit justice, or culture?'
'Uncultured; and the other unjust.'
'Very good. And what do we call that which does not admit dying?'
'Un-dying.'[183]

'And soul does not admit death?'

'No.'

'So soul is un-dying.'

'Yes, it is un-dying.'

'Well,' said Socrates, 'can we say that that has been proved? What do you think?'

'Most completely, Socrates.'

Section Q: The argument is concluded. What is 'un-dying' cannot surely perish; therefore it must withdraw.

'Here is another question for you, Cebes. If the uneven were necessarily imperishable, would not three be imperishable?'

106a

'Of course.'

'Then again, if what is un-hot were necessarily imperishable, when you applied heat to snow, would not the snow withdraw still intact and unmelted? It could not cease to exist, nor on the other hand could it remain where it was and admit the heat.'

'That is true.'

'In the same way I assume that if what is un-cold were imperishable, when anything cold approached fire, it could never go out or cease to exist; it would depart and be gone unharmed.'

'That must be so.'

b

'Are we not bound to say the same of the un-dying? If what is un-dying is also imperishable, it is impossible that at the approach of death soul should cease to be. It follows from what we have already said that it cannot admit death, or be dead; just as we said that three cannot be even, nor can odd; nor can fire be cold, nor can the heat which is in the fire. "But," it may be objected, "granting (as has been agreed) that odd does not become even at

c

the approach of even, why should it not cease to exist, and something even take its place?" In reply to this we could not insist that the odd does not cease to exist – because what is un-even is not imperishable; but if this were conceded, we could easily insist that, at the approach of even, odd and three retire and depart. And we could be equally insistent about fire and heat and all the rest of them, could we not?'

'Certainly.'

'So now in the case of the un-dying, if it is conceded that this is

also imperishable, soul will be imperishable as well as un-dying.
Otherwise we shall need another argument.'   *d*

'There is no need on that account,' said Cebes. 'If what is un-
dying and eternal cannot avoid destruction, it is hard to see how
anything else can.'

'And I imagine that it would be admitted by everyone,' said
Socrates, 'that God at any rate, and the Form of Life, and
anything else that is un-dying, can never cease to exist.'

'Yes indeed; by all men certainly, and even more, I suppose, by
the gods.'

'Then since what is un-dying is also indestructible, if soul is   *e*
really un-dying, surely it must be imperishable too.'

'Quite inevitably.'

'So it appears that when death comes to a man, the mortal part
of him dies, but the un-dying part retires at the approach of death
and escapes unharmed and indestructible.'

'Evidently.'

'Then it is as certain as anything can be, Cebes, that soul is un-
dying and imperishable, and that our souls will really exist in the
next world.'

'Well, Socrates,' said Cebes, 'for my part I have no criticisms,
and no doubt about the truth of your argument. But if Simmias   *107a*
here or anyone else has any criticism to make, he had better not
keep it to himself; because if anyone wants to say or hear any
more about this subject, I don't see to what other occasion he is to
defer it.'

*Section R: Socrates gives his view of the nature of the universe and
of the soul's fate after death. The material is myth-like, and
comparable with 'myths' of the after-life with which the Gorgias
and Republic conclude. It makes no profession of ascertainable
literal truth. It has clearly been composed specifically for the
Phaedo, in such a way as to reflect the gulf between the hazy
world of sensation and the clear world of the intellect that the rest
of the work has already pointed to. It also suggests an enormous
gap between the painful or at least unattractive environment
which awaits the common man after death and the bright visions
of a higher world which await the philosopher. It therefore per-
forms a protreptic purpose, encouraging Socrates' followers to go*

*on with their mission after his death so that they may look
forward to the day when they may follow him.*

'As a matter of fact,' said Simmias, 'I have no doubts myself
either now, in view of what you have just been saying. All the
b same, the subject is so vast, and I have such a poor opinion of our
weak human nature, that I can't help still feeling some misgivings.'

'Quite right, Simmias,' said Socrates, 'and what is more, even if
you find our original assumptions convincing, they still need more
accurate consideration. If you and your friends examine them
closely enough, I believe that you will arrive at the truth of the
matter, in so far as it is possible for the human mind to attain it;
and if you are sure that you have done this, you will not need to
inquire further.'

'That is true,' said Simmias.

c 'But there is a further point, gentlemen,' said Socrates, 'which
deserves your attention. If the soul is immortal, it demands our
care not only for that part of time which we call life, but for all
time; and indeed it would seem now that it will be extremely
dangerous to neglect it. If death were a release from everything, it
would be a boon for the wicked, because by dying they would be
released not only from the body but also from their own wickedness together with the soul; but as it is, since the soul has emerged
as something immortal, it can have no escape or security from evil
d except by becoming as good and wise as it possibly can. For it
takes nothing with it to the next world except its education and
training; and these, we are told,[184] are of supreme importance in
helping or harming those who have died at the very beginning of
their journey to the other world.

'This is how the story goes. When any man dies, his own
guardian spirit, which was given charge over him in his life, tries
to bring him to a certain place where all must assemble, and from
which, when they have been sorted out by a process of judgement,
they must set out for the next world, under the guidance of one
e who has the office of escorting souls from this world to the
other.[185] When they have there undergone the necessary experiences
and remained as long as is required, another guide brings them
back again after many vast periods of time.

'Of course this journey is not as Aeschylus makes Telephus

describe it. He says that the path to Hades is straightforward, but   108a
it seems clear to me that it is neither straightforward nor single. If
it were, there would be no need for a guide, because surely nobody
could lose his way anywhere if there were only one road. In fact, it
seems likely that it contains many forks and crossroads, to judge
from the ceremonies and observances of this world.[186]

'Well, the wise and disciplined soul follows its guide and is not
ignorant of its surroundings; but as for the soul which is deeply
attached to the body – after a long infatuation with it and with the   b
visible world, as I said before – it is only after much resistance and
suffering that it is at last forcibly led away by its appointed
guardian spirit. And when it reaches the same place as the rest, the
soul which is impure through having done some impure deed,
either by setting its hand to lawless bloodshed or by committing
other kindred crimes which are the work of kindred souls, this
soul is shunned and avoided by all; none will company with it or
guide it; and it wanders alone in utter desolation until certain   c
times have passed, whereupon it is borne away of necessity to its
proper habitation. But every soul that has lived throughout its life
in purity and soberness enjoys divine company and guidance, and
each inhabits the place which is proper to it. There are many
wonderful regions in the earth; and the earth itself is neither of the
kind nor of the size that the experts suppose it to be; or so I'm led
to believe.'[187]

'How can you say that, Socrates?' said Simmias. 'I myself have   d
heard a great many theories about the earth, but not this belief of
yours. I should very much like to hear it.'

'Why, really, Simmias, I don't think that it calls for the skill of a
Glaucus [188] to explain what my belief is; but to prove that it is true
seems to me to be too difficult even for a Glaucus. In the first
place I should probably be unable to do it; and in the second, even
if I knew how, it seems to me, Simmias, that my life is too short
for an explanation of the required length. However, there is no
reason why I should not tell you what I believe about the appear-   e
ance of the earth and the regions in it.'

'Well,' said Simmias, 'even that will do.'

'This is what I believe, then,' said Socrates. 'In the first place, if
the earth is spherical and in the middle of the heavens, it needs
neither air nor any other such force to keep it from falling; the   109a

uniformity of the heavens and the equilibrium of the earth itself are sufficient to support it.[189] Any body in equilibrium, if it is set in the middle of a uniform medium, will have no tendency to sink or rise in any direction more than another, and having equal impulses will remain suspended. This is the first article of my belief.'

'And quite right too,' said Simmias.

b 'Next,' said Socrates, 'I believe that it is vast in size, and that we who dwell between the river Phasis[190] and the pillars of Hercules[191] inhabit only a minute portion of it; we live round the sea like ants or frogs round a swamp; and there are many other peoples inhabiting similar regions. There are many hollow places all round the earth, places of every shape and size, into which the water and mist and air have collected. But the earth's true surface is as pure as the starry heaven in which it lies, and which is called 'ether' by c most of our authorities. The water, mist and air are the dregs of this ether, and they are continually draining into the hollow places in the earth. We do not realize that we are living in its hollows, but assume that we are living up on top of the earth. Imagine someone living in the depths of the sea. He might think that he was living on the surface, and seeing the sun and the other heavenly bodies through the water, he might think that the sea d was the sky. He might be so sluggish and feeble that he had never reached the top of the sea, never emerged and raised his head from the sea into this world of ours, and seen for himself – or even heard from someone who had seen it – how much purer and more beautiful it really is than the one in which his people live. Now we are in just the same position. Although we live in a hollow of the earth, we assume that we are living on the surface, and we call the air heaven, as though this were the heaven through which the stars move. But the truth of the matter is the same, that we are too e feeble and sluggish to make our way out to the upper limit of the air. If someone could reach to the summit, or grow wings and fly aloft, when he put up his head he would see the world above, just as fishes see our world when they put up their heads out of the sea; and if his nature were strong enough to keep looking,[192] he would recognize that that is the true heaven and the true light and 10a the true earth. For this earth and its stones and all the regions in which we live are marred and corroded, just as in the sea everything is corroded by the brine, and there is nothing worth mentioning that grows there,[193] and scarcely any degree of perfect formation, but only eroded rocks and sand and measureless mud, and messy swamps wherever there is earth as well; and nothing is in the least worthy to be judged beautiful by our standards. But the things above excel those of our world to a degree far greater still. If this is the right moment for a story,[194] Simmias, it will be worth your while to hear what it is really like upon the earth which lies beneath the heavens.' **b**

'Yes, indeed, Socrates,' said Simmias, 'it would be a great pleasure to us, at any rate, to hear this tale.'

'Well, my friend,' said Socrates, 'the earth's true surface, viewed from above, is supposed to look like one of those balls made of twelve pieces of skin,[195] variegated and marked out in different colours, of which the colours we know – the ones which artists use – can give only a hint; but there the whole earth is made up of **c** such colours, and others far brighter and purer still. One section is a marvellously beautiful purple, and another is golden; all that is white of it is whiter than chalk or snow; and the rest is similarly made up of the other colours, still more and lovelier than those which we have seen. Even these very hollows in the earth, full of water and air, assume a kind of colour as they give off reflections **d** amid the different hues around them, so that there appears to be one continuous patchwork of colours. The trees and flowers and fruits which grow upon this beauteous earth are proportionately beautiful. The mountains too and the stones have a matching degree of smoothness and transparency and their colours are lovelier. The pebbles which are so highly prized in our world – the jaspers and rubies and emeralds and the rest – are fragments of these stones; but there everything is as beautiful as they are, or **e** finer still. This is because the stones there are in their natural state, not damaged by decay and corroded by salt water as ours are by the sediment which has collected here, and which causes disfigurement or disease to stones and earth, and likewise to animals and plants. The earth's true surface is adorned not only with all these stones but also with gold and silver and the other metals, for many rich veins of them occur in plain view in all parts **111a** of the earth, so that to see them is a sight for the eyes of the blessed.

'There are many kinds of animals upon it, and also human beings, some of whom live inland, others round the air, as we live round the sea,[196] and others in islands surrounded by air but close to the mainland. In a word, as water and the sea are to us for our

b purposes, so is air to them; and as air is to us, so the ether is to them. Their climate is so temperate that they are free from disease and live much longer than people do here; and in sight and hearing and understanding and all other faculties they are as far superior to us as air is to water or ether to air in clarity.

'They also have sanctuaries and temples which are truly inhabited by gods; and oracles and prophecies and visions and all other kinds of communion with the gods occur there face to face.[197]

c They see the sun and moon and stars as they really are;[198] and the rest of their happiness matches this too.

'Such is the nature of the earth as a whole and of the things that are round about it. But there are many places within the earth itself, all around it wherever there are hollow regions;[199] some of these are deeper and more extensive than that in which we live, others deeper than our region but with a smaller expanse, some

d both shallower than ours and broader. All these are joined together underground by many connecting channels, some narrower, some wider, through which, from one basin to another, there flows a great volume of water, monstrous unceasing subterranean rivers of waters both hot and cold; and of fire too, great rivers of fire; and many of liquid mud, some clearer, some murkier, like the rivers in

e Sicily that flow mud before the lava comes, and the lava stream itself. By these the several regions are filled in turn as the flood reaches them.

'All this movement to and fro is caused by an oscillation inside the earth, and this oscillation is brought about by natural means, as follows.

'One of the cavities in the earth is not only larger than the rest,

112a but pierces right through from one side to the other. It is of this that Homer speaks when he says

Far, far away, where lies earth's deepest chasm;[200]

while elsewhere both he and many other poets refer to it as Tartarus. Into this gulf all the rivers flow together, and from it they flow forth again; and each acquires the nature of that part of

the earth through which it flows. The cause of the flowing in and b
out of all these streams is that the mass of liquid has no bottom or
foundation; so it oscillates and surges to and fro, and the air or
breath that belongs to it does the same; for it accompanies the
liquid both as it rushes to the further side of the earth and as it
returns to this. And just as when we breathe we exhale and inhale
the breath in a continuous stream, so in this case too the breath,
oscillating with the liquid, causes terrible and monstrous winds as
it passes in and out. So when the water retires to the so-called c
"lower" region the streams in the earth flow into those parts and
irrigate them fully; and when in turn it ebbs from there and rushes
back this way, it fills our streams again, and when they are filled
they flow through their channels and through the earth; and
arriving in those regions to which their ways have been severally
prepared, they make seas and lakes and rivers and springs. Then
sinking again beneath the ground, some by way of more and d
further regions, others by fewer and nearer, they empty themselves
once more into Tartarus, some much lower, some only a little
lower than the point at which they were drawn off; but they all
flow in at a level deeper than their rise. Some flow in on the
opposite side to that on which they came out, and others on the
same side; while some make a complete circle and, winding like a
snake one or even more times round the earth, descend as far as
possible before they again discharge their waters. It is possible to e
descend in either direction as far as the centre, but no further; for
either direction from the centre is uphill, whichever way the
streams are flowing.

'Among these many various mighty streams there are four in
particular. The greatest of these, and the one which describes the
outermost circle, is that which is called Oceanus.[201] Directly opposite this and with a contrary course is Acheron,[202] which not only
flows through other desolate regions but passes underground and 113a
arrives at the Acherusian Lake, where the souls of the dead for the
most part come, and after staying there for certain fixed periods,
longer or shorter, are sent forth again to be born as living
creatures. Halfway between the two a third river tumbles forth,
and near its source emerges into a great place burning with sheets
of fire, where it forms a boiling lake of muddy water greater than
our sea.[203] From there it follows a circular course, flowing turbid

b and muddy, and as it winds round inside the earth it comes at last to the margin of the Acherusian Lake, but does not mingle with the waters; and after many windings underground, it plunges into Tartarus at a lower point. This is the river called Pyriphlegethon, whose fiery stream belches forth jets of lava here and there in all parts of the world. Directly opposite to this in its turn the fourth river breaks out, first, they say, into a wild and dreadful place, all

c leaden grey, which is called the Stygian region, and the lake which the in-flowing river forms is called Styx. After falling into this, and acquiring mysterious powers in its waters, the river passes underground and follows a spiral course contrary to that of Pyriphlegethon, which it meets from the opposite direction at the Acherusian Lake. This river too mingles its stream with no other waters, but circling round falls into Tartarus opposite Pyriphlegethon; and its name, the poets say, is Cocytus.

d 'Such is the nature of these things.[204] And when the newly dead reach the place to which each is conducted by his guardian spirit, first they undergo judgement to determine those who have lived well and holily, and those who have not. Those who are judged to have lived a neutral life set out for Acheron, and embarking in those vessels which await them, are conveyed in them to the lake; and there they dwell, and undergoing purification are both absolved by punishment from any sins that they have committed, and rewarded for their good deeds, according to each man's deserts.

e Those who on account of the greatness of their sins are judged to be incurable – people who have committed many gross acts of sacrilege or many wicked and lawless murders or any other such crimes – these are hurled by their appropriate destiny into Tartarus, from whence they emerge no more.[205]

'Others are judged to have been guilty of sins which, though, great, are curable; if, for example, they have offered violence to

114a father or mother in a fit of passion, but have spent the rest of their lives in penitence, or if they have committed manslaughter after the same fashion. These too must be cast into Tartarus; but when this has been done and they have remained there for a year, the surge casts them out – the manslayers down Cocytus and the offenders against their parents down Pyriphlegethon. And when, as they are swept along, they come past the Acherusian Lake, there they cry aloud and call upon those whom they have killed or violently abused, and calling, beg and entreat for leave to pass *b* from the stream into the lake, and be received by them. If they prevail, they come out and there is an end of their distress; but if not, they are swept away once more into Tartarus and from there back into the rivers, and find no release from their sufferings until they prevail upon those whom they have wronged; for this is the punishment which their judge has appointed for them.

'But those who are judged to have lived a life of surpassing holiness — these are they who are released and set free from imprisonment in these regions of the earth, and passing upward to *c* their pure abode, make their dwelling upon the earth's surface. And of these such as have purified themselves sufficiently by philosophy live thereafter altogether without bodies, and reach habitations even more beautiful, which it is not easy to portray — nor is there time to do so now. But the reasons which we have already described provide ground enough, as you can see, Simmias, for leaving nothing undone to attain during life some measure of goodness and wisdom; for the prize is glorious and the hope great.

'Of course, no reasonable man ought to insist that the facts are *d* exactly as I have described them. But that either this or something very like it is a true account of our souls and their future habitations — since there is certainly evidence that the soul is deathless — this, I think, is both a fitting contention and a belief worth risking; for the risk is a noble one. We should use such accounts to enchant ourselves with;[206] and that is why I have already drawn out my tale so long.

'These are the reasons, then, for which a man can be confident about the fate of his soul — as long as in life he has abandoned those *e* other pleasures and adornments, the bodily ones, as foreign to his purpose and likely to do more harm than good, and has devoted himself to the pleasures of acquiring knowledge, and so by adorning his soul not with a borrowed beauty but with its own — with self-control, and goodness, and courage, and liberality, and truth — has *115a* settled down to await his journey to the next world. You, Simmias and Cebes and the rest, will each make this journey some day in the future; but "for me the fated hour" (as a tragic character might say) "calls even now". In other words, it is about time that I took my bath. I prefer to have a bath before drinking the poison, rather than give the women the trouble of washing me when I am dead.'

Section S: Socrates' last moments, and the release of his soul.

b   When he had finished speaking, Crito said, 'Very well, Socrates. But have you no directions for the others or myself about your children or anything else? What can we do to please you best?'

'Nothing new, Crito,' said Socrates; 'just what I am always telling you. If you look after your own selves, whatever you do will please me and mine and you too, even if you don't agree with me now. On the other hand, if you neglect yourselves and fail in life to follow the track that we have spoken of both now and in

c   the past, however fervently you agree with me now, it will do no good at all.'

'We shall be keen to do as you say,' said Crito. 'But how shall we bury you?'

'Any way you like,' replied Socrates, 'that is, if you can catch me and I don't slip through your fingers.' He laughed gently as he spoke, and turning to us went on: 'I can't persuade Crito that I am this Socrates here who is talking to you now and marshalling all the arguments; he thinks that I am the corpse whom he will see

d   presently lying dead; and he asks how he is to bury me! As for my long and elaborate explanation that when I have drunk the poison I shall remain with you no longer, but depart to a world of happiness that belongs to the blessed, my words seem to be wasted on him though I console both you and myself. You must give an assurance to Crito for me – the opposite of the one which he gave to the court which tried me. He undertook that I should stay; but you must assure him that when I am dead I shall not stay, but

e   depart and be gone. That will help Crito to bear it more easily, and keep him from being distressed on my account when he sees my body being burned or buried, as if something dreadful were happening to me, or from saying at the funeral that it is Socrates whom he is laying out or carrying to the grave or burying. Believe me, my dear friend Crito: misstatements are not merely jarring in their immediate context; they also have a bad effect upon the soul. No, you must keep up your spirits and say that it is only my body that you are burying; and you can bury it as you please, in

116a whatever way you think is most proper.'

With these words he got up and went into another room to bathe; and Crito went after him, but told us to wait. So we waited, discussing and reviewing what had been said, or else dwelling upon the greatness of the calamity which had befallen us; for we felt just as though we were losing a father and should be orphans for the rest of our lives. Meanwhile, when Socrates had taken his bath, his children were brought to see him – he had two *b* little sons and one big boy – and the women of his household – you know – arrived. He talked to them in Crito's presence and gave them directions about carrying out his wishes; then he told the women and children to go away, and came back himself to join us.

It was now nearly sunset, because he had spent a long time inside. He came and sat down, fresh from the bath, and he had only been talking for a few minutes when the prison officer came in, and walked up to him. 'Socrates,' he said, 'at any rate I shall *c* not have to find fault with you, as I do with others, for getting angry with me and cursing when I tell them to drink the poison – carrying out the magistrates' orders.[207] I have come to know during this time that you are the noblest and the gentlest and the bravest of all the men that have ever come here, and now especially I am sure that you are not angry with me, but with them; because you know who are responsible. So now – you know what I have come to say – goodbye, and try to bear what must be as easily as *d* you can.' As he spoke he burst into tears, and turning round, began to go away.

Socrates looked up at him and said, 'Goodbye to you, too; we will do as you say.' Then addressing us he went on, 'What a charming person! All the time I have been here he has visited me, and sometimes had discussions with me, and shown me the greatest kindness; and how generous of him now to shed tears at my departure! But come, Crito, let us do as he says. Someone had better bring in the poison, if it is ready prepared; if not, tell the man to prepare it.'

'But surely, Socrates,' said Crito, 'the sun is still upon the *e* mountains; it has not yet gone down. Besides, I know that in other cases people have dinner and enjoy their wine, and sometimes the company of those whom they love, long after they receive the warning; and only drink the poison quite late at night. Please don't hurry; there is still plenty of time.'

'It is natural that these people whom you speak of should act in that way, Crito,' said Socrates, 'because they think that they gain by it. And it is also natural that I should not; because I believe that I should gain nothing by drinking the poison a little later – I should only make myself ridiculous in my own eyes if I clung to life and hugged it when it has no more to offer. Come, do as I say and don't make difficulties.'

At this Crito made a sign to his slave, who was standing nearby. The slave went out and after spending a considerable time returned with the man who was to administer the poison; he was carrying it ready prepared in a cup. When Socrates saw him he said, 'Well, my good fellow, you understand these things; what ought I to do?'

'Just drink it,' he said, 'and then walk about until you feel a weight in your legs, and then lie down. Then it will act of its own accord.'

As he spoke he handed the cup to Socrates, who received it quite cheerfully, Echecrates, without a tremor, without any change of colour or expression, and said, looking up bull-like[208] from under his brows with his usual steady gaze, 'What do you say about pouring a libation from this drink? Is it permitted, or not?'

'We only prepare what we regard as the normal dose, Socrates,' he replied.

'I see,' said Socrates. 'But I suppose I am allowed, or rather bound, to pray the gods that my removal from this world to the other may be prosperous. This is my prayer, then; and I hope that it may be granted.' With these words, quite calmly and with no sign of distaste, he drained the cup in one draught.

Up till this time most of us had been fairly successful in keeping back our tears; but when we saw that he was drinking, that he had actually drunk it, we could do so no longer; in spite of myself the tears came pouring out, so that I covered my face and wept broken-heartedly – not for him, but for my own calamity in losing such a friend. Crito had given up even before me, and had gone out when he could not restrain his tears. But Apollodorus,[209] who had never stopped crying even before, now broke out into such a storm of passionate weeping that he made everyone in the room break down, except Socrates himself, who said: 'Really, my friends, what a way to behave! Why, that was my main reason for sending away the women, to prevent this sort of discordant behaviour; because I am told that one should make one's end in a reverent silence. Calm yourselves and be brave.'

This made us feel ashamed, and we controlled our tears. walked about, and presently, saying that his legs were heavy, down on his back – that was what the man recommended. The man (he was the same one who had administered the poison) kept his hand upon Socrates, and after a little while examined his feet and legs; then pinched his foot hard and asked if he felt it. Socrates said no. Then he did the same to his legs; and moving gradually upwards in this way let us see that he was getting cold and numb. Presently he felt him again and said that when it reached the heart, Socrates would be gone.

The coldness was spreading about as far as his waist when Socrates uncovered his face – for he had covered it up – and said (they were his last words): 'Crito, we ought to offer a cock to Asclepius.[210] See to it, and don't forget.'

'No, it shall be done,' said Crito. 'Are you sure that there is nothing else?'

Socrates made no reply to this question, but after a little while he stirred; and when the man uncovered him, his eyes were fixed. When Crito saw this, he closed the mouth and eyes.

This, Echecrates, was the end of our comrade, who was, we may fairly say, of all those whom we knew in our time the bravest and also the wisest and the most just.

POSTSCRIPT

When the Narnia of C. S. Lewis is destroyed and like some shadow-land yields to a new and brighter Platonic Narnia beyond (in *The Last Battle*), it perplexes some young readers, inspires others, and produces in others a mixed reaction. Plato's Theory of Ideas has both inspired and puzzled his readers for centuries. It is an integral part of the philosophy of his middle period, and has links with his psychology, epistemology, ethics and theology. Most in evidence in the *Phaedo* is the connection between the Theory of Ideas and the doctrine of immortality (i) in the final argument for immortality, (ii) in the Argument from Similarity and (iii) via the Theory of Recollection. The contrast between Ideas and particulars provides the basis for the distinction, early in the work, between the real philosopher and the ordinary man; it also lies behind the contrast between our regions of the earth and its true and beautiful surface in the myth. Thus it colours the work throughout. The pursuit of the Ideas and the cleansing of that part of us most akin to them recurs like a refrain, making it particularly difficult for those out of sympathy with this theme to read the work with an open mind.

Nowhere in his writings does Plato openly expound this theory. The *Phaedo* already assumes that we are quite familiar with it (76d, 100b), and we can only assume that a significant number of his intended readers (or listeners) had heard a good deal about it. If those readers were essentially the members of his own school, then the assumption is understandable, but I doubt whether he can have envisaged such a restricted market for a work that contains both propaganda and apologetic. A wider public would have known something about Plato's philosophy from (i) his earlier published works, (ii) the published works of rival intellectuals such as Antisthenes and Isocrates, and (iii) the references to it in the comedy of the day.

Taking his earlier published works first, it should have been possible for an alert reader to extract from them the rudiments of the theory. As in the *Euthyphro*, when Plato sought to define certain ethical qualities he did so in such a way as to emphasize the oneness of the concept, the need that it should embrace all instances of the quality and exclude everything that did not instantiate it. He emphasized that what he required was some formula which would capture the quality without offering examples or lists of things where the quality could be found. Thus, as a direct result of his Socratic searches for definition, he was led to seek an identifiable unity which was *different* from the instances, one of them or all of them.

Furthermore he was led to demand that these qualities which he sought to define should be real. Justice, temperance, courage and holiness, indeed virtue as a whole, were thought to be something real, which belonged to a man and deeply influenced how he acted. The value of discussing them was tied up with their reality and their potency. Justice in particular had long been thought to be not merely the property manifested in just acts, but rather a powerful principle deeply embedded in the workings of the universe. Courage had long been considered a potent force within the individual, a possession which in many cases became the salvation of his city.

One of the problems was the fact that the instances from which the Idea was distinguished were often not very convincing. Socratic definition had sought to isolate a quality and see it in its own right, away from such imperfections as its instances might display. Nobody imagined that justice itself, as cosmic force or motivational factor in the mind of the true politician, could ever be unjust. But what human being had never shown signs of injustice? The Socratic dialogues present to the reader many instances of humans with a reputation for fine qualities, but who are so portrayed as to seem to fall short of the ideal. In the *Gorgias* and *Meno* the search for a man of real virtue, past or present, is singularly unsuccessful, unless it be Socrates himself. Perhaps, then, there were no real instances of some of these qualities – or not at least since Socrates was alive. In that case could it be that justice, courage, piety, etc. simply ceased to exist or diminished in stature just because Socrates had died? Was virtue any less a legitimate and real object of study at a time when there was no genuine instance of it? Ought it not to be what it is, entirely independent of the few who seem capable of putting it into approximate practice?

The split between the ideal and the physically actual in ethics was mirrored also in the sphere of mathematics, an area of increasing concern from the end of the *Gorgias* and the *Meno* on. The *Phaedo* makes much of the example of equality, never fully instantiated (or so it was thought) in the physical world. Mathematical Ideas are more difficult for us to envisage than for Plato, for he was used to Pythagorean theory which saw basic arithmetic notions as representative of something not only really existent in the physical world but really a force within it. The cosmic power of geometrical equality is expounded in the *Gorgias* (508a), for instance. Mathematics also provided particularly credible examples of meaningful concepts that remained ever the same regardless of how imperfectly they were instantiated in the physical world.

From the Socratic search for definitions of ethical concepts and an increasing interest in pure mathematics Plato's Theory of Ideas was developing. It is possible that the *Hippias Major*, which displays such an interest in the theory of definition as would suggest the formation of an ontology of definable concepts, represents a middle stage between the ontologically more naive definition dialogues (assumed to have been written early) and the developed Theory of Ideas in the *Phaedo* (see Paul Woodruff, *Plato: Hippias Major*, Oxford, 1982).

Even so it would have been a surprise for the average reader of the *Phaedo* to encounter the Theory of Ideas represented as a much-discussed theme of (Plato's) Socrates. Ideas *as a class of realities* are simply not discussed in the dialogues until now, unless perhaps the accepted chronology of the dialogues is mistaken. It is likely, therefore, that much of the discussion had arisen from others' impressions of what Plato's treatment of his *definienda* implied. Had he been criticized by rivals or mocked by the comedians for what he seemed to have in mind when seeking definitions of qualities which made no reference to the bearers of those qualities? Certainly there exist fragments of Antisthenes and of Middle Comedy which seem to be mocking Plato's Ideas, and whereas the former's criticism might not provoke widespread reaction the comedian's voice was heard by many and might rapidly fan rumours about some peculiar theory held by Plato. And whereas a lesser thinker might trim his sails, Plato could only be expected to embrace with relish the consequences of his search for entities unchanged by the decay of physical realities. Yes, he did believe in perfect, unchanging and eternal realities to which the things of this world could only hope to approximate. They were, in fact, the very goal of his philosophy, and, he thought, of all true philosophy.

The *Phaedo* then is an admission by Plato of the importance of these supposed realities to him and to all that he stood for. How much metaphysical dogma attaches to the Theory at this stage is unclear, and there must have been many details of it which Plato had failed to satisfy himself on – among them, no doubt, the range of things which might be expected to have Ideas, an issue which the *Parmenides* (130b ff.) still fails to clarify. In the earlier part of the *Phaedo* the Ideas seem to surface in a natural manner, a manner which helps make the overall thrust of Plato's views seem unsurprising. But the rigid two-world ontology of the Argument from Similarity cannot fail to emphasize the remoteness of the Ideas from everything which the ordinary man is aware of, and the project of explaining the state of things in terms of the Ideas (100b ff.) – in terms of such static and non-physical entities – would probably have shocked many early readers. The particulars are not only named as they are because of the Ideas, they *are* what they are because of them.

Plato has now passed beyond the stage of allowing his Theory to emerge gently and in the way most conducive to winning acceptance. He wants the Theory to sound increasingly remote, farther and farther from the ordinary man's world of experience. A theme initially introduced with the relatively innocent appeal to man's belief in a real justice (65d) develops into an explanation of the world in terms utterly foreign to us – foreign to us, but not to the Socrates who stands at the verge of the next world. We should not complain that this is so; Plato is taunting us, holding out notions which are as yet beyond our reach. Even now he is not presenting us with a fully articulated philosophy; he is inviting us to seek further, warning us also, perhaps, that the goal of this search is not to be realized in this life but in a world to come.

One major question is the link between the explanation of phenomena in terms of Ideas and their explanation in terms of an Intelligent God which 'Socrates' had previously been searching for. The explanation in terms of Ideas in fact brings back into consideration forces such as fire and heat, which 'Socrates' had earlier rejected as candidates for properly explaining the world. If the final approach to causation is to satisfy him it must relate somehow to *purpose*, to the intelligent design of the universe. Furthermore, at 99c–d, Socrates sees his method of tackling the problem via the Ideas as a 'secondary approach', a phrase which would normally suggest the use of oars as a second-best alternative to sails at a time when the wind fails. The destination remains the same, but the ideal course to the destination lets you down, and so you revert to a more laborious means of propulsion. There is no help for 'Socrates' for the simpler journey to the Mind which organized the universe, and we are thus obliged to work our way back to it.

The first step on the path is to establish *why* any particular thing will come to have the property P; Socrates demands that we explain it in the first instance with reference to its participation in P-ness. The focus is not upon sundry ingredients, not themselves P, which have been physically required for the acquisition of P, but rather upon the property itself – for if x is P (Simmias is tall, for instance) because some Intelligence demands it be P, then it does not help us understand that Intelligence if we focus upon other features of x which are not themselves P (Simmias's head, for example, or eight centimetres). Intelligence has required that P-ness come to be in x, and therefore *something* must be present in x, or come to belong to x, which *brings* P-ness *with it or which entails* P-ness. In the physical world Intelligence works through physical means to bring about the various facets of its design, through fire to bring about heat, through soul to bring about life. If an odd number of rulers is important to the design of a government, then a number such as three or five will be chosen to bring it about. Intelligence works out what properties need to be present, and then what can be relied upon to bring them. The Ideas are the design-elements of the universe (explicitly so in the *Timaeus*), and the Designer reasons out how, when and where they will come to be present in it.

No doubt the virtues of justice, temperance, courage and wisdom are likewise seen as part of the universal purpose, instantiated where possible in the individual according to the design employed by Intelligence. How do they come to be instantiated? Presumably by the introduction of something into the soul whose presence necessarily entails these virtues. For Socrates, one supposes, that something would in each case have been moral knowledge; but for Plato, perhaps, it was becoming some fundamental orderliness (*Gorgias* 507–508), linked closely with the study of the order of the heavens (*Timaeus* 90a–d). Mathematical properties are there seen as contributing to the universal design, so it is no suprise that Ideas of such properties as equal or odd appear regularly in the *Phaedo*.

There can be no surprise, then, that the philosopher is keen to apply his mind to the Ideas. If they are the design-elements of the universe, part of the universal plan which the world is striving to realize, their loveliness will be prior to the loveliness of any earthly thing, which, for some portion of its limited life, may strive to instantiate them. They are not subject to the limitations of earthly matter, so that they do not merely reflect the plan; they are just as one would plan them to be. By studying them the philosopher has access to the very mind which organizes the universe.

NOTES

General Introduction

1. For instance, there is cross-examination of a witness in Andocides' speech *On the Mysteries*, written within a year of the trial of Socrates.
2. See Diogenes Laertius 3.49, probably drawing on Aristophanes of Byzantium whose arrangement of the corpus emphasized dramatic elements. See Chapter 4.iv of my *Thrasyllan Platonism*.
3. The Penguin translation of Xenophon's Socratic works has recently been updated and revised by Robin Waterfield (1990).
4. Some fragments of Aeschines have been included as an appendix to the Penguin volume *Plato: Early Socratic Dialogues*, ed. T.J. Saunders (1987). Saunders's introduction should be consulted for a fuller discussion of the nature of Socratic questions and conversations.
5. 'One should not believe Aristotle . . . when he says in the first book *On Poetics* (a mistake for *On Poets*) that dramatic dialogues had been written even before Plato by Alexamenos of Teos.'
6. The fact that a single slave is invited to read an entire dramatic dialogue at *Theaetetus* 143c confirms that such works were not normally acted out by a plurality of readers.
7. The important exception here is the *Laches*. Though 'dramatic', half the dialogue is over before the main philosophic conversation begins.
8. For a different view, see Gregory Vlastos, 'The Socratic Elenchus', in *Oxford Studies in Ancient Philosophy* 1 (1983), pp. 27–74.
9. Whereas Plato doubts if they are any more of a reflection than facts (*erga*), this is because facts as ordinarily conceived are viewed by Plato as a reflection of the true world in much the same way. *Logoi* and *erga* are both reflections of a single original (cf. *Republic* 509–511).
10. The term for mathematical computation (*logismós*) is employed as a general term for 'reasoning' after the *Meno*, a work which makes much use of mathematics.
11. For this rationale, see Diogenes Laertius 3.57, and the anonymous *Prolegomena to Plato's Philosophy* 25. The 'paradigm' notion explains why these works should be separated from a work set immediately before the *Euthyphro* (*Theaetetus*) together with works set between it and the *Apology* (*Sophist*, *Politicus*).
12. One might argue, likewise, that the *Crito* had done much to explain Socrates' readiness to die; certainly Crito's major speech shows that

Plato is already responding to criticism of Socrates' uncompromising tactics during and after the trial (45e), and the whole work justifies his readiness to face death rather than commit an act of injustice.

13. For Isocrates in his speech *Against the Sophists* of *c.* 390 B.C., shortly before the *Euthydemus*, clearly has Socratic practitioners of eristic in mind.

14. At times this has resulted in a split in the figure of Socrates even within Platonic dialogues, most notably in the split between the surface-Socrates and the notorious *alter ego* of the *Hippias Major*. Also note the presence in the trio *Theaetetus–Sophist–Politicus* of young men one of whom has the same name as Socrates and the other the same physical features.

15. He does seem to set himself up as something of an expert in 'erotics' at *Symposium* 177d, etc., and *Lysis* 204c.

16. In addition to the *Apology*, see *Theaetetus* 150c–151d.

17. For a spirited defence of the view that Socratic irony is not outright dishonesty, see G. Vlastos, 'Socratic Irony', *Classical Quarterly* 37 (1987), 79–95. My own view would be somewhat less extreme than that of Vlastos.

18. See here G. Vlastos, 'Socrates' Disavowal of Knowledge', *Philosophical Quarterly* 35 (1985), 1–31.

19. There is much discussion of the possibility that the virtue of *sophrosyne* (self-control, orderliness) might be a matter of self-knowledge and/or the ability to recognize knowledge/ignorance.

20. *Theaetetus* 150c–151d; *Apology* 33c.

21. Note that Socrates also attributes his expertise in 'erotics' to God; *Lysis* 204c.

22. *Symposium* 216c.

23. cf. *Apology* 39c.

24. See *Euthyphro* 11b–c, which is less than conclusive in its support for the tradition. The story in the *Theaetetus* that his mother was a good midwife should not be taken as indicative that his mother had a career; see Tarrant, *Classical Quarterly* 38 (1988), 116–22.

25. Note that the *Parmenides* depicts Socrates at around the age of twenty conversing with Parmenides and Zeno the Eleatics, but this work does not appear to be trying to tell us anything about Socrates and the story may have been invented to suit Plato's dramatic purposes. In any case Socrates is not in charge of the argument here.

26. He tells us in the *Cratylus* (384b–c) that he was unable to afford Prodicus's fifty-drachma course, and had to settle instead for the one-drachma course.

27. The earliest instance of this mentioned in the *Symposium* (220b–d) actually took place on this Thracian campaign.

28. *Laches* 181a–b, 188c–189b; *Symposium* 220d–221b.

29. See *Apology* 21a.

30. See particularly *Euthydemus* 272c, where an allusion to Ameipsias's play is highly probable.

31. Here I am indebted to the work of Paul A. Vander Waerdt, whose own Chapter 2 in his collection *The Socratic Movement* (Cornell U.P., 1993) may usefully be consulted.

32. Note that the agnosticism of Protagoras (fr. 4) suits the Socrates of the play less well than the more overt 'atheism' of Prodicus (fr. 5).

33. In Archelaus there seems to be no appreciable separation of Intelligence from the material principles and no appreciable cosmic role for it as a result.

34. See, for instance, the edition of K.J. Dover (Oxford, 1968).

35. *Hippias Major*, 283c ff., *Protagoras* 342c ff., etc. – passages full of irony, but also *Crito* 52e.

36. *Protagoras* 319b ff., *Crito* 52b.

37. *Platonic Piety* (New Haven and London, 1990), p.20.

Euthyphro

1. On this question, see the general introduction, p.xv.

2. Euthyphro, Cephalus, Charmides, Laches and Theaetetus. The reader may in each case find himself thinking that Socrates is a better example of that quality.

3. Cephalus sees justice as truthfulness and paying debts (*Republic* 331b–d); Charmides sees prudence as orderly and peaceable conduct (*Charmides* 159b, getting closest to giving a universal definition), Laches sees courage as staying in line and facing the enemy (*Laches* 190e), Theaetetus sees knowledge as the mathematical sciences and also demiurgic arts, while Euthyphro sees prosecuting religious offenders as being piety.

4. Euthyphro's 'approved by the gods' is not much help unless what is approved is necessarily good; Laches' 'endurance' does not at first exclude rash endurance; Charmides' 'sense of shame' misses the point that shame is sometimes bad; Polemarchus's 'helping friends and harming enemies' allows justice to be a source of harm; Theaetetus's 'perception' fails to capture the rightness of knowledge.

5. The level of irony follows a similar pattern: sharpest in *Laches* and *Euthyphro*, less so in *Charmides* and *Republic* 1, mild indeed in *Theaetetus*. Note that the 'narrative' works provide an additional level of irony; Socrates can tell the story ironically as well as speaking ironically to the interlocutor.

6. Besides the three, the *Laches* has also the two old men, and *Republic* 1 has Cephalus, Glaucon and Cleitophon.

7. Note that the well-known comparisons in the *Meno* (80a–b) and the *Apology* (30e) are with *animals*, the sting-ray and gadfly respectively.

8. This is pretty obvious in the *Laches*, where Socrates actually complains that Nicias's definition really applies to the whole of virtue (199e).

9. Again, the *Laches* presents as interlocutors two generals whose very natures incline them to the two sides of courage that constantly shine

through in the dialogue: simply soldiering on and carefully planning one's campaign.

10. Compare 5d, 6d–e.

11. Compare *Meno* 75c–d for the need to define anything in terms which the other person will understand.

12. The King Archon ('the King' for short) was nothing like a monarch, but was known as such because his functions had once been a monarch's duty; he was that one of the nine archons entrusted with oversight of religious law, which included cases of homicide (a religious crime) as well as impiety. His Porch was in the Agora.

13. It is difficult to be certain about who Euthyphro was, whether there could be any truth in the story of his prosecuting his father (which seems (i) far-fetched and (ii) chronologically problematic), or, if he was not an actual person with the tendencies of our character, why Plato would depart here from his normal habit of employing speakers who had really existed. A 'Euthyphro' is mentioned also in the *Cratylus* as being a seer who is inclined to be 'carried away' (in a religious manner) with etymologizing (396d). It has become fashionable to make something of the literal meaning of the names of Plato's interlocutors; the present name has associations with a 'straight' or 'orthodox' mind, which seems apposite but proves nothing.

14. A gymnasium which took its name from the precinct of Apollo Lyceius, in which it was set. Elsewhere in Plato we learn that it is a frequent haunt of Socrates (*Symposium* 223d), and meet his conversations there (*Lysis* and *Euthydemus*).

15. The difference is between private cases and a public indictment or *graphe*.

16. Meletus was not an uncommon name, but it is tempting to identify the present one with, for example, the one who accused Andocides of impiety, also in or around 399 B.C., or the poet mentioned by Aristophanes at *Frogs* 1302. There is no reason to assume that the present Meletus would have agreed with Socrates that he was an 'unknown', for there is a touch of malice in Plato's words. Andocides' accuser is probably the author of speech 4 of 'Lysias', and the religious attitudes taken there bear a striking resemblance not just to the attitude expected from the accuser of Socrates, but also to the attitude taken here by Euthyphro!

17. The corruption charge seems to have been more serious than that of religious innovation. For the exact charge see *Apology* 24b–c, Xenophon, *Memorabilia* 1.1.1, and Diogenes Laertius 2.40.

18. A good Socratic sentiment: note the attention given to education in the ideal state of *Republic* 2–3.

19. This part of the charge, which is actually rather ambiguous, spoke of Socrates' failure to accept (whether for outward recognition or inner belief) the gods of the city, and of his introduction of other strange new divinities. See *Apology* 24b–c, Xenophon *Memorabilia* 1.1.1. Suggestions of Socrates' religious unorthodoxy are recurrent in

Aristophanes' play *Clouds*, where it is not a matter of his personal divine sign but of his physicalist explanation of phenomena usually associated with gods.

20. On the divine sign, see *Apology* 31c–d and 40a; it appears from these references that it was a kind of inner voice that 'told' Socrates not to do certain things that he might otherwise have done. It is never represented as a god, but it is called here a *daimonion* or 'divine thing': the singular of the term used in the charge to refer to Socrates' 'new divinities'. Euthyphro immediately thinks of the divine sign because it is a form of prophecy which makes Socrates akin to himself.

21. Socrates thinks of the sophists and of the animosity which many Athenians felt towards them: see *Protagoras* 316c–d and Anytus at *Meno* 91c.

22. For Socrates' generosity and failure to charge a fee (as the sophists did) see *Apology* 33a–b. This clearly set Socrates apart from the sophists in Plato's mind.

23. Note the ironic inaccuracy of Euthyphro's predictions.

24. The humour is aided by the fact that the Greek verb for 'prosecute' also means 'chase'; while we talk of 'going on a wild goose chase' the Greeks simply spoke of 'chasing a flying thing'.

25. Debate continues as to whether the historical details are plausible. The large Aegean island of Naxos would appear to have been outside Athenian control since 404 B.C. If so, then one must explain the judicial delay or posit either anachronism or the total invention of the story by Plato. Tredennick favoured this last possibility. There are grave doubts as to whether such a case could have any hope of success under Athenian law. On the other hand it suits Plato perfectly in so far as it takes religious orthodoxy to its logical (and unorthodox) conclusion, contrasting well with Socrates' mild but acknowledged unorthodoxy. It is particularly important that Socrates too was sometimes represented as turning son against father, as in the closing stages of Aristophanes' *Clouds*, and by the unnamed 'accuser' at Xenophon, *Memorabilia* 1.2.49–51. Euthyphro's 'piety' is really a much greater threat to the bond between father and son.

26. The Interpreter was an official, apparently the senior member of a board of three, who advised on how to tackle matters of religion, especially religious pollution.

27. Exactly what Meletus would have thought of Euthyphro's attitudes is important to the interpretation here; clearly it would suit Plato's polemical purposes well if Meletus did subscribe to similar beliefs to Euthyphro's. That is a distinct possibility if he is to be identified with the Meletus who prosecuted Andocides; see note 16 above.

28. Plato now uses the term *idea*, by which Plato refers to the entities of his notorious Theory of Ideas in the middle period dialogues. How technical its use is here is a matter of some controversy. But Plato's message would of course have been intelligible to his audience even without their being familiar with this theory. The word is related to a verb of vision, and suggests a recognizable mark.

29. Literally the 'one who commits injustice'; this is significant, as holiness is later to be viewed as a subdivision of justice.

30. The references here are to well-known tales in Hesiod's *Theogony* (126 ff., 453 ff.): Uranus (Heaven) imprisoned his children deep in the body of Gaia (Earth) until Kronos, the youngest of them, was able to attack and castrate him; Kronos tried to avoid having his own throne usurped by a child by swallowing his offspring, but his wife Rhea tricked him into swallowing a stone rather than Zeus, his youngest son, causing him to vomit and so return his older children. Zeus subsequently did overpower Kronos, and imprisoned him.

31. The tactic of appealing to myths concerning the gods and heroes in order to justify personal behaviour is mocked by Aristophanes at *Clouds* 1047–1070; it is seen as particularly dangerous by Plato himself at *Republic* 378b, where these very examples of Uranus, Kronos and Zeus are being considered.

32. It is difficult to believe that Socrates is genuinely interested in the possibility that Euthyphro might be right. Belief that *all* such myths were literally true would not have been widespread (like 'creationism' among modern Christians), and intellectuals like Xenophanes and Heraclitus had for a century been openly criticizing the acceptance of the myths of Hesiod and Homer.

33. Principally Hesiod and Homer: strife between gods supporting the Greeks and others supporting the Trojans is prominent in Homer's *Iliad*.

34. Every fourth year the Panathenaea was celebrated particularly lavishly, and a robe was embroidered for the statue of Athena Polias. The Robe became almost a symbol for Athens herself. Evidently Socrates has reservations about the representation upon it of the battle between gods and giants.

35. A procession escorted the Robe up to the Acropolis. The statue itself was in the Erechtheum.

36. The term used here is *eidos*, another of Plato's terms for his Ideas, often translated 'form' or 'Form'.

37. Now the term *idea* recurs. Note that it seems to be with reference to the one 'idea' that both things holy and things unholy are recognized.

38. The word translated 'observe' means literally 'look away to' and is regularly used by Plato in connection with the Ideas as standards for comparison. The word translated 'means of comparison' is the origin of our word 'paradigm'; it is also regularly used in connection with the Platonic Ideas.

39. It is a doctrine of the *Gorgias* (454c–455a) that merely telling somebody something that is right does not amount to teaching and does not bring about knowledge even if the other person accepts the belief; teaching requires an explanation justifying the views stated.

40. The argument becomes clumsier in English, for 'divinely approved' translates the single word *theo-philes*. Tredennick's 'god-beloved' and 'god-hated' appear to me to be too much like terms of emotion.

41. At first sight a totally unnecessary question – but the reason for it will soon be evident.

42. See note 30, above. Zeus would approve of imprisoning one's father, perhaps, but would Kronos, whom he imprisoned?

43. Hephaestus took revenge upon his mother Hera, who had thrown him out of heaven because he was lame; as God of metalworkers, he created for her a golden throne carefully designed so that she would not be able to escape from it. This is another Homeric tale (*Iliad* 18, 394–405) to which Plato has strong objections (*Republic* 378d).

44. Mitigating circumstances and diminished responsibility were not then able to secure avoidance of punishment.

45. Plato is constantly conscious of the fact that one had to state one's case in court in a limited space of time, which was measured by the *clepsydra*. Compare *Gorgias* 455a.

46. Socrates believes that any real god will act and think *rationally*; thus acts would be approved by them according to rational principles. Holiness is here seen as being a possible explanation of why the gods might universally approve certain actions. Their quarrels would arise when deeds are neither holy nor unholy.

47. I have tried here to keep as close as possible to the flavour of the argument. 'Being carried', etc. denotes the *state* of having something done to one, whereas 'gets carried', etc. denotes the *action* that one is at the receiving end of. I strongly suspect that Plato had his motives for not wishing to express himself with perfect clarity here, for he is not saying much more than that action by the subject is the reason for the object having something done to it, not vice versa.

48. The problem here is that 'being approved', unlike 'being carried', is not an obvious case of having something done to one; it might rather be a case of having acquired a property. In this case Plato would see the state of acquiring the property as being due to some process which results in property acquisition.

49. Plato bases his claim on the difference between the two concepts; though his claim is strongly worded for rhetorical effect, he does not in fact maintain that there is a fundamental difference between *things* which are divinely approved and *things* which are holy. The terms may indeed have the same extension (if *x* is holy, the gods will approve it, and if the gods approve *x* then it is divinely approved), but they do not have the same meaning.

50. Unless the *Euthyphro* is much later than is usually supposed, or has been revised later, then there is little doubt that the terminology of essence and accident is as yet non-technical.

51. Daedalus was a figure of divine ancestry (descended from Hephaestus) who was an archetypal inventor and sculptor prominent in Minoan and Mycenaean mythology. *Qua* sculptor, he is associated with the carving of limbs which were separated from the main body of the statue for most of their length, thus suggesting the ability to move freely. Since trades were conventionally passed from father to son,

stonemasons traced their ancestry back to Daedalus, while Socrates was the son of a stonemason.

52. It is fundamental to Socratic dialectic that the responder will be held responsible for the course of the argument; compare *Meno* 82e–85b.

53. A mythical king of Lydia, of proverbial wealth; ancestor of the house of Atreus; offender of the gods, and sufferer of eternal punishment as a result.

54. In the *Protagoras* it is argued that everything holy is *ipso facto* just and everything just is *ipso facto* holy (331a–e).

55. Stasinus, probable author of the *Cypria* (fr. 24). If not Stasinus, then the author is unknown.

56. Literally 'planted': there is perhaps some kind of distinction between a primary creator and a secondary propagator. Text and translation are uncertain.

57. The Greeks had a view of number which was strongly influenced by geometry, and the Greek here talks of 'scalene' number (odd) and 'isosceles' number (even); these terms belong not to triangles as they would today, but to a pair of lines united at the top (like two sides of a triangle), or two 'legs'. The even number 6 can be represented by two legs of length 3, but, since the Greeks did not recognize fractions, the odd number 7 would be represented by legs of uneven length, such as 3 and 4.

58. Justice towards animals is seldom recognized by the Greeks; exceptions would usually involve some special doctrine, like the Pythagorean doctrine of transmigration, by which a soul, after leaving the human body, might enter an animal one. In this case the animal which one maltreats could turn out to be one's own ancestor.

59. In the latter part of the dialogue Socrates is clearly directing the thrust of his attack against the conventional notion that the gods require certain duties to be performed by men. They will either want something because they are improved by it (implying that they are lacking it unless we comply); or because it contributes to some end which they have in view (still implying that they need us); or they want it because it pleases them, either for some rational reason (which Euthyphro should be able to explain) or because of some whim.

60. The word translated 'marvellous', being a *pan*-compound, is almost certainly ironical. Though Socrates tends to hammer this question, we should not suppose that an answer to it will solve the problem of what holiness is; rather we should recognize that Socrates pours scorn on the idea that we can contribute to the gods' work (or happiness) in any way whatsoever.

61. Although suggestions of some kind of providential governance of the world do recur in both Plato and Xenophon's Socratic writings, this is rather a strong statement to be coming from Plato's Socrates. The emphasis is usually on man's own power to do himself some good, and upon knowledge being the means to achieve this – but Socrates' words are tailored to achieve approval from Euthyphro.

62. Proteus was an old sea-god who would not willingly yield up information, and was able to transform himself into all kinds of beasts if trapped. He had to be tied and held fast during his magical contortions in order that he might be subdued and yield the information required. See Homer, *Odyssey* 4. Plato again makes use of the Proteus analogy at *Euthydemus* 288b and *Ion* 541e.

63. Tredennick notes that Socrates now credits Euthyphro only with thinking that he knows. This should not, however, be taken as an indication that Socrates' attitude to Euthyphro's claims has changed; Socrates can hardly say, 'I know well enough that you know . . .'

64. Of course Socrates' final speech is ironical, but there is some substance in it. Those who prided themselves on their religious knowledge were not able to give as persistent a questioner as Socrates any sure guidance about matters divine such as could have averted his condemnation for impiety.

Apology

1. See Ledger (1989), p.223.

2. An important exception is now Brickhouse and Smith (1989), pp.48 ff.

3. Anytus was the politician of the team, a good democrat whom Plato portrays in the *Meno* as an implacable opponent of the sophists; Meletus was theoretically chief prosecutor, as the *Euthyphro* shows; Lycon is little known, though 24a suggests that he was a frequent speaker in the courts, who could therefore somehow 'represent' the orators.

4. The great losses in manpower suffered by Athens in the final decade of the Peloponnesian War meant that there were far fewer old men performing jury service than would have been the case when Aristophanes' *Wasps* was written (422 B.C.). Whether these 'untrue accusations' predate the representations in that comedian's *Clouds* in 423 B.C. we cannot tell.

5. This is a simplified picture of the 'Socrates' of the *Clouds*. It is crucial to the plot that Socrates' school harbours personifications of the weaker and the stronger argument, the former of which knows how to win unjust cases (112–18); inside the school the students are busy studying both heavenly and underground phenomena (187–94).

6. This was reasonable: Presocratic theories on the workings of the universe were offered as an *alternative* to making them the work of traditional gods.

7. It is clear to all that Aristophanes is meant; it may be an intentional slight to mention him only as an afterthought here.

8. It is important to note that the speeches in many important Athenian trials were timed by the water-clock (*clepsydra*), equal time being allotted to defence and prosecution. It seems difficult to reconcile Socrates' attitude here with the notion that there may have been

further speakers who spoke for the defence, though Plato's version of Socrates' speech is not so very long when one bears in mind that there were three speakers for the prosecution (23e).

9. The tone of this paragraph is hesitant, and the repeated verbals (translated 'must') suggest tasks that Socrates might prefer to have avoided.

10. A comic touch which many would find inappropriate, satirizing the old prejudices by casting them in the solemn form of a legal charge. In this 'charge' we see three mistaken views of Socrates: that he is a physical philosopher, that he is a sophist and that he is a professional teacher.

11. Aristophanes' *Clouds* introduces a Socrates who is swung out above the set suspended from the crane (218). His first full line (225) has him proclaim that he is treading the air and looking askance at the sun. In lines 227–234 he gives an absurd biological explanation of why he needs to be up high.

12. Another jest, with the serious purpose of depicting Meletus as one who would prosecute somebody at the drop of a hat.

13. The *Phaedo* speaks of a period in which Socrates *was* interested in Presocratic philosophy (96a–98b), and it is uncertain how early this would have been. Surely not all the jury could have been too young to have experienced this side of Socrates? The reason why Socrates is able to make this appeal is because such theories had never been discussed publicly as this was too dangerous. For this very reason it was easy enough for Athenians to suspect Socrates of engaging in such things privately. Notice that he does not *deny* that he had discussed them; he denies that he has any expertise in them, something of which he was certainly convinced.

14. Suggestions that Socrates took a fee are present in Aristophanes' *Clouds* (98, 876, and possibly 1146), but here Socrates never expresses any real interest in money and is just as poor as ever. Plato likes to distinguish the true philosopher from the sophist on the grounds that the sophist takes a fee: which would have been difficult for him if Socrates had done so. This would not have excluded the acceptance of gifts from wealthy patrons (as when he is ready to take their money to pay his fine at 38b).

15. Gorgias claimed only to be a teacher of rhetoric, and is sometimes not credited with the title 'sophist'; however, in so far as he was much travelled, gave public demonstrations of his art, and offered for a fee private lessons designed to lead to the political success of the pupil, he resembled the sophists. Among these, Prodicus and Hippias were the two most celebrated, after Protagoras; both of them were contemporaries of Socrates, and probably better known at Athens than their forerunner. Prodicus was an expert in language, a little pedantic perhaps but interesting enough for Socrates to have taken a modest course with him (*Cratylus* 384b) and to have been otherwise associated with him (e.g. *Clouds* 361). Hippias was a polymath, whose pompousness is treated mercilessly in Plato's works.

16. Callias inherited a huge fortune (200 talents: *Lysias* 19.48) from Hipponicus, and was notorious for the manner in which he went about spending it – much of it on sophists (*Cratylus* 391b). He acts as simultaneous host to Protagoras, Prodicus and Hippias in Plato's *Protagoras*. He is also the host figure of Xenophon's *Symposium*.

17. Evenus is less well known than the sophists so far mentioned, a man versed in various forms of literary composition, an inventor of oratorical devices and moreover a poet (*Phaedrus* 267a). The treatment of him as a philosopher at *Phaedo* 61b–c is ironic. There is a later tradition that he taught Socrates poetry.

18. One cannot sensibly comment on the fee without knowing the duration of the course. Isocrates *Against the Sophists* 3, with minor socratics in mind, thinks 300–400 drachmae ridiculously little to ask when one promises all but immortality. Diogenes Laertius (9.52) says that Protagoras had charged 10,000 drachmae.

19. To call a god as witness is a grotesque idea that is unlikely to have found favour. The Delphic oracle, sacred to Pythian Apollo, god of prophecy among other things, was the supreme authority in the Greek world. However, it had fallen out of favour at Athens by its apparent bias towards the other side during the Peloponnesian War, and it is very doubtful whether the Athenians would have been so impressed by the oracle's reply as Socrates is. Its advice could be sought on all matters, great and small. It is not known when Chaerephon visited it, and Xenophon's account (*Apology* 14) says that the oracle made Socrates supreme in the moral virtues instead of in wisdom.

20. Chaerephon features as a kind of apprentice of Socrates in the *Gorgias*, and is mentioned several times in Aristophanes' *Clouds* as being the other leader of Socrates' school. He is mocked there for his feeble appearance and his interest in entomology, and may have played an even greater role in the version originally staged (fr. 139 *Poetae Comici Graeci*). He occurs also in *Wasps* and *Birds*. Elsewhere in comedy he appears as a cheat and/or thief. It is unlikely that a mention of this favourite butt of comic humour (democrat or not) would have done anything to raise the tone of Socrates' case.

21. Socrates refers to the establishment and overthrow of the rule of the Thirty Tyrants (404 B.C.), when the democratic party was banned, but returned after capturing the Piraeus.

22. We meet this brother, Chaerecrates, in Xenophon's *Memorabilia* 2.3.

23. We may deduce from this that the oracular response preceded Socrates' investigations, which in turn preceded his unpopularity. He is unpopular by 423 B.C., something which Aristophanes capitalizes on rather than causes.

24. Socrates' unorthodox beliefs are now in evidence. He cannot accept that the gods will engage in any dishonourable conduct, such as lies. Yet deception among the gods is frequent in Greek myth. Moreover Socrates appears to be laying down rules for divine conduct in much the same way as he will impose moral rules upon the jury.

25. A favourite oath of Socrates; at *Phaedrus* 236e he offers to swear by the plane-tree he sits under. It is doubtful whether his use of pseudo-oaths would have been perceived as having any bearing on the question of his impiety.

26. With these words Socrates manages to compare his superficially meddlesome tasks with the Labours of Heracles; a jury might have seen this as either mockery or arrogance or both.

27. It is important to note that the poet traditionally had the role of teacher in Greece, and Greeks expected to learn from them. Greek education gave great weight to the study of Homer and other poets.

28. Plato's *Ion* shows Socrates exposing a rhapsode's reliance upon such inspiration (as opposed to knowledge); the *Phaedrus* sees it as characteristic of lover, faith-healer, true prophet and true poet (244a ff.); and the *Meno* explains political virtue too as dependent upon correct opinion derived from quasi-divine inspiration akin to that of the seer.

29. A much-respected class of person among the democrats of Athens.

30. Compare Charicles at Xenophon, *Memorabilia* 1.2.36 and Thrasymachus at *Republic* 337a.

31. Helping the gods is another odd idea, as *Euthyphro* 15a shows.

32. It is important to Socrates' case that he should not have been seeking such followers.

33. Meletus's connection with the poets is unclear; it may be that we should associate him with the figure mentioned by Aristophanes at *Frogs* 1302.

34. Anytus was a prominent politician under the revived democracy, and is represented as being prejudiced against sophists and the like at *Meno* 89c–95a.

35. We know little about Lycon, but later tradition continued to connect him with the orators.

36. See note 8, above. Note that there is an implied criticism of Athenian court procedure here.

37. This is not word for word. The corruption charge has here been put first, though it followed the atheism charges in the actual affidavit: see Xenophon, *Memorabilia* 1.1.1, and Diogenes Laertius 2.40 (from Favorinus).

38. Terminology translated 'give attention' here and elsewhere in the cross-examination puns crudely on Meletus's name, whose root (*mele-*) suggests somebody who cares or pays attention to something.

39. Note that the Assembly was open to all adult male citizens; Socrates himself could have attended. He had in fact been a member of the Council, whose membership numbered 500. Meletus's assent, which is no doubt given so that he should seem to be a committed supporter of democratic ideals and institutions, thus takes an unreasonably optimistic view of the numbers able to improve young men.

40. It is a common Socratic theme that 'nobody errs willingly', i.e. that all crimes are committed as a result of some ignorance. But to found an argument on his own somewhat paradoxical doctrine (how can a court accept that nobody willingly commits a crime?) is a dangerous tactic.

41. Compare Anytus's fanatical avoidance of sophists at *Meno* 91c.

42. Meletus is in a quandary: he may very well be aware that there was a wealth of sophistic arguments designed to show that anything one believed could not be false or non-existent (see *Euthydemus* 283c ff.), but what his charge means is that Socrates does not believe in any god *which can be credited as such*, though he does introduce *divinities of his own imagining, which accordingly do not exist*. The jury would feel considerable sympathy for Meletus, knowing very well what was meant, as presumably Socrates did too. Rather than admit Socrates believes in gods and be forced to admit that there exist gods in which Socrates believes, he opts to defend the position that Socrates has no belief in any god.

43. A leading question, since the sun and moon, though often involved in myth and cult, are hardly typical 'gods' in the Greek anthropomorphic mould, nor are they gods associated specially with Athens. Socrates is inviting Meletus to make the error of attributing Anaxagorean theories to him.

44. Anaxagoras, a generation older than Socrates, is reputed to have been banished from Athens at some time, probably *c.* 450 B.C., in part because of his seemingly irreligious doctrines which gave physical rather than divine explanations of many features of the universe. Socrates was often associated in antiquity with Anaxagoras's pupil Archelaus. He believed that the sun was a huge incandescent stone, the moon similar but not ablaze, since it was illuminated by the sun. See Diels-Kranz, *Die Fragmente der Vorsokratiker* 59A42.

45. Normally an area within a Greek theatre used for the chorus's dances during a performance. It might have been used for other purposes at times. However, we are told that such a name was also given to an area within the *agora* at Athens, which might seem a more likely location for trading in books.

46. *Daemones*: a less specific term than 'gods', often used of some supernatural power which is unidentified by the speaker or not recognized by Greeks as a god in the normal sense, but nevertheless able to be applied to the gods.

47. This might have an appearance of orthodoxy, but in fact the term *daemon*, translated 'supernatural being', can be used for a host of mysterious powers (fate, fortune, dead souls, etc.).

48. Socrates finishes with a rhetorical flourish, but with a sentence whose complexity and opacity can only contribute to an impression of deviousness.

49. Note the shock tactic of 28a, the anonymous objection at 28b, the favourable comparison of oneself with others at 28c–d, and the mention of military service at 28e.

50. Achilles, hero of the *Iliad*, from which Socrates now gives a paraphrase of 18.94–106.

51. *Iliad* 18.96.

52. The three campaigns at which Socrates is known to have served as a

hoplite. The fighting around Potidaea in 432 B.C., just before the outbreak of the Peloponnesian War, was intense, and Socrates' friends are surprised to see him back (*Charmides* 153b); he saved Alcibiades there, and again showed great gallantry at Delium in the disaster of 424 B.C. (*Symposium* 220d). Plato does not refer elsewhere to Socrates fighting at Amphipolis. A battle at Amphipolis, like Potidaea a Thracian settlement, took place in 422 B.C., but Burnet doubts whether an elderly Socrates could have served in a small select force then. Fighting also took place there in 437 B.C.

53. Note that this is not a real option for the court – the notion is introduced so that Socrates can make his priorities clear.

54. A radical idea, unlikely to convince the jury, and likely to be taken as a gesture of defiance. Socrates sometimes believes that the only significant way of helping or harming a man is to give or take away knowledge (*Euthydemus* 292b, *Protagoras* 345b). As we see from the *Phaedo* (97d), Socrates believes in a rationally governed universe, in which evil will not triumph over good.

55. It was normal for a defendant to insert a catalogue of his own and his family's services to the city.

56. Members of each tribe were selected for duty by lot, and each tribe took its turn to serve as presidents (or *prytaneis*) for one month. At this time they had a great deal of extra executive power.

57. The Athenians fought a sea-battle at Arginusae in 406 B.C., where victory was marred by the failure (owing to a storm) to recover the bodies. It was decided illegally to try all the generals responsible for this calamity (only eight in fact, of whom two were not present, having fled Athens) by a single vote.

58. The Tholos, where the Thirty had their headquarters, but which was generally used by the *prytaneis*.

59. There may once again be a play on the name of Meletus here; it has been argued that Socrates may be alluding to the fact that Meletus had himself taken part in the arrest of Leon; see H. Blumenthal, *Philologus* 117 (1973), 169–78, and J.J. Kearney, *Classical Quarterly* 30 (1980), 296–98. See also note 60, below.

60. It is interesting that one of their names was Meletus (Andocides, *On the Mysteries* 94), a man who took part in the prosecution of Andocides for religious crimes. Scholars have often thought that this Meletus could not possibly have been the prosecutor of Socrates, but see previous note.

61. The effect of this passage is to liken Socrates to the soothsayers, who were held in very little honour during the Peloponnesian War, being satirized mercilessly in comedy, and suffering from a mood of general scepticism as to the efficacy of trying to keep the gods on one's side. Compare the treatment Euthyphro had experienced (*Euthyphro* 3b–c).

62. The interlocutor in *Crito*.

63. A prominent Socratic who wrote dialogues of which significant fragments remain. See Saunders (1987).

64. Demodocus and Theages appear in Plato's (?) *Theages*.

65. Prominent in the *Republic*, along with Plato's other brother Glaucon.

66. Narrator of the *Symposium*; he also appears in the *Phaedo*.

67. Homer, *Odyssey* 19.163; implying that one has all the usual human connections.

68. Lamprocles, Sophroniscus and Menexenus.

69. J. Burnet (*Plato's Euthyphro, Apology of Socrates and Crito* (Oxford, 1924), p. 147) finds here a reference to the practice of *prokrisis*, or selection prior to lot, but it is difficult to be sure that the language is technical.

70. i.e. a crime against the gods, as contravening an oath.

71. If the number of the jury was the reputed 500 or 501 and 30 is not a round figure, then the vote was 280 to 220 or 221.

72. Socrates is mocking Meletus still. The total of votes cast against Socrates was less than three fifths, and he divides the number by three, attributing just over ninety votes to each speaker.

73. As provided for victors at the Olympic and perhaps other games, and for certain representatives of eminent families, etc. Socrates is clearly being most provocative in proposing a considerable state honour as his punishment.

74. Socrates' belief that nobody does wrong willingly does not elsewhere lead to the view that nobody deserves to be punished: indeed *Gorgias* 474–481 argues that it is better for a man who has erred to submit to punishment.

75. A reference to the eleven magistrates in charge of prisons, etc.

76. This is confirmed by the *Crito* (52c), and the accusers would almost certainly have been satisfied with it.

77. i.e. they will think Socrates is using his 'irony': I have tried to translate in such a way as to suggest both evasion and playfulness.

78. Said by Xenophon (*Oeconomicus* 2.3) to have been about a fifth of his entire property.

79. The fine proposed is finally a large one, but the jury now know that he will not be bearing the brunt of it himself. What kind of punishment will it be?

80. How paradoxical this would have sounded to a jury who had no doubt felt Socrates to be the most impudent offender they had come across and the least willing to bow to the authority of the court.

81. One should remember during this section that the *dikasts* were both jury and judges, so a true juryman will also be a true judge, judging truly.

82. It is generally assumed that Socrates has Orphic and/or Pythagorean ideas in mind here; the belief in some kind of after-life was of course common, but the more orthodox Greek view made this a dismal half-life which could not be welcomed. One may compare ideas on the after-life which emerge in the *Phaedo*. *Gorgias* 493a–d certainly has an Orphic/Pythagorean myth of the after-life in mind; *Meno* 81a–b thinks of a specific type of person as holding relevant beliefs in the

after-life, though it is to be emphasized that their views also allow for the return of souls to this world. No such provision is made in the *Apology*.

83. The King of Persia was seen by the Greeks as a paradigm of worldly happiness.

84. A traditional triad of just men who were rewarded with the role of underworld judges, and who feature in the myth of judgement at the end of the *Gorgias* (523c ff.). There is an implication that Socrates will find much in common with these traditionally just figures!

85. An agricultural divinity, associated with the cult of Demeter and Kore. He may take the place of Minos in Athenian representations of the underworld judges, for Minoan Crete had been considered an unjust enemy of Athens.

86. Musaeus and Orpheus were seen as the supreme bards of the Orphic religion; Hesiod and Homer were of course the two supremely influential Greek epic poets, who also had considerable influence on the shape of religious beliefs. Note the somewhat immodest assumption that Socrates will readily be able to mix with the great figures who shaped Greek religion.

87. Both in a sense victims of the wily Odysseus. Palamedes was supposed to have been tried and executed on false treason charges (a story from the *Cypria*), while Ajax committed suicide after losing the 'trial' for the arms of Achilles. Socrates is now succeeding in comparing himself with two heroes of the Trojan War period!

88. Agamemnon (Greek leader in the Trojan War, who had to sacrifice his daughter in order to sail), Odysseus (famed for worldly cunning) and Sisyphus (a Corinthian king famed for unscrupulous cleverness, and subsequently doomed to eternal punishment in Hades) were all figures in whom Socrates might expect to find character defects and unsound moral reasoning.

Crito

1. See, in particular Kahn (1981).

2. This may be the wrong term, for theories of social contract generally involve an agreement between the citizens; Socrates' agreement has been made with the city and its laws, not with citizens and legislators.

3. See, in particular, H. Thesleff, 'Platonic Chronology', *Phronesis* 34 (1989), 1–26, with note 76.

4. This is not explained by the fact that Socrates is chatting to a respected friend; he can be ironical enough when talking to Crito in the *Euthydemus*.

5. On this, see the general introduction, p. xxii.

6. Socrates is not eliciting statements from Crito for the purpose of demonstrating an inconsistency in his belief that he, Socrates, should escape.

7. Thesleff, loc cit., note 76. Polycrates appears not to have been writing early in the 390s B.C.

8. *Crito* uses the learned verbal forms in *-teon* far more frequently than any other Platonic work. A high rate normally characterizes later dialogues, though also *Republic*. All these forms except one group of four occur in this section.

9. See Ledger, *Recounting Plato* (1989), p.185.

10. Allen in his conclusion (1980, p.111) emphasizes that legal obligation 'rests essentially neither on force nor on a set of rules fixed in the nature of things or in the mind of God'. It is rather a powerful moral obligation resting on the twin premises that one must not return injustice and one must abide by just agreements.

11. Crito, like other friends of Socrates, had been visiting him regularly in prison. Though the death sentence is normally carried out without delay, the annual sea-mission to Delos to celebrate the victory of Theseus over the Minotaur and Minoan Crete had left on the day before Socrates' trial. No execution could take place until the ship returned, giving Socrates plenty of time to escape if he desired – a perfectly normal occurrence. Undoubtedly discussions about the desirability of escape would have taken place. P. Köln 205 preserves fragments of another writer's dialogue on this same issue.

12. It seems that Crito had been tipping the jailer.

13. See note 11, above; also *Phaedo* 58a–c.

14. The nearest point of Attica to Delos, about thirty miles south-east of Athens.

15. Homer, *Iliad* 9.363, slightly altered; the line implied that Achilles was going *home* to Phthia, and its use here suggests that Socrates is returning to his real home.

16. *Epieikestatoi*: the term used is suggestive of those who have a degree of superiority, and since it is often opposed to the qualities of the masses (e.g. in Aristotle and Thucydides), it can suggest a willingness to criticize popular politics and beliefs.

17. Compare *Politicus* 303a on the weakness of democracy as an agency for good or for evil.

18. The doctrine that knowledge is the only real good, and ignorance the only real evil. See above, p. 205, note 54.

19. Simmias and Cebes will be the principal interlocutors in the *Phaedo*.

20. Crito is observing, in a non-technical manner, that their interests and the moral course are in agreement. It is a well-known Socratic theme that one's interests *always* coincide with morality – thus what is bad for one coincides with what is morally dishonourable (cf. 49b).

21. A striking personification of argument (*logos*), anticipating the striking personification of the Laws later.

22. Already we have the picture of a Socrates who adheres to certain tenets (or at the very least hammers certain themes), who stands in contrast to the 'Socrates' familiar from the aporetic dialogues. However, the tenets are for himself, not necessarily something to be imposed on

others; the reader should judge from what follows how far Socrates' tenets accord with expectations derived from other dialogues which have been read.

23. It is true they do 'revert' – to an issue which seemed to have been adequately if briefly tackled before (44c–d).

24. The view that all people's opinions are equally correct is not supposed to be ridiculous, but is indeed associated with Protagoras at (e.g.) *Theaetetus* 152b.

25. The notion that arguments are not once and for all conclusive, but have to be repeated and tested in a variety of situations throughout life, seems typical of Socrates, as evidenced particularly by the discussion with Callicles in the *Gorgias* (481 d ff.).

26. This seems a strange lapse on the author's part, for there had been great initial care to contrast Socrates' coolness with Crito's agitation.

27. Socrates has in mind that entity normally translated as 'soul' (as *Republic* 609b ff. shows), but there is a curious reluctance to use the usual word here.

28. Again a striking personification.

29. Such sentiments have occurred less explicitly at 44d; they are also typical of Callicles in the *Gorgias* (e.g. 486b–c).

30. The democracy was notorious for changing its mind after the imposition of a death sentence. One example is the change of heart after the illegal trial of the generals after Arginusae (*Apology* 32b); another famous case is the changed decision over the Mytileneans in Book 3.36 ff. of Thucydides.

31. It is clear from 54a that Socrates does not regard the bringing-up of sons as a matter of indifference; perhaps also, from 45a, that he does not regard expense as such.

32. Plato's theory of punishment tends to regard just punishments as being for the good of the person punished, e.g. *Gorgias* 476d ff.; punishment is never rightly undertaken for the purpose of revenge, *Protagoras* 342b. Compare also *Republic* 332b–336a: the good man does not harm his enemy.

33. This seems unusually pessimistic for Socrates; his elenchus assumes some glimmer of the correct moral principles in all of us, and he is not shy of tackling a Callicles or a Thrasymachus. Does the Socrates of the *Crito* preach only to the semi-converted?

34. The constancy of Socrates' beliefs is again emphasized in the *Gorgias* (e.g. 482a–c, 508c–509a).

35. There is ambiguity in the Greek: it could mean 'Ought one to fulfil all that one agrees . . . to be just', and even as translated there are two interpretations, one supposing that the unjust mechanics of agreement invalidate the contract, the other supposing that it is unjust terms that will do so. Does the contract have to be justly made? And do the terms have to be just to be binding, or do they merely have to have been agreed to be just? The latter interpretation would tend to make the condition redundant – one does not agree to terms which one considers

unfair in any case. Furthermore the speech of the Laws will later emphasize the fairness of the agreement which Socrates has allegedly made with them – the fairness both of its terms and of the way in which it was made. In fact Athenian contract law does routinely make the validity of the contract subject to its fairness – to there being *cause* for the agreement and to the terms not requiring anything itself unjust. See Allen (1980), p. 87. Compare Kraut (pp. 29–33), who resists a tendency which he finds in Allen to *conflate* the injustice of the mechanics of an agreement and the injustice of its terms (p.32 and note 11).

36. We have here the important notion that a single violation such as that contemplated is not just a challenge to the one law which is thereby not correctly applied, but to the whole system of law. See Allen (1980), pp. 84–5.

37. The language resembles that of a formal charge, here brought against the city.

38. Strictly speaking, the comparison between the Laws and one's parents is not intended to supply an additional premise for the argument that escape would constitute an injustice, but to emphasize the *magnitude* of the injustice being contemplated. It does, however, also help to establish how fair and reasonable Socrates' 'contract' with the Laws had been.

39. Preparing the way for seeing the Laws as a kind of parent. However, what is at issue now is more a matter of tradition than formal law, so that the Laws come to stand for the whole cultural system according to which the city operates. Notice how the argument depends upon the Laws being regarded as a single body of law and tradition such that no part can be disregarded without damage to the whole.

40. 'Music' here covers the whole literary side of a traditional Greek education. Even in *Republic* 2 Socrates still thinks that 'music' and gymnastics together constitute the best basic education, but he has severe criticisms of details of the 'musical' part.

41. It is important that Socrates was regarded (ever since the *Clouds*, where Pheidippides learnt to justify the beating of his father and mother) as one who encouraged disrespect for one's parents. The charge appears to have been revived by Polycrates (Xenophon, *Memorabilia* 1.2.49), in company with the charge that he encouraged disrespect for the established laws (ibid., 9).

42. It is clear that the Laws consider the obvious time for scrutinizing the 'contract' to be the age of seventeen, when the Athenian male was formally confirmed in his citizenship by a process of *dokimasia*. See Kraut, p.154.

43. The personification now has the unfortunate consequence of picturing the Laws as tyrants, and the liberty-conscious Athenians as a willingly enslaved people. Their fear of a benevolent tyrant would of course be that he would not always be giving the same kind of orders, and one wonders what Socrates' response ought to be if the Laws radically

changed their methods of operation. Admittedly the Athenians can try to alter the Laws if they find them operating badly (if that is not to destroy the Laws with whom one is now contracted), but a tyrant's subjects are also able to try to influence his rule.

44. Here the reader should reflect on how realistic this choice would have been for the average Athenian. Would there be anywhere for him to go where he could expect laws of a substantially different kind?

45. It is unclear whether these words should be in the text, and whether they refer to the Isthmian Games.

46. For Socrates' military service, see *Apology* 28e.

47. A curious idea, implying that one only reproduces in congenial surroundings. That view is in fact espoused by Plato at *Symposium* 206e ff. Note that Socrates is hardly exceptional in having raised three children in Athens!

48. It is difficult to deny the implication that the jury would have accepted a proposed penalty of exile.

49. This rhetorical phrase generally strengthens the claim being made, since what is so in deed is superior evidence to what is so in word. In this case, however, a verbal agreement would have been much better evidence.

50. Kraut (p.30) finds here three reasons which might have made the 'contract' invalid: (i) compulsion, (ii) trickery, (iii) time-pressure.

51. It is odd exaggeration that Socrates should be thought to have had this option from the moment of birth rather than from the age when such matters became his responsibility (which would give a period of just over fifty years).

52. It is Plato's *Laws*, not any Socratic text, which comes immediately to mind as an example of respect for the Spartan and Cretan legal codes.

53. Both charges seem to have been made against Socrates by Polycrates in his literary *Accusation of Socrates*, and were possibly linked, see note 41, and for the rare word 'destroyer', Themistius *Oratio* 23, 296b–c.

54. Likewise Xenophon says that Critias (said by Polycrates to be Socrates' pupil) learnt lawlessness in Thessaly. But Socrates' claim seems insensitive to Crito's links with that place.

55. Apparently a proverbial expression for pointless indulgence, which serves to underline Socrates' derogatory attitude towards Thessaly.

56. Reading ⟨καὶ⟩ before μή.

57. For the judges of the Underworld, see *Apology* 41a, *Gorgias* 523c.

58. The distinction is not without problems; can the Laws, who are even given a human voice, be seen in isolation from the legislators and judges who administer them? Can the State, of which the Laws are professedly a part, be an entity separate from the people who comprise it? Further, if the citizens have judged in accordance with the law, then either (i) Socrates has not been wronged, or (ii) the Laws are implicated in the wrong he has been done but if the citizens have not judged in accordance with the law, how can Socrates be seeking to avoid lawful punishment?

59. Surely Socrates cannot return an injustice to the Laws, if they have acted justly; but can he really be returning an injustice to his fellow-men either, if he has no contract with them and has no intention of harming them? Perhaps there is the notion of repaying *the Laws* for an injustice which *men* committed in their name.

60. The reference is to those experiencing a Corybantic trance, and the idea is that the sound of the ritualistic music rings on in one's ears even when it has stopped; though oriental, these rites were quite acceptable at Athens, as *Euthydemus* 277d shows.

Phaedo

1. Diogenes Laertius 2.105.

2. See most notably Ronna Burger, *The Phaedo: a Platonic Labyrinth* (1984).

3. In fact Plato rejects this view in later works such as *Republic* 9, *Timaeus* and *Philebus*. He sees much intellectual activity and some naturally pleasant sensations as independent of prior pain, and also recognizes that there are some pleasures (such as those of smell) which are not preceded by any perceptible lack – or by pain, if it is agreed that all pain must be perceptible.

4. She did this so that the weaving should never be completed, in order that she might delay marrying one of her suitors.

5. Compare *Gorgias* 494a–c.

6. Compare *Euthyphro* 9c–11b.

7. Thus the notion that man's stay on earth is a kind of captivity in which the gods are our beneficent masters (62b) has considerable illustrative value. Strictly Socrates ought to believe that the gods are sanctioning his release from the body at this time if he is to justify his own conduct. That this was his belief is best illustrated by Apology 40a–c and *Crito* 54c.

8. The problem here is whether, when the soul adopts a new body, it can continue to be viewed as the same person. Plato would credit it (at least if it has entered a human body) with the ability to recollect what it learnt in its discarnate life, but the continuity seems much less strong than between the discarnate life and its *previous* embodiment.

9. See Bostock (1986), pp. 25–30.

10. Teiresias was a prophet whose earthly blindness had brought new powers of divine vision.

11. Aristotle, *Nicomachean Ethics* 10.2.

12. Though orthodox Pythagoreans saw numbers, etc., as basic physical entities.

13. This vector can be either another Idea or a physical substance; soul too can be a vector, and this seems to fall under some other heading – possibly 'non-physical substance'.

14. Again I think there is a hint of Presocratic physics lurking in the

background, giving the appeal more power over Plato's audience. It was a principle that anything existent could not simply vanish into nothing; change must leave behind it something changed. Now ceasing to live would seem to involve one of two things: either (i) passing into non-existence, or (ii) becoming dead. Presocratic physics would seem to ban (i); but the soul is such that it cannot take on the attribute 'dead', so (ii) is also impossible. Hence assuming the soul is subject to the same rules as the entities of physics (as the metaphysician must), it cannot 'die' in either of the two imaginable ways.

15. It is important to realize that the Greeks, even if they expected some kind of life after death, as clearly Phaedo does, tended to assume that it would deprive all ordinary humans of much that was worthwhile. It would be a dark, damp semi-existence below rather than anything akin to the Christian Heaven. Socrates is therefore quite unusually reconciled to death.

16. See *Apology* 34a for Apollodorus; on the blending of pleasure and pain, see the introduction to *Phaedo*.

17. The latter is Crito; see *Apology* 33d. On Epigenes and Aeschines, see 33e.

18. Antisthenes was perhaps the senior Socratic, and had great influence upon the subsequent cynic school.

19. Ctesippus features in the *Euthydemus* and *Lysis*.

20. Menexenus features in the *Menexenus* and *Lysis*.

21. We may only speculate on Plato's absence from the discussion.

22. Simmias and Cebes are the chief Interlocutors in this work, and have Pythagorean connections; Euclides and Terpsion are met in the prologue to the *Theaetetus*, and the former was responsible for developing the Megarian philosophy, which paid much attention to subtle argument.

23. See *Apology* 37c.

24. Xanthippe has the reputation of being a very difficult woman, in part owing to her portrayal by Antisthenes in Xenophon's *Symposium* 2.10. Other sources mention a woman named Myrto as having also been a wife of Socrates.

25. In the *Gorgias* (493a–500a) pain is not conceived as pleasure's opposite, indeed the argument at 495e ff. relies upon their not being opposites; pleasure and pain diminish simultaneously (as one slakes one's thirst, etc.), while opposites can neither wax nor wane simultaneously. Pain is there regarded as an underlying lack, pleasure as the process by which it is restored. Hence Plato's reluctance to state here that pain is simply pleasure's opposite. There appear to be changes, however, to the *Phaedo*'s theory.

26. On pleasure and pain alternating, see the introduction to *Phaedo*, p. 97.

27. See *Apology* 20b and note.

28. *the arts*: – literally 'music', but embracing all creative activity overseen by the Muses, especially poetic activity. One of the verbs used is also

commonly used for *composing poetry*, and would naturally be taken this way when coupled with 'music'. Socrates now suspects that the words are to be taken in this literal sense.

29. It is (Delian) Apollo's festival, Apollo is the god of prophetic dreams, and the Muses are also closely connected with Apollo, so that he, if any god, would be connected with the composition of poetry. Hence Socrates' prologue is addressed to Apollo.

30. On this section, see the introduction to *Phaedo*, pp. 97 ff., 'Desiring death and suicide'.

31. A prominent Pythagorean of the time, of whom a number of fragments survive, some generally accepted as authentic. His sect had been expelled from Italy, and he settled in Thebes, where Simmias and Cebes had come into contact with him.

32. Probably the prohibition of suicide. For alternatives of interpretation here see Gallop, pp. 79–83.

33. The relativity of 'good' is a major sophistic theme, associated with Protagoras at *Protagoras* 334a–c. If one applied it only to the *physical* condition, circumstances, or experiences of the individual, Plato would be in agreement.

34. Cebes is supposed to have concluded that death is better for some people. These would normally and uncontroversially be persons so bad or unfortunate that death is a boon; so to have reached that conclusion Cebes does not have to accept that philosophers are better off dying because of the attraction for them of the after-life.

35. To judge from *Gorgias* 493a ff. the Orphics told a number of stories about life and death which were allegorically interpreted by the Pythagoreans. Naturally one would expect material familiar to the Pythagoreans to be used in a conversation with Cebes and Simmias.

36. I have preferred this translation to Tredennick's 'guard-post', which appears to interpret the Greek word as an outpost in which the people are designated the task of *guarding*. Most modern interpreters see the reference here as being to a place in which prisoners are *guarded*. In fact the Orphics believed that life on earth was a punishment for the soul, and the penalty was a kind of imprisonment, as *Cratylus* 400c shows. It is apparent that Socrates will not commit himself to the idea that we are being punished; the obligation not to escape results from God's generosity to his human serfs.

37. It is quite conventional to think of the gods of the Underworld as a different group from the Olympians, of whom Socrates' closest god, Apollo, was one.

38. A way of making a strong but guarded assertion typical of 'Socrates' in the early-middle dialogues; cf. *Gorgias* 508e–509a, *Meno* 98b.

39. Medical writers at this time explained physical processes mostly in terms of hot, cold, wet and dry. No doubt the hemlock is thought of as freezing its victim, and heat will thus be seen as an antidote.

40. Assent to this proposition is natural enough for the Greek (who would be used to the idea of some shadow of the former person journeying at

death to Hades), and it has a tremendous influence over the course of the argument hereafter. Thus Socrates is often accused of having prejudged the issue; but the notion that something has 'left' the body at death is natural, 'soul' frequently means just 'life' (which is the thing most naturally thought to leave), and any important physical change would naturally be interpreted as admixture or separation according to late Presocratic physics. Socrates assumes the loss of a life-giving ingredient, but he is not assuming that this ingredient itself coheres as a functioning entity after leaving the body.

41. It is perfectly normal for Plato to be questioning whether these 'pleasures' are properly so called. We learn from the *Protagoras* (353c ff.) that the long-term effects are often painful rather than pleasant.

42. Particularly Xenophanes, fr. 34–35, Epicharmus, fr. 12, and Parmenides, fr. 7. But still, it must be admitted that nothing there explains how Plato can hope to avoid clarifying his reasons for his low estimation of the senses in the *Phaedo*, and it would be dangerous to suppose that his reasons are the same as those of 'the poets'. What he shares with them is the belief that the senses cannot penetrate to that deeper reality which will explain the world, but it is likely that his reasons are linked with his own Theory of Ideas, and concern the alleged failure of any object of sensation to perfectly exemplify any of the various attributes (e.g. holy, equal, cold) which are accredited to them.

43. i.e. taste, smell and touch.

44. The language recalls Socrates' dismissal of the jailer's concerns about his body in favour of his own desire for philosophical discussion (63e).

45. The Platonic Theory of Ideas (eternal, unchanging, perfect principles of various qualities which occur imperfectly in this world) now makes its first appearance. The philosopher aims to understand these things in their own right so far as is possible. In the middle-period dialogues they feature as the true objects of knowledge, since we cannot fully know what is changing, and their instantiations in the physical world are subject to change. See also the postscript on the Theory of Ideas.

46. Rejecting, as is usual, the textual emendation proposed by Burnet in his Oxford Classical Text.

47. Keeping the full text of the Oxford Classical Text, and interpreting approximately as Gallop does.

48. This may be a surprise, for withdrawal from the body does not entail finding ourselves in the presence of other souls. We know that Socrates expects to meet other fine souls after death (63b), but we do not know why. However, there was a tendency to envisage similar physical substances finding their way naturally to the same strata of the universe, and if the rule can be extended to soul then there might be a particular place where soul in its pure state will naturally come to reside – whereas, if it were contaminated with substances that seek a lower place, it would be held back nearer to earth.

49. This recurrence of the 'body-prison' theme of 62b indicates why Socrates finds the image attractive. It is not that the soul has committed

an offence to get there, but rather that the body is, for the philosopher, an exceedingly restrictive place.

50. The text refers explicitly to the younger partner in a male-to-male homosexual relationship, for whom, as the *Symposium* demonstrates, erotic passion was more likely to be felt by a Greek male than for any other; a classic case of a lover dying a certain death on behalf of a dead beloved would be that of Achilles for Patroclus (*Symposium* 179e; where, however, the relationship is inverted). *Symposium* 204–212 also makes much of the similarity between this erotic love and the philosopher's love of wisdom. The terminology here is most appropriate to erotic love. Hence it is possible, though not certain, that the reference to wives and sons should be deleted (with Verdenius). The words could easily be a gloss – the result of an attempt to impose upon the text the moral expectations of a later age.

51. It is important here that 'philosopher' literally means 'lover of wisdom'.

52. It is customary for Plato in his middle period to see men as falling into three basic types: those who pursue basic physical needs (in which case they are likely to value money highly), those who pursue honour, and the 'philosophers' who pursue wisdom. Such a division operates in the *Republic*, particularly in Book 8, where it goes hand in hand with the tripartite division of the human soul. I have understood the text in such a way as seems to accord with that theory, for whereas it is clear why a body-lover should be a lover of money (money enabling him to fulfil his bodily desires), there is no special connection between love of the body and love of prestige. If I am right, the money-lover is in fact the conventionally temperate man, or the oliogarchic man of *Republic* 8, who controls desires with a view to wealth, while the prestige-lover is the conventionally brave man.

53. For the theory of 'popular virtues' and their difference from the philosopher's virtue, see the introduction to *Phaedo*, pp. 102 ff., 'Popular and Socratic Morality'.

54. Dialogues traditionally placed at the end of the early period begin to make this distinction between the popular conception of the virtues and the virtues as they ought theoretically to be, e.g. *Meno* 88b–c, *Euthydemus* 281c; see also *Phaedo* 82a–b.

55. The text here is most difficult to interpret; Burnet's omissions achieve nothing, and I have tried to translate the full manuscript text, aiming at what must be the overall sense. The reader should be aware that many different translations might be offered.

56. How popular justice is similar to temperance and courage is unclear; *Republic* seems to suggest that in the popular view the point of fairness and cooperation between friends is to harm enemies most effectively. The archetypes of unthinking justice and temperance at 82b are bees, wasps and ants, not to mention moderate humans – those showing these 'virtues' within their communities but not perhaps beyond them.

57. The emblem here is the *narthex* or fennel-rod tipped with ivy, carried by the worshippers of Dionysus; the devotees are his *bacchae*.

58. There are reports that the Heraclitean Cratylus had been a substantial influence upon Plato in his younger days, and the radical theory of perpetual change painted by Cratylus can have left little room for anything to endure within this universe, let alone soul. Thus Plato is beginning by tackling a hostile and influential position from within, bringing out those aspects of it which are helpful for his own present position. Heracliteanism remains a moderate influence over Plato's picture of the phenomenal world.

59. It is important to realize the nature of the beliefs which Socrates is attempting to counter. Cebes is not suggesting that the soul becomes non-existent, but that without the body to hold it together (and being an insubstantial sort of thing) it no longer coheres and no longer forms any discernible entity. This agrees with the picture of death as a parting of soul and body, and it also marks the soul as an entity that is thought of in semi-physical terms, for at the very least its existence is spatio-temporal. What Socrates has to prove, therefore, is that the soul *coheres* even without the body.

60. There is a clear reference here to the *Clouds* of Aristophanes, where comic terminology incorporating this idea of 'playing about' (*adoleschia*) is in evidence.

61. Probably a reference back to the 'Orphic' ideas of 63c and 69c, though the pluperfect tense might have made this plainer. It would also be possible to translate 'which we (are able to) remember'. The 'other world' is given its conventional name of Hades by Plato, but the important thing is that there should be *some* location capable of housing disembodied souls.

62. Cf. particularly *Meno* 81a–c, with the quotation from Pindar there, which, like the work of other inspired poets, is supposed to reflect the doctrine of certain priests and priestesses.

63. Note the proposition which Socrates feels he must prove: that there are identifiable soul-entities located elsewhere, capable of animating new bodies here.

64. Tredennick used the translation 'generation' rather than 'coming to be'; but generation seems to apply to new subjects, not to new predicates which become true of the same subject. The Greek verb *gignesthai* can be used of (i) a subject coming into existence or being born, (ii) something coming to be so, and (iii) a subject becoming *F* where *x* is a predicate.

65. Notably absent from the examples of opposites are those specially associated with the Pythagoreans, such as one and many, odd and even, limited and unlimited, yet they would not present Socrates with any special problems.

66. This answer seems to be hasty. Cebes ought to have said 'being inanimate' perhaps, for to say 'dead' tends to imply not just the absence of lite but the absence of life from something which has

previously lived. But these objections may be misdirected if the argument is being intentionally conducted in a Heraclitean framework. Firstly Heraclitus had spoken of death to various kinds of element in such a way that would not imply its animation (B36), and secondly the shifting nature of reality was such that it could always be said of any two basic physical substances, X and Y, that the X now present was dead Y and the Y now present was dead X.

67. The conclusion is scarcely justified without further argument. There may first need to be something 'dead' if it is to acquire the attribute 'living', but it has not been shown that this something is soul, nor that, if it were, it would be in Hades.

68. The 'again' is natural, because of the implication of a previous life in the contentious word 'dead'. For us even the idea of 'coming to life' is awkward, as we think of the child as alive from the beginning. It was at birth, for the soul was traditionally associated with breath. Whether it could be thought of as 'dead' before it takes its first breath is less likely.

69. Whether they have agreed that living *souls* come from dead *souls* is very dubious, and yet this was what they needed to prove.

70. Here begins a supplementary argument, designed to make it certain that there must be a process of rebirth opposite to the process of death.

71. Endymion was, according to myth, an attractive male loved by the Moon; in most versions he is blessed with eternal sleep.

72. Anaxagoras (fr. 1) began his book with this idea, which depicts a kind of primeval chaos, in which everything (except mind, the separative agent) formed an undifferentiated mass.

73. This is of course what one would naturally believe today. But if one believes in some life-force, a life-force which deserts when the creature ages and dies, one will surely want to postulate a means by which that life-force can be implanted and grow in the young. Note that there is some uncertainty concerning text and translation at this point.

74. This is surely due to Plato's conception of 'recollection' as an essential element in the educational process. Like Simmias, the reader must be made aware of his forgotten inner consciousness.

75. The readership is evidently supposed to be familiar with this doctrine, which had probably been outlined already in the *Meno* (81–86).

76. 'Learning' is generally regarded by Plato as the acquisition of knowledge proper (not just correct opinion), as something which renders the learner able to explain what he learns, and as a result of the activities of some 'teacher' rather than of personal discovery.

77. There is deliberate play on the notion of recollection. As in the *Meno*, it is plain that Meno himself is recollecting (being taught) something during the recollection episode, so too Simmias is 'recollecting' something during the recollection episode here.

78. The 'correct explanation' (*orthos logos*) is something that is considered possible for all those who have knowledge; cf. 76b.

79. Such a diagram had been employed in the *Meno* to help Meno's slave 'recollect' basic facts of geometry.

80. So far Plato seems to have been wanting to remind us what it is like to be reminded of something, in order that we may ask ourselves whether we do not undergo a similar experience when we 'learn'. It seems now, however, that he is keen to nip in the bud any sophistic objections to his 'Recollection of Ideas' theory based upon the same or a different dilemma. The Ideas are such that they must have some qualities (e.g. being perfectly what they are) that the corresponding particulars cannot have, but nevertheless it is only to the extent that particulars *resemble* a given Idea that they come to acquire its 'name': e.g. it is only because a given circle resembles the Idea of the circle that it comes to be called a circle at all.

81. At this point the Theory of Ideas returns.

82. This is surely a natural admission for anybody with a background in Pythagoreanism and geometry to make.

83. Socrates is here setting up a paradox: we seem to acquire knowledge of an Idea from our experience of the particulars; yet (whereas we think any concept involving predicates $A, B, \ldots N$ must derive from experience of things with the predicates $A, B, \ldots N$) the Idea differs by at least one predicate from any particular one could name.

84. (i) Is Plato saying that the sticks appear equal to two different people or in two different respects or to two different things, or (with a variant textual reading) at two different times. (ii) Is Plato here seriously concerned with a lack of true equality in the *physical* world or in the *phenomenal* world? Are any two sticks automatically unequal in their own right, or is it enough for Plato that we can examine any two sticks from angles (literal or metaphorical) which will make them appear unequal? Certainly the emphasis here seems to be on different *impressions* which these equal things give, not on the precise reason for the two impressions being different.

85. The Greek actually uses the odd expression 'the equals themselves'. Usually Plato would use such terminology *in the singular* to refer to the Ideas, but the Ideas seem always to be one. He could easily have taken a geometrical example such as square or circle which would not have involved any difficulty with the implied duality in the notion itself; it is possible, therefore, that Plato hopes this example may help to teach us something additionally about metaphysics, in which case he is deliberately distinguishing between 'equals themselves' and 'equality'. Therefore I am tempted by the proposal of R.S. Bluck (*Phronesis* 4, 1959, 5–11) to see a reference here to something analogous to the 'largeness in us' from 102d ff., to whatever it might be about the two 'equal' sticks which really is equal. However, there is no immediate significance for *Plato's* metaphysics; we are concerned with what *anybody* might or might not imagine. It is natural to envisage *something* about each of two roughly equal sticks which is indeed equal; but nobody would try to persuade themselves that whatever it is about them that is equal (*de dicto*) is really unequal. For similar impossibilities without obvious invocation of the Theory of Ideas, cf. *Theaetetus*

190b–c. There is no need to emend the text, as Bostock (1986, p. 82) does.

86. It is true that equal sticks do not strike us as being 'inequality' either, and so there is no outright conflict here. For this reason translations like the present one have worried commentators, for Plato would seem to be making a point not strictly relevant to the argument. What we have here, however, is a classic case of irony designed to underline the absurdity of any such notion.

87. See note 80, above.

88. The way in which the particulars 'fall short' of the Ideas is again a matter of controversy. The notion has been prepared by the example of remembering a person from his portrait, and appreciating how close the resemblance is (73c–74a). Again I think that we should remember that the audience has a Pythagorean background, and that the principal example being used has much mathematical significance. Pythagoreans, with their love of musical theory, and mathematicians in general would have taken little convincing of the tendency of particulars to exemplify only imperfectly the concepts which they were discussing. One may mention that Bostock (1986) sees a difficulty in that Plato could not have seen the number of any five coins, for instance, as being imperfectly equal to that of any five other coins, but Plato would simply have seen this as the equality of *numbers*, not of coins – the numbers of the two groups of coins being 'what were actually equal' about the groups, not their precise weight and colouring, nor even their denomination.

89. Tredennick believed that it was the notion of equality which was referred to here, but this makes poor sense in the context.

90. There already (since 74d) seems to be a dynamic teleological notion of the instances in this world all striving in as much as they can for the perfection of their respective Ideas. For teleology, see 97c ff.

91. 'Equals' here is not in the text, but a Greek might easily supply it.

92. Strictly it must be before we first used our senses *in this comparative way* that we should have had to have knowledge of the standard of comparison. Must we assume that our *earliest* awareness of earthly equals was such that we knew their deficiencies? Perhaps Plato is talking of our earliest *recognition of equals as equals*, thinking that we cannot even label two things 'equals' until we can measure them against equality itself; for otherwise it would be open to us to hold that our notion of equality is derived from earlier sensations of equality, such as were not accompanied by any recognition of deficiency.

93. Certainly we had the faculties, but does Plato want to imply that we actually recognize things through them at this stage?

94. Commentators since Hackforth recognize that this alternative is shortly to be rejected; the other alternative appears at 75e3.

95. Commentators note problems of applying the deficiency principle to these examples. It is unclear how an elephant could fail to be bigger in

every respect and from all angles than a mouse! However, it is not clearly required for the argument that *all* physical attributes should *always* be imperfect.

96. Tredennick with good reason interprets the Greek *logon didonai* ('to give an account') as 'to give an explanation'. It is sometimes interpreted more technically as meaning to give a definition or to give proof, but the Greek really falls short of either meaning, and it seems unreasonable, if I saw my brother commit murder, to say that I didn't know this unless I can define it (what, precisely?) or prove it!

97. This pessimistic statement is often contrasted with the suggestion at 74b that we know what actual equality is. It seems here that it may only be Socrates and a few others who can pass a stringent test of knowledge, whereas human beings in general 'know' equality in a much weaker sense. The Theory of Recollection naturally encourages two different senses of 'know', one applying to the subconscious presence of pre-natal 'knowledge', and the other used only for fully recollected knowledge. Note how at *Meno* 85c–86a the slave is at one moment spoken of as having right opinion (not yet knowledge), and at another as having knowledge (85d9–12). For more detail, consult Bedu-Addo (1991), who emphasizes the harmony in Plato's epistemology from the *Meno* to the *Republic*.

98. Socrates is taking more than one step at a time. We have not been shown that the previous existence was non-bodily, though there would be a regress if it had been of the same bodily kind: our perceptions there too would rely on background knowledge from a previous existence. If intelligence is required to apprehend the Ideas, then of course our souls would have had to be intelligent in the life that brought them their knowledge of the Ideas.

99. Gallop, p. 134, shows that Simmias's admission of defeat is premature. There is in fact no reason why a theory of latent knowledge should have *ever* before been fully known; we could perhaps have acquired something akin to a dim memory at birth based on no prior experience.

100. How much is Socrates claiming here? That the two doctrines stand and fall together? He has only argued from the existence of (known) Ideas to the pre-existence of souls, though it is clear that immortality of souls would not be an attractive prospect for Socrates without the existence of the Ideas (and thus that his discussion would indeed be a waste of time). Could Plato have thought that it could be proven that if the Ideas don't exist the soul must be mortal? It is more likely, I submit, that the final sentence (76e5–7) is a gloss on the previous ones, whose language it follows very closely. Simmias's reply might have been taken by a later editor to imply the biconditionality thesis (whereas it is doubtful whether it does so), and Socrates' question altered to imply it too.

101. The joke has some philosophical purpose, inviting the reader to reflect on the type of insubstantial and fragmented entity likely to become dissipated before the similarity argument.

102. It emerges from 114d that the 'myth' is the kind of enchantment which Socrates can offer for this purpose.

103. On this section, see the introduction to *Phaedo*, p. 106.

104. These assumptions underlie the physics of the atomist Democritus, whose 'atoms' are literally unsplittable particles, and thus the permanent material stuff of the universe.

105. It appears now that Plato is associating his Ideas with the things of which Socratic dialectic used to seek a definition. This would legitimize the attempt to see Socrates himself as an exponent of the Ideas. However, some commentators, including Hackforth, interpret the clause as a reference to proofs of existence rather than quests for definitions.

106. It is standard doctrine in the *Phaedo* that particulars take their 'name', i.e. any descriptive attribute which applies to them, as a result of their (partial) conformity with the Idea that is properly so called (cf. 102a–b). Justice, for instance, would be perfectly 'just', whereas any instance of a just act or just person would acquire the name 'just' in a secondary sense from Justice itself. Hence, while there can be no change to what Justice is, there can be considerable change in a just man and in his degree of conformity with Justice.

107. This seems to be qualified later at 81d, but it is really only the bodily impurities of a bad soul which make the ghost invisible there.

108. The shift in terminology suggests that it is no longer the soul's similarity to the Ideas which is being claimed, but rather its similarity to the gods which are also (almost by definition) eternal.

109. The last words seem to amount to a strong qualification, but soul has not been proven to be totally invariable, etc., only very like what is invariable. This is more in harmony with later developments in Plato's theory of soul, which no longer see it as uniform; furthermore it is created from various elements at *Timaeus* 35a–b, and the same work regards all things which are thus created as being technically dissoluble, even if they are never actually destroyed.

110. Egyptian mummification procedures were well known, and are discussed in detail by Herodotus in Book 2. Plato himself was clearly fascinated by a great many Egyptian customs and beliefs, and was accused in his own day of plagiarizing Egyptian ideas.

111. There is a pun here, and possibly an attempt to derive Hades from *Aides* (unseen), though *Cratylus* 404b forcefully rejects this derivation.

112. The last attribute may seem less expected, but there has been a suggestion that the soul is also like the gods running through the similarity argument from 79e; Bostock indeed regards this as an independent analogy (1986, p. 118).

113. Gallop remarks on the difficulty of reconciling this talk of ghosts with the notion of an immaterial soul; it is indeed the kind of notion which would most easily suggest the blending of a material soul with a material body. But we should not suppose that Plato's view of

immateriality is such as to imply the absence of spatial attributes, e.g. of shapelessness. Plato repeatedly uses spatial terms in describing the soul and its experiences.

114. Plato now brings in the theory of transmigration of souls, including transmigration from one species to another. Simmias and Cebes, as Pythagoreans, are unlikely to voice any great surprise, though it does not suit the philosophic purpose of the dialogue well. Plato is arguing for *individual* immortality, and it is hard to see how *my* soul can remain my soul if it becomes that of an ant or a kite; in particular Plato is arguing that the essential nature of a human soul is to be rational, and all such creatures were thought of as lacking the potential for rationality. Surely Plato would not have wanted to allow that my soul can be destroyed *qua* human soul, losing its most valuable power along with its humanity. We should allow for considerable irony in what he says at this point, and note the constant reference to what is 'likely', i.e. to what has some affinity with the truth rather than being altogether true. In the myth at the end of the work the souls of the bad are punished in a region below us rather than above or around the tombs, and they remain very much human souls.

115. Primarily sexual assault here, since food, drink and sex are a common trio. Other kinds of assault are covered under 'injustice', below.

116. See the introduction to *Phaedo*, pp. 102 ff., 'Popular and Socratic Morality'. It is interesting that these people who practise ordinary virtue seem to be included among the inferior souls who can appear as ghosts around the graveyards, and are reincarnated in such lifeforms as bees or ants.

117. A single type of man, the *Republic's* 'timarchic' type; see, on the lover of prestige, 68c.

118. As I interpret the Greek, the particular case of a property '*p*' is seen as (i) other than the Idea '*P*', (ii) housed in some thing other than '*P*', and (iii) apprehended via some cognitive organ other than the soul.

119. See above, 68e ff.

120. On this section, see the introduction to *Phaedo*, p. 96, 'Pleasure and Release'.

121. The life of alternating pleasure and pain is conceived as having great crests and troughs, which reason smooths out.

122. On the swan-song, see the general introduction, p. xxii.

123. On the Eleven, see *Apology*, 37c.

124. Tredennick translated 'we Pythagoreans', but it is not clear that this is a reference to his own school rather than to people in general.

125. Here is the part of the theory that has the most impact. Cebes is accepting, as Plato often appears to be accepting, the validity of Heraclitean flux theory as applied to physical things. Hence the body is not the same now as it was two minutes ago, nor indeed can it accurately be called the same body. The bodies which the longerlasting soul wears out are not the bodies of different individuals

living in different centuries, but the succession of bodies that the individual has experienced during his *one* bodily life. The soul may in fact have resembled the tailor/weaver in as much as it is perpetually occupied with the renewal and replacement of its own clothes, its body, since the soul is traditionally the force behind nutrition and growth.

126. The two primary reasons for scepticism in the ancient world were the suspicions that (i) things are not of such a nature as to be known, and (ii) even if things are inherently knowable, men do not have the required cognitive ability to know them.

127. Whereas the shaving-off of hair was normally a sign of grief, it had been for the Argives a sign of determination, after a heavy defeat by Sparta, to recover the territory which had been lost to them. See Herodotus 1.82.

128. Alluding to one of Plato's favourite myths in which Heracles, when fighting the hydra, is attacked also by a huge crab, and has to call on Iolaus as his helper; cf. *Euthydemus* 297b–d.

129. i.e. while Socrates lives; the hemlock is drunk at dusk.

130. An early written example is to be found in the *Dissoi Logoi*, a sophistic compendium. Plato's own *Euthydemus* portrays two sophists who specialize in confusing people by producing opposite arguments. The present passage suggests that such techniques might also be combined with a belief in the Heraclitean flux theory (cf. Aenesidemus in Sextus Empiricus, *Pyrrhonian Hypotyposes* 1.210). Argument for both sides was also a technique practised either for exercise or for display by writers of forensic speeches.

131. The tidal channel between Euboea and the Greek mainland, famous for its strong alternating currents.

132. Socrates persists with his well-known theme that knowledge is the only truly good thing, ignorance the only truly bad one. Hence if he lives on, he will be right, and that will be good for him; while if he perishes completely, he will be wrong, and he will be deprived of what's bad for him!

133. That this is an independent argument may legitimately be doubted, but the point emerges in such a way as to make it more difficult, psychologically, to accept Simmias's theory.

134. Anticipating Socrates' use of the Ideas in the application of his hypothetical method; 100a ff.

135. Another description for the Ideas; there is an allusion back to 75d. See above, 76e, for the apparent interdependence of the theories.

136. This, and Socrates' three previous contributions, supply premises vital for the *final* argument against the attunement theory, beginning at 94b. Why they are placed here is unclear, though it may be that Plato wishes to go over various beliefs about the soul which he thinks Simmias will assent to *before* determining a direct line of attack. In this way the dialogue seems to develop in a manner more reminiscent of natural conversation. Plato's Socrates often elicits premises well before they are actually used.

137. The text, in which I follow Hackforth, is difficult at this point. The manuscript reading would make any attunement such as to be no more or less of an attunement than any other, but the 'universal' reading is not necessary for the argument. Cf. Bostock (1986), p. 128.

138. I take it that the proponents of the attunement theory would agree that it is the soul, not some bodily organ like the brain, which is the controlling factor here, and that the control is such as to keep the organism in tune. Plato's own *Republic* would not regard the physical desires as simply the work of the body, but rather as a function of a different part of the soul; this, however, does not make the argument work any less effectively against Simmias's theory as long as Simmias regards the body as the motive force behind the desires. If Simmias were to postulate a rational soul which resisted the appetitive soul, then he would make his psychical attunement out of tune with itself!

139. *Odyssey* 20, 17–18.

140. The appeal to Homer's authority looks almost like another argument. Why does Plato here think that such an appeal can help? Probably because Simmias had treated the attunement doctrine as an *endoxon*, as something with widespread support among people expected to be right. To find Homer disagreeing with the doctrine would be to undermine this claim of support among men who matter.

141. Harmonia was the legendary wife of Cadmus, revered founder of Thebes, who was said to have brought the alphabet to Greece; but the word *harmonia* is that which has been used for an attunement throughout.

142. Notice the way Socrates brings out this aspect of Cebes' conception of the soul's role, compatible to some degree with the notion that the body has become a labour of love for which the soul eventually sacrifices itself.

143. See the general introduction, p. xxvi.

144. I think it dangerous to retain the translation 'cause'; the word has a wide semantic range, and to translate 'cause' is to make the theory developed by Socrates to replace Presocratic physics into a quasi-physical theory itself. In view of the considerable influence of the Presocratics on the *Phaedo* in general, however, we should be prepared to detect possible parallels with Presocratic causation theories in Socrates' substitute for it.

145. It is crucial here that the verbs for 'coming-to-be' and 'being' have both an absolute sense, when a thing comes into existence and continues that existence, and another sense in which they take the complement: x comes-to-be warm, is warm, etc. The latter can also be taken as a case of warmness coming-to-be or existing. Socrates is interested not only in how men come-to-be but also how they come-to-be wise, i.e. how wisdom comes-to-be.

146. These were the theories of Archelaus (an Athenian with whom Socrates is often associated, who was much influenced by Anaxagoras).

147. This seems to be a case of thought and knowledge coming-to-be.

148. The theories on thought derive from the Presocratics Empedocles, Anaximenes, Heraclitus and Alcmaeon of Croton.

149. It should be noted that what Socrates is seeking to explain is the coming-to-be not of the man, but of the attribute 'big' as applied to him – how he came-to-be big. We should perhaps associate the present theory with Anaxagoras (cf. Diels-Kranz, *Die Fragmente der Vorsokratiker* 59A46), though Socrates has yet to meet his mind theory. The theory could have been commonplace.

150. Another instance of the coming-to-be of the attribute 'bigger'. Naturally, when the Greeks said 'taller *by a head*', using the dative case of the word for head, they did not mean that this head was a *reason* for something's being taller, even though the dative case sometimes did indicate a cause or reason. Socrates is ironically suggesting that, if the Presocratic view of causation were correct, there *should* be something 'in' the tall man, the greater number, and the larger size which is responsible for the tallness or largeness or double quantity – much as there might be water in something, making it damp. He may have been influenced by Anaxagoras, who believed that the seeds of all basic properties were to be found in any physical conglomerate at all (fr. 4).

151. A glance at Presocratic physics will help explain Socrates' difficulty, which is a case of F-ness being caused by both x and y, where x is the opposite of y. If *the hot* were adduced as the reason for fever, it would be odd if in other circumstances *the cold* were said to be the reason for fever.

152. See the general introduction, p. xxvi.

153. The flat earth was generally a feature of Ionian cosmologies, the spherical earth (occupying the centre) of Italian and Sicilian cosmologies.

154. The books were easy to procure and inexpensive (*Apology* 26d–e).

155. There is a pun here.

156. Natural choices; cf. *Crito* 53b. The idea that these bodily substances would act as an independent intelligence is here for humour's sake, as the oath tends to confirm.

157. The *Timaeus* distinguishes the auxiliary reason, which most people think a real reason, from the true reason, which is intelligence (46c ff.). It could in fact be claimed that this work is Plato's own attempt to work out the implications of Anaxagoras's doctrine along the lines required here by Socrates.

158. The vortex and the kneading-trough are two prominent terms (which suffer a change in terminology owing to their gender) in Aristophanes' *Clouds*, though there is no direct link between them in the extant play. Socrates is being amusing here, for it strikes him as odd that anybody should use a quick thing like a vortex to keep the earth stable, or support a substantial thing like a kneading-trough on a base of insubstantial air.

159. To believe in Atlas, the giant who holds the world upon his shoulders, would by this time be an indication of gullibility.

160. At first sight the comparison suggests that Socrates is aware that he has just suffered a case of 'blindness' as a result of lifting his eyes away from the darkness of the world of the physicists straight up to the blazing light of Anaxagoras's Intelligence principle (eclipsed by the way in which Anaxagoras had himself used it). There would then be an important parallel between the way in which Anaxagoras's Intelligence (which always pursues the good) is here conceived, and the way in which the Idea of the Good can be compared with the Sun in *Republic* 6–7. Socrates, however, attributes the threatened mental 'blindness' not to the brightness of Anaxagorean Intelligence, but rather to the use of the senses to try to understand the physicists' world directly (96c, 99e). This may be because the soul is blinded by the *darkness* of an alien sensory world in much the same way as the senses are blinded by strong light (cf. 83a).

161. This is perhaps a denial that the approach through the senses is a direct approach to reality rather than an assertion that theory approaches it directly. The things of the senses have the status of an image or reflection of the Ideas in the *Republic*, though this doctrine is not explicit in the *Phaedo* (Bostock (1986), 90–92). If Socrates is committed to the concept of an Intelligence which *works out* what is best according to theory before trying to realize it physically, it is not surprising that he should see theory as a potentially more direct approach to the reasons for things.

162. 'Lay down' translates the verb related to the noun 'hypothesis', hence Socrates is now explaining what is known as his 'hypothetical method'. It is naturally compared with the account of a hypothetical method at *Meno* 86c ff. Bostock (1986 p. 166) shows how that passage actually employs the method (described at *Phaedo* 101d–e) of justifying one hypothesis on the basis of a more fundamental one, and also treats the method as a second-best approach to the subject.

163. For the notion that the Theory of Ideas is already much talked of, see 76d.

164. The language of 'participation' (i.e. having a portion of) is frequently used to describe the particular's relation to the Idea in the middle-period dialogues, but will be much criticized in the *Parmenides*. The metaphor should not be taken to suggest that the particular has some fixed percentage of some finite stock of (e.g.) Beauty in the world, but rather that it only possesses incomplete Beauty.

165. Socrates tries to avoid technicalities which do not affect the argument. Note, however, that Plato's theory covers both simple predicates such as 'large' and relations such as 'larger' or 'equal' which are more difficult to think of as being 'in' the object. Indeed Plato was interested in the mechanics of sensation at this time, and may have been somewhat under the influence of a Protagorean view of sensation which we meet at *Theaetetus* 156, whereby all predicates are relations

in so far as they are dependent upon a unique relation between object and perceiver. When a white thing is perceived the 'whiteness' itself emerges in the mid-stream reaction between eye and surface, is carried to the surface, and makes it 'white'. Hence the object's being white is secondary to (indeed causally dependent on) the coming of whiteness to it, but it may be more accurate to speak of its being associated with whiteness than its having whiteness inside it.

166. There is the assumption here that where X and Y are opposites, something possessing the property Y could not be the cause of anything coming to have the property X. The assumption would be typical of Greek medicine: if the doctor wants to bring about a moister or warmer body he does not give it dry, very cold nourishment, for that will make it drier and colder still. Plato assumes that the principle has a wider application; for another relevant passage see *Theaetetus* 199d, where it seems absurd that one's knowledge can make one ignorant.

167. There is a problem in the text at this point. The verb translated 'hold fast to' is repeated fom above. Various emendations are proposed. 'Refuse to answer' suggests that this should have been the verb for asking a question, with the addition of a preposition.

168. Literally 'higher' hypothesis; it is difficult to explain the phrase without reference to the hierarchy of 'hypotheses' leading up to the Idea of the Good as 'unhypothetized principle' in *Republic* 6, 510–11. Plato also speaks of a hypothetical method which he has taken over from the mathematicians at *Meno* 86c–87b, another passage which ought hopefully to be related to this present one. That passage used the term 'hypothesis' for a condition which if it obtained would make something else to be so. Here Socrates has been suggesting that F will be true of x if there is an F-ness which x participates in. If the truth of the 'hypothesis' were questioned, one would have to produce another condition which, if it applied, would make the original hypothesis true. Thus 'hypothesis' is being used for a logical reason (a sufficient condition), as opposed to the mechanical reasons and motivational reasons that have been earlier discussed.

169. One thinks naturally of Euthydemus and Dionysodorus in Plato's *Euthydemus*, as well as the persons accused at 90c of abusing argument. The error described, however, is not a known technique of such sophists.

170. The Idea; the terminology is deliberately varied.

171. This claim is generally regarded as excessive. It would, however, be perfectly justified if Socrates were here employing a quasi-Protagorean theory of sensation, whereby the various non-essential predicates of a thing are not strictly embodied 'in' a thing at all, but result rather from the way the perceiver views that thing (and in some cases *in relation to what* he views it), only coming to be 'in' it as a result of that interaction between viewer and object, as at *Theaetetus* 156.

172. I have enclosed the preposition in inverted commas because its

significance has been a matter of controversy. While it is clear that Plato is referring to a quality *as it is associated with* humans, etc., 'in' is the standard way of referring to a property which belongs to something, and it may not have any metaphysical significance. Hence whether Plato is operating with three metaphysical levels, so that he has not only tall things and a transcendent Idea of Tallness but also tallness immanent in us, is not entirely clear. Above all it is not clear whether 'tallness in us' implies more than the tallness that human beings *envisage* as being in us.

173. See the Argument from Opposites, section C above.

174. Plato does not here mean the Idea of the Opposite, but the Idea of any quality which has another quality opposite to it.

175. By 'that which is in Nature' Plato again means the Idea. Similar language is also found in *Republic* 10 (597b–598a) and the *Cratylus* (389a–d). The expression ought to remind one of how far Plato intends his theory to offer an alternative to Presocratic physics. The Ideas are somehow more 'natural' than particulars in so far as they always follow their own nature.

176. The theory that particulars derive their name from the Idea. This relates to Simmias 'coming to be described as' small or large (102c) and to 78e, and is a regular part of Platonic theory. Of course Plato does not attempt to say that (e.g.) white things are 'white' in the same way as the Idea of White is 'white'.

177. There has been considerable debate here as to whether Plato is now talking about Ideas of Snow and Fire, immanent forms, or just the fire and snow with which we are all familiar. In the absence of any trace of language which might identify them as Ideas, it is best to assume that Plato was content to have us think of ordinary fire and snow. The reason why *ordinary* snow must never be hot is that it must be accompanied by the immanent form 'cold' (thus participating in the Idea of Cold), not because it is itself immanent in some subject.

178. Following what seems to be a physical example, we now come to a mathematical one, as if it made no difference to Plato what sorts of thing are able to have these essential properties and so resist the opposite properties. In some ways this is an advantage because it excuses him from first discussing in great detail what sort of thing the soul in particular is. The number three, however, is here treated rather as an immanent form, able to belong to (e.g.) three pencils and requiring them to participate in the Idea 'Odd'.

179. One might profitably consider what happens to the 'three' in three pencils when a fourth pencil is added to make them even in number. Clearly we cannot have a case of three any longer.

180. The term translated 'approach' suggests also hostility, as if the approach were that of an advancing enemy. Note that the term 'Forms' is now, and in some cases hereafter, unlikely to apply specifically to the transcendent Platonic Idea, which is fixed and immobile. It is the heat in something which would approach the cold in something else.

181. There is uncertainty here. One might also translate 'which are compelled by whatever gets a hold on them . . .'. Translation here is often thought to be crucial for the interpretation of the whole passage, and as I translate it there is thought to be an implication that these things, in so far as they get a hold on others, must be Ideas themselves. I think it would be truer to say that they must be either Ideas or immanent forms, and there is a strong weighting towards the latter: wherever an immanent form 'fire' or 'three' enters upon a block of wood or a family of geese, then there will be hot wood (excluding 'cold') or three geese (excluding 'even').

182. A third word (*morphê*) for a 'Form' or 'Idea' now appears, though we seem now to be focusing on the immanent presence of the Idea.

183. 'Un-dying' does not yet mean immortal, but 'unable to receive death or the state of being dead'.

184. Socrates reverts once again to 'Orphic' tales of the after-life.

185. This was one of the traditional roles of Hermes, though it would be uncharacteristic of Plato to be concerned with the name.

186. Plato often gives myth-like material an aetiological role, making it explain features here in the life that is familiar to us. The translation 'ceremonies' is uncertain; most manuscripts have the unnecessarily specific 'sacrifices'.

187. Myth-like material is frequently treated by Plato as a matter of belief rather than knowledge; cf. *Gorgias* 524a, *Republic* 621c. Note that although it is here implied that Socrates has been convinced *by somebody*, Simmias's response shows that the reader is not intended to find this theory at all familiar.

188. Not to be identified with certainty, but references to the skill of Glaucus were proverbial, and variously explained in antiquity.

189. Socrates' response to the Presocratic theories satirized at 99b–c.

190. On the east side of the Black Sea, and the eastern boundary of the world as known to the Greeks.

191. The Straits of Gibraltar at the western end of the Mediterranean.

192. As eyes are not able to withstand watching the eclipsing sun (99d–e), so only the philosophic mind is thought of as able to withstand the intellectual light of the upper regions.

193. Plato is probably thinking of the absence of flowering and fruiting plants, not of a lack of vegetation generally.

194. A *mythos*, or 'myth'; however, the Greek term is not quite as technical as its English equivalent. That Socrates feels that the 'story' is only now beginning indicates a slight difference in status between the preliminary description of the earth (based perhaps on Socrates' conviction of how things ought to be if the world is organized for the best) and the more fanciful details which are to follow.

195. Balls made in the shape of a regular dodecahedron, with twelve surfaces each of which is a regular pentagon. Plato's Demiurge used this shape for the cosmos as a whole at *Timaeus* 55c.

196. The 'humans' referred to here live in a 'golden age' type of environ-

ment; another way in which Plato's 'myth' draws on typical themes of Greek mythology.

197. i.e. they do not rely on the mediacy of a priest, priestess or seer for information about the future, nor upon dreams rather than waking visions.

198. Knowledge of the heavenly bodies was seen in early Greek philosophy as the pinnacle of human cognitive effort. Hence it is a fitting climax here.

199. There now begins an account of the underworld designed to harmonize both with Socrates' 'geography' and with empirical observations concerning things underground, particularly concerning volcanic activity, tides, and underground rivers. Again Socrates is demonstrating his interest in matters of importance for the Presocratics, though approaching them from a different angle.

200. *Iliad* 8.14. Tartarus is mentioned at line 481.

201. The mythical river encircling the world.

202. Acheron, Cocytus and Pyriphlegethon are all mythical underworld rivers. So is Styx, which here becomes a lake.

203. The Mediterranean.

204. The basic geography of Socrates' world has now been described. We pass on to the journey through it of various kinds of disembodied soul.

205. There seems to be some inconsistency between this and the Argument from Opposites; the latter demands that all souls which leave this earthly state should eventually return, whereas incurable criminals, and people of exceptional holiness too, will not do so.

206. A reference to the confidence-inspiring 'enchantment' process of 78a.

207. The orders of the Eleven, whose servant the officer was.

208. See the introduction to *Phaedo*, p. 96.

209. See above, p. 59a.

210. The significance of these words has been much discussed. As Asclepius is god of healing, it ought to suggest that Socrates' soul has been healed; also there may be a hint of criticism of Pythagoreans such as Simmias and Cebes, who normally reject all maltreatment of animals as their souls may be one's own ancestors: but Socrates might claim that one is injuring only the body.

SELECT BIBLIOGRAPHY

Literature on Plato is extensive. I have confined myself here to mentioning a number of works written in English, usually quite recent, which the reader may find to be of assistance. For information on more extensive bibliographies, please refer to p.381 of the Penguin volume entitled *Plato: Early Socratic Dialogues* (ed. T. J. Saunders, 1987), but note also the appearance of a more recent extensive bibliography on Socrates:

KATZ, Ellen L., and NAVIA, Luis E., *Socrates: an Annotated Bibliography* (London and New York, 1988).

ADKINS, A. W. H., *Merit and Responsibility* (Chicago and London, 1960).
ALLEN, R. E., 'Law and Justice in Plato's *Crito*', *Journal of Philosophy* 69 (1972), 557–67.
– *Socrates and Legal Obligation* (Minneapolis, 1980).
– *Plato's Euthyphro and the Earlier Theory of Forms* (New York, 1970).
ANNAS, Julia, 'Plato's Myths of Judgement', *Phronesis* 27 (1982), 119–43.
ARIETI, J. A., 'A Dramatic Interpretation of Plato's *Phaedo*', *Illinois Classical Studies* 11 (1986), 129–42.
BALLARD, E. G., *Socratic Ignorance: an Essay on Platonic Self-Knowledge* (The Hague, 1965).
BARKER, Andrew, 'Why did Socrates Refuse to Escape?', *Phronesis* 22 (1977), 13–28.
BEDU-ADDO, J. T., 'Sense-experience and the Argument from Recollection in Plato's *Phaedo*', *Phronesis* 36 (1991), 27–60.
BOSTOCK, David, *Plato's Phaedo* (Oxford, 1986).
– 'The Interpretation of Plato's *Crito*', *Phronesis* 35 (1990), 1–20.
BRICKHOUSE, Thomas C., and SMITH, Nicholas D., *Socrates on Trial* (Oxford, 1989).
– 'Socrates and Obedience to the Law', *Apeiron* 18 (1984), 10–18.
– 'A Matter of Life and Death in Socratic Philosophy', *Ancient Philosophy* 9 (1989), 155–66.
BURGER, Ronna, *The Phaedo: a Platonic Labyrinth* (New Haven, 1984).
BURKERT, Walter, *Greek Religion* (Cambridge, Mass., 1985).
CALVERT, Brian, 'Plato's *Crito* and Richard Kraut', in S. Panagiotou (ed.), *Justice, Law and Method in Plato and Aristotle* (Edmonton, 1987).
COHEN, Marc S., 'Socrates on the Definition of Piety', *Journal of the History of Philosophy* 9 (1971), 1–13.

DORTER, Kenneth, 'Socrates on Life, Death and Suicide', *Laval Théologie et Philosophie* 32 (1976), 23–41.

– *Plato's Phaedo: an Interpretation* (Toronto, 1982).

DOVER, Kenneth J., *Aristophanes' The Clouds* (Oxford, 1968).

– *Greek Popular Morality in the Time of Plato and Aristotle* (Berkeley and Los Angeles, 1974).

FREDE, Dorothea, 'The Final Proof of the Immortality of the Soul in Plato's *Phaedo* 102a–107a', *Phronesis* 23 (1978), 24–41.

FRIEDLÄNDER, Paul, *Plato* (trans. H. Meyerhoff), 3 vols. (New York, 1958–69).

GALLOP, David, *Plato's Phaedo* (Oxford, 1975).

GILL, Christopher, 'The Death of Socrates', *Classical Quarterly* 23 (1973), 25–8.

GOSLING, J. C. B., *Plato* (London and Boston, 1973).

– 'Similarity in *Phaedo* 73 seq.', *Phronesis* 10 (1965), 151–61.

GULLEY, Norman, *The Philosophy of Socrates* (New York, 1968).

GUTHRIE, W. K. C., *A History of Greek Philosophy*, vols. 3 and 4 (Cambridge, 1969, 1975). Volume 3 is also available in two separate paperbacks, entitled *Socrates* and *The Sophists* (Cambridge, 1971).

HACKFORTH, R. M., *Plato's Phaedo* (Cambridge, 1955).

IRWIN, Terence H., *Plato's Moral Theory* (Oxford, 1977).

KAHN, Charles, 'Did Plato write Socratic Dialogues?', *Classical Quarterly* 31 (1981), 305–20.

– 'Problems in the Argument of Plato's *Crito*', in *Nature, Knowledge and Virtue*, ed. T. Penner and R. Kraut (Edmonton, 1989), 22–44.

KERFERD, G. B., *The Sophistic Movement* (Cambridge, 1981).

KRAUT, Richard, *Socrates and the State* (Princeton, 1983).

LEDGER, Gerard, *Recounting Plato* (Oxford, 1989).

MCPHERRAN, Mark, 'Socratic Piety in the *Euthyphro*', *Journal of the History of Philosophy* 23 (1985), 283–309.

MONTUORI, Mario, *Socrates, Physiology of a Myth*, trans. J. M. P. and M. Langdale (Amsterdam, 1981).

– 'The Oracle given to Chaerephon on the Wisdom of Socrates', *Kernos* 3 (1990).

MORGAN, Michael, *Platonic Piety* (New Haven and London, 1990).

NAVIA, Luis E., *Socrates: the Man and his Philosophy* (Lanham, New York and London, 1985).

RANKIN, H. D., *Sophists, Socratics and Cynics* (London, 1983).

ROBINSON, Richard, *Plato's Earlier Dialectic* (Oxford, 1953).

ROBINSON, T. M., *Plato's Psychology* (Toronto, 1970).

ROSEN, Frederick, 'Piety and Justice in Plato's *Euthyphro*', *Philosophy* 43 (1968), 105–16.

SAUNDERS, T. J. (ed.), *Plato: Early Socratic Dialogues* (Penguin, 1987).

SEESKIN, Kenneth, *Dialogue and Discovery: a Study in Socratic Method* (Albany, 1987).

STONE, I. F., *The Trial of Socrates* (Boston, 1987).

TARRANT, Harold, 'Midwifery and the *Clouds*', *Classical Quarterly* 38 (1988), 116–22.

TAYLOR, A. E., *Plato: the Man and his Work* (London, 1960).

– *Socrates* (Garden City, 1953).

TAYLOR, C. C. W., 'The End of the *Euthyphro*', *Phronesis* 27 (1982), 109–18.

TELOH, Henry, *Socratic Education in Plato's Early Dialogues* (Notre Dame, 1986).

TREDENNICK, Hugh, and WATERFIELD, Robin (eds.), *Xenophon: Conversations of Socrates* (Penguin, 1990).

VANDER WAERDT, Paul A., *The Socratic Movement* (Ithaca, 1993).

VERSÉNYI, Lazlo, *Holiness and Justice: an Interpretation of Plato's Euthyphro* (Lanham, New York and London, 1982).

VLASTOS, Gregory (ed.), *The Philosophy of Socrates* (Garden City, 1971).

– 'Socrates on Obedience and Disobedience', *Yale Review* 42 (1974), 517–34.

– 'The Socratic Elenchus', *Oxford Studies in Ancient Philosophy* 1 (1983), 27–58.

– 'Socrates' Disavowal of Knowledge', *Philosophical Quarterly* 35 (1985), 1–31.

– 'Socratic Irony', *Classical Quarterly* 37 (1987), 79–95.

– 'Is the "Socratic Fallacy" Socratic?', *Ancient Philosophy* 10 (1990), 1–16.

– *Socrates, Ironist and Moral Philosopher* (Cambridge, 1991).

WEST, T. G., *Plato's Apology of Socrates* (Ithaca and London, 1979).

WOOZLEY, A. D., *Law and Obedience: The Arguments of Plato's Crito* (London, 1979).

INDEX

READ MORE IN PENGUIN

In every corner of the world, on every subject under the sun, Penguin represents quality and variety – the very best in publishing today.

For complete information about books available from Penguin – including Puffins, Penguin Classics and Arkana – and how to order them, write to us at the appropriate address below. Please note that for copyright reasons the selection of books varies from country to country.

In the United Kingdom: Please write to *Dept. EP, Penguin Books Ltd, Bath Road, Harmondsworth, West Drayton, Middlesex UB7 0DA*

In the United States: Please write to *Consumer Sales, Penguin Putnam Inc., P.O. Box 12289 Dept. B, Newark, New Jersey 07101-5289*. VISA and MasterCard holders call 1-800-788-6262 to order Penguin titles

In Canada: Please write to *Penguin Books Canada Ltd, 10 Alcorn Avenue, Suite 300, Toronto, Ontario M4V 3B2*

In Australia: Please write to *Penguin Books Australia Ltd, P.O. Box 257, Ringwood, Victoria 3134*

In New Zealand: Please write to *Penguin Books (NZ) Ltd, Private Bag 102902, North Shore Mail Centre, Auckland 10*

In India: Please write to *Penguin Books India Pvt Ltd, 11 Community Centre, Panchsheel Park, New Delhi 110017*

In the Netherlands: Please write to *Penguin Books Netherlands bv, Postbus 3507, NL-1001 AH Amsterdam*

In Germany: Please write to *Penguin Books Deutschland GmbH, Metzlerstrasse 26, 60594 Frankfurt am Main*

In Spain: Please write to *Penguin Books S. A., Bravo Murillo 19, 1° B, 28015 Madrid*

In Italy: Please write to *Penguin Italia s.r.l., Via Benedetto Croce 2, 20094 Corsico, Milano*

In France: Please write to *Penguin France, Le Carré Wilson, 62 rue Benjamin Baillaud, 31500 Toulouse*

In Japan: Please write to *Penguin Books Japan Ltd, Kaneko Building, 2-3-25 Koraku, Bunkyo-Ku, Tokyo 112*

In South Africa: Please write to *Penguin Books South Africa (Pty) Ltd, Private Bag X14, Parkview, 2122 Johannesburg*

READ MORE IN PENGUIN

A CHOICE OF CLASSICS

Hesiod/Theognis	**Theogony/Works and Days/Elegies**
Hippocrates	**Hippocratic Writings**
Homer	**The Iliad**
	The Odyssey
Horace	**Complete Odes and Epodes**
Horace/Persius	**Satires and Epistles**
Juvenal	**The Sixteen Satires**
Livy	**The Early History of Rome**
	Rome and Italy
	Rome and the Mediterranean
	The War with Hannibal
Lucretius	**On the Nature of the Universe**
Martial	**Epigrams**
	Martial in English
Ovid	**The Erotic Poems**
	Heroides
	Metamorphoses
	The Poems of Exile
Pausanias	**Guide to Greece (in two volumes)**
Petronius/Seneca	**The Satyricon/The Apocolocyntosis**
Pindar	**The Odes**
Plato	**Early Socratic Dialogues**
	Gorgias
	The Last Days of Socrates (Euthyphro/ The Apology/Crito/Phaedo)
	The Laws
	Phaedrus and Letters VII and VIII
	Philebus
	Protagoras/Meno
	The Republic
	The Symposium
	Theaetetus
	Timaeus/Critias
Plautus	**The Pot of Gold and Other Plays**
	The Rope and Other Plays